KT-198-662

ed on or before

30130503909209

OR 6.93

Women, Celibacy
and Passion

BY THE SAME AUTHOR

REFLECTING MEN at twice their natural size
(with Dale Spender)
JUST DESSERTS: Women and Food

SALLY CLINE

Women, Celibacy and Passion

The South East Essex
College of Arts & Technology
CR
Carnarvon Road   Southend on Sea   Essex   SS2 6LS
Tel: Southend (0702) 220400   Fax: Southend (0702) 432320

ANDRE DEUTSCH

This book is dedicated to Ba Sheppard.

It is also for Dale Spender, Sheila McIlwraith, Wendy Mulford for their literary strengths.

First published in Great Britain 1993 by
André Deutsch Limited
105-106 Great Russell Street
London WC1B 3LJ

Copyright © 1993 Sally Cline
All rights reserved

The author has asserted her moral right.

CIP data for this title is available
from the British Library.

ISBN 0 233 98804 1

Printed in Great Britain by
St Edmundsbury Press, Bury St Edmunds, Suffolk

305.4CLI   X41504

CONTENTS

ACKNOWLEDGEMENTS   vi

INTRODUCTION   **Celibacy is not Hereditary**   1

CHAPTER ONE   **Genital Messages**   23

CHAPTER TWO   **Genital Manipulations**   37

CHAPTER THREE   **Celibacy Begins in the Mind**   71

CHAPTER FOUR   **Spirituality? A Simple Life? Or Just Sheer Spite?**   91

CHAPTER FIVE   **Convent Girls and Impossible Passions**   118

CHAPTER SIX   **Celibacy is More Than Chastity**   143

CHAPTER SEVEN   **Perpetual Virgins**   165

CHAPTER EIGHT   **Endangered Species**   191

CHAPTER NINE   **Celibate Sisters**   215

CHAPTER TEN   **Creative Solitude**   227

CONCLUSION   **A Passion for Celibacy**   253

NOTES   256

BIBLIOGRAPHY   266

INDEX   274

ACKNOWLEDGEMENTS

A vital acknowledgement goes to the many women in North America and Great Britain who talked with me and offered their accounts of celibacy and passion. Their names have been altered but their voices and views weave through these pages.

The Royal Literary Fund awarded me a literary merit grant which enabled me to live, during a very difficult period, so that I could finish this book. Marjorie Allen's financial patience and support have been constant. To both I am deeply indebted.

In North America I thank for hospitality, interview organization, research facilities, contacts and discussions, Bernie Lucht, (Canadian Broadcasting Corporation, Toronto) Doreen Brule (Canadian Broadcasting Corporation, Ottawa), Anne Gurnett (New Jersey), Kathy Mullen, Rob Hess, Graham Metson (Montreal), Kate McKenna and Alisa Hornung Weyman (Toronto). In Halifax, Nova Scotia I thank Carol Millett, Keith Loudun, Barbara Cottrell, Shelley Finson (some exciting spiritual debates) and most particularly Adele McSorley who read and wittily revised the penultimate draft, and had some fascinating Catholic ideas, and Betty Ann Lloyd who asked me if I wanted challenge or affirmation, and when I lied, gave me both every day for a week on a red clay beach in Nova Scotia. In Ottawa, Cheryl Lean, my former radio partner, now a quicksilver lawyer, gave me a Macintosh, a speedy bike, a summer's workspace, and her own inimitable brand of chiselled clarity.

In Great Britain lengthy audio-typing was patiently endured and meticulously transcribed by Aliye Seif Al Said who also shared her charming house, and gave me computer space, as did Julia Ball in her art-filled studio, during the book's final stage. Rhiannon James produced an impeccable bibliography in record time; Margaret Wright contributed useful historical research; Lowana Veal spent

patient hours on the index; Polly Stokes did the bulk of the typing/
printing at high speed with her usual humour and unselfishness.
Jude Emmanuel gave me typing space, hospitality, and Jewish
Feminist insights. Liz Hodgkinson's provocative ideas on celibacy
were immensely helpful.

For encouragement and stimulating talks I thank Carol Jones and
Anne Christie. For keeping my health in order I thank Joel Jaffey,
and for getting my shelves and desks back in order I thank Martin
Graves, both made the writing possible. For discussions on Buddhism
and spirituality I thank Alison West, Stella King and Sarah Patterson.
Sarah read innumerable drafts and was always constructive and
compassionate, and opened up my mind to alternative viewpoints.
I thank Em (Marion) Callen for reading the lengthy final draft and
for subsequently offering me a challenging new approach to celibacy.
For always 'being there' after so many years, I thank my friend
Kathy Bowles.

In Cornwall, yet again, I thank Jean Adams for the inspiring writing time at her superb Sunset Heights. In Scotland, for
organizing interviews, arranging research schedules, and offering
me hospitality, I thank Jen Kitzinger, Diana Mutimer, Michael
House, and most of all my ex-editor and friend Sheila McIlwraith
without whose extraordinary patience and critical help in reading
and re-reading and setting to rights the first chapter, I might never
have progressed to the second!

Dale Spender worked with me on large portions of an early
version, my debt to her is incalculable. My literary agent Tessa
Sayle regularly offered me sparky ideas and affectionate support.
This means a lot. My publisher Tom Rosenthal has never been too
busy to help or talk to me. Esther Whitby, my longtime friend, and
editor throughout most of the book, was reassuring, dependable, and
skilfully critical. Clare Chambers, my new editor, herself a writer,
has an author's imaginative feel as well as an editor's tough, clear
mind.

My family, extended family, and intimates, have as always been
a source of strength, personally and professionally. Cousin Joan
Harris offered continuous interest and excellent meals; Caroline
Hill gave me hospitality and even her own room; Elsie Sheppard
has been enthusiastic and supportive throughout. Aunt Het (Harriet)
Shackman lit up most days with her attention, her concern, her
stimulating comments, her unconditional affection. Cousin Jonathan
Harris, a first class chef, became a first rate removal firm and moved

me, the computer, the work, and the books, to and from five houses, accompanying the journeys with wonderful meals and provocative ideas. Cousin Jane Shackman organized the bibliography, transcribed dozens of audio tapes, read drafts, and spent a year with me in delightful Leys Avenue debating extreme and often hilarious versions of celibacy.

In Leys Avenue, lovely Vic Smith with her irrepressible spirits and intellectual acuteness, recharged my sometimes weary batteries, and kept me on my toes about what passion and celibacy mean to young women.

I thank Carol Kendrick for consistent hospitality and for her constant communications that reduced our distance, for her endless patience in reading several chapters many times, and for bringing joy and laughter into a writer's routine. I thank Ba Sheppard, who for fourteen years has given me emotional support and the intellectual space to grow and write, who this time gave me a year's freedom in her own home to wrestle with celibacy, a subject on which we don't agree, and to complete the book dedicated to her.

Every day I want to thank Wendy Mulford not just for the original idea of celibacy, but for the loan of her attic and the gift of her friendship. Every day it is her writerly understanding that sustains me.

Finally I want to thank my electric daughter Marmoset Adler for the remarkable way she has arranged interviews, researched topics, produced data, posted me news cuttings, exchanged ideas and offered me perpetual encouragement. She helped with this book perhaps more than she realized. Love and gratitude.

Cambridge, March 1992

Author's note.

My most memorable and bizarre conversations on celibacy were with Angela Carter on a long train journey we took together. Angela died 16 February 1992 just as I had finished the chapter on solitude and death. She died at the height of her own powers but her books will continue to inspire. I should like to remember her originality, brilliance and *kindness* here, and to feel that perhaps some of her quirky and magic vision might unexpectedly surface through my use of some of the ideas we debated on passion and celibacy.

INTRODUCTION

Celibacy is not Hereditary

'SEX has been domesticated, stripped of the promised mystery, added to the category of the merely expected. It's just what is done, mundane as hockey. It's celibacy these days that would raise eyebrows.'[1]

Celibacy raises eyebrows because it is an act of rebellion against the sacred cow of sexual consumerism.

This is a consumer society. An assumption built into it is that we should all be eager consumers of sexual activity. Women in particular should consume and accept sexual congress along with beauty products, diet regimes, low wages and violent inflictions, as part of a contemporary cultural system which aims to checkmate power in aspiring women's lives.

Like militarism today, meat yesterday, fur coats the day before, sexual intercourse and general genital thrashing about, are things a woman is expected to purchase – if she can afford the price. Some women have decided the price is too high, the rewards simply do not justify it. Other women have suggested there are no rewards at all.

Most books on the subject of sex suggest that a woman's failure to tone up her genitals regularly will lead her into an advanced state of sickness or offer her early warning signals of the onset of madness. This book does not take that line. It suggests that sexual activity (preferably with men, best of all with a husband), seen as mandatory from the purchase of the wedding ring to the loan of the invalid chair (and beyond, oh yes beyond!) may not be the only or the best way to achieve exultation.

Although all forms of sexual, and especially genital activity are seen as more productive than positive abstention, a specific emphasis is put on penile enhancement, both actual and symbolic.

Should you still misguidedly think that the joys and problems attached to the male penis are insignificant, or none of your concern, let me draw your attention to a recent news cutting which reported that China had 'solved a world medical problem' because a Chinese surgeon, Long Daochu, had achieved a medical breakthrough in the field of penis enlargement. He was now able to lengthen a little man's penis by two to three inches and double its circumference to more than five inches 'without dampening its sensitivity and erectness'.[2] A cultural vision that sees such a miniature medical matter as the solution to a world medical problem is a male genital perspective whose ideas of grandeur necessitate mandatory penis empowering.

As Germaine Greer aptly pointed out in her book *The Change: Women, Ageing and the Menopause*, although for a woman to be unwanted may also mean she is free, such women who refuse even to try to empower the penis are seen as old bats, old bags, crones, mothers-in-law, and castrating women.[3]

Greer was focusing on women over fifty, but, as Dale Spender and I discovered in an earlier study, not enabling the penis, not reflecting male sexual values, will bring severe penalties to women *of any age*.[4] This is because not buying into the ideology I have termed the Genital Myth means not accepting the fictions of the male power elite who socially control women's lives when they prescribe sexually active behaviour and symbolic penis enhancement.

In the past celibates, who did not accept the conditions of the genital myth of their age, if they were female, were seen as women who disturbed the social order. Today, celibacy for women has that curious stigma, that faint odour of displeasing oddness, that the terms 'green' and 'veggie' once had. Think back. Remember when green politics were seen as 'deprivation' or 'eccentricity'. I remember when being a vegetarian and being against nuclear weapons was seen as being deficient. 'But what about steak? Won't you miss it?' I was asked. 'What about our safety? Don't you want your country to feel secure?' I was hectored. In exactly the same ill-informed way, people still say: 'What about sex? How do you manage?'

Today green politics are seen as a passionate but thoughtfully sound boycott of commercial consumerism and worldwide environmental damage. Our kitchen sinks and toilet bowls shine with eco-friendly products which reflect (at least superficially) our acceptance of a politics once seen as weird and untenable. The decision not to engage in irresponsible politics is an undeniable political statement.

Similarly, celibacy as the decision not to engage in sexual acts is undeniably a *sexual* statement. That too will be seen as heretical. How can you be making a sexual statement if you are not 'doing it'? As for writing about not doing it – communicating, nay disseminating, sacrilegious messages – this can only be regarded as damnable impiety. Celibacy is of course not merely a sexual statement, it is also a political statement. Celibacy is the bright green politics of the sexual forum. And for many women celibacy is an area where the grass is greener.

No wonder people raise eyebrows. No wonder the term 'celibacy', at least when it is applied to women, is explosive. I discovered at the start of the research that even writing about it provokes strong reactions. The first occurred when I told my ex-lover that I was engaged on a book about celibacy.

'Celibacy? *Celibacy!* I can't see that being popular. It's certainly not something I'm interested in.'

I had noticed. I had not had much interest in it myself in those days. Laughing at the memory of what sexual consumers we had both been, I turned back to the computer.

The second reaction occurred when a doctor friend took me to a hospital consultant's Christmas party. The room was filled with intelligent, articulate, noisy medical men and women. Enthusiastically, she introduced me to group after group, saying warmly, 'Sally is writing a book about celibacy in women.' A shocked silence fell upon each group in turn. A couple of women said 'Oh goodness'. One man said he knew a great deal about celibacy in men. Most of the medics searched in vain for any appropriate words to keep the conversation going. Mainly they stayed silent or turned away. It was as if she had told them I was researching into a rare and stigmatized terminal illness; although I suspect I should have received a more positive response if she had.

The third response to the subject I was studying occurred in the small Cornish fishing village where I was staying with a writer friend to work on the book. When it was time for her to return to the city, she bought me a farewell present from the boathouse stores. It was one of those teatowels that offer a set of zany mottoes, each illustrating the law that says anything that can go wrong will go wrong. She thought I might find at least one motto applicable to my life or work. Emblazoned across the centre of the teatowel was the message: 'Celibacy is not hereditary'.

However droll the disguise, the subtext of the message was

serious: celibacy is today assumed to be in the nature of a disease; it is perceived as something to be wary of (be grateful that you cannot inherit it); it is viewed as outside the normative experience of both sexes, and in the case of women, any form of celibacy is seen as something that needs a remedy, but self-chosen celibacy is seen as an impossible possibility.

This is the more extraordinary as celibacy, hardly a novel notion, has an ancient and esteemed tradition, especially for men; and in many societies earlier than our own, has been regarded as a more elevated ideal than sexual activity. Celibacy, certainly for men, sometimes for women, was seen as healthy at a point when coitus was seen as injurious to health.

In the early Christian world a self-controlled ascetic celibacy was derived from the concept of sin and atonement. Male restraint in cohabitation, and lifelong sexual continence were seen as Christian virtues. According to a ruling made by a Hamburg District Court in 1981, the Christian faith was founded on the person of Jesus Christ who is defined as the Redeemer whose life was devoid of all sin and pleasure. By 'pleasure' the Court was referring to just one in particular, the physical sensual pleasure known popularly as 'sex'. Thus by linking sexual pleasure closely with sin it endorsed an earlier Catholic view that sexual pleasure cannot be devoid of sin.

For theologians, Jesus's alleged disapproval of sexual pleasure, which had repercussions for Christian marriage, led logically to the establishment of a celibate priesthood. In the year 385 AD for instance, Pope Siricius, a great Mariologist and despiser of matrimony, strongly influenced the growth and esteem for celibacy by describing it as a 'crimen' (crime) for priests to have sexual intercourse with their wives after ordination. As the majority of priests were married at this point, this new respectable practice of celibacy hit them hard. When Pope Siricius, in a letter to Himerius, the Spanish Bishop of Tarragona, in 385 AD, further condemned sexual conduct as 'obscoena cupiditas' or vile lechery, both priests and lay people began to accept that celibacy was virtuous and sex was not.[5]

The Ancient World too found celibacy not merely commendable but also healthy. Unlike those of Christianity, their theories on the subject did not derive from concepts of sin and atonement but were based largely on medical considerations. In the sixth century BC, Pythagoras is reported as saying that men should devote themselves to sex only in the winter, never in the summer, and only sparingly with due moderation in spring and autumn. Sex, it seems, was dreadfully injurious to health at all times, in all seasons. He suggested that the best time to make love was when a man wished to weaken himself through loss of semen.[6] Women on the other hand did not sustain a loss of energy resulting from the emission of semen, so sexual intercourse was somewhat less harmful to them. However, in general the Ancient World in that period saw the sexual act as dangerous, difficult to control, debilitating and detrimental to health.

Celibacy was seen as the reverse. Positive, powerful, and constitutionally healthy. This view was shared by Xenophon, Plato, Aristotle and the physician Hippocrates in the fourth century BC. Hippocrates believed that the retention of semen was the key to physical strength, that excessive loss of semen wasted the spinal marrow and resulted in death. In the second century AD Emperor Hadrian's personal physician, Soranus of Ephesus, stated that sexual activity led to a dangerous squandering of energy, that the only justification for it was reproduction, and that permanent celibacy was the way forward to a healthy life.[7]

Michel Foucault in his *History of Sexuality* surveying the sexual critics of the Ancient World discovered that sexual activity became increasingly condemned during the first two centuries AD. Doctors recommended abstinence and celibacy for increased vitality, and later the philosophers of Stoa (from whence we get the term 'stoic' meaning impassive) disparaged all sexual activity outside marriage, called marriage itself into question, subordinated its structure to total abstinence from carnal passion, and elevated celibacy to a position of the highest regard.[8]

Celibacy, then, was set against marriage, and indeed its original and primary meaning was quite simply 'unmarried', derived in the seventeenth century from the Latin 'caelebs', meaning unmarried. It was only a secondary meaning that suggested 'one who has taken a religious vow of chastity'.[9] With its sense of being single, and operating on one's own, the root meaning of celibacy is connected with self-determination rather than with genital or non-genital activity.

While celibate women today are trying to return to the interpretation of celibacy as independent singleness, they are up against the forces of the genital myth which firmly interpret it as nothing more than genital abstention.

It is indeed ironic that an ancient view of celibacy as a positive singlehood conferring wisdom, health and spiritual power on its followers, has been overturned by a twentieth century society satiated with sex. Subscribing to the genital myth, today's market place ideologues offer female capitalist consumers the idea that it is sexual activity which promotes salubrity, emotional fulfilment, and even transcendental bliss.

The myth works in various ways on the psyches of individual women so that their joint purchasing powers may be open to sexual (and commercial) coercion. One way is the promotion of sexual activity as an essential ingredient in standards of beauty, youth and femininity. Not to be sexually active suggests a woman is ugly, old or unfeminine. A focus on appearance or youth keeps women in a constant state of anxiety and distracts them from the main issues in the ongoing struggle against oppression. Mandatory heterosexual consumption as integral to this way of thinking keeps women in line by keeping their attention firmly fixed on men. Compulsory congress has always been a smart move on the divide-and-conquer frontlines of attack. Never more so than now when women have made so many gains in legal and social directions.

Constant sexual availability to men, and a prescriptive and rigorous programme of sexual activity, is linked to the new orthodox dogmas concerning age and weight. As the second wave of feminism broke through impediments to gain and regain legal and reproductive rights, as it encouraged women to breach the power structure at every level, so did eating disorders rise, women's size shrink, cosmetic surgery increase and bypass all other medical areas in terms of growth, and compulsory sexual congress become the way for women to assert anxiously that they were still 'real women' in men's eyes.[10]

Another way the genital myth works is by viewing all aspects of sexual activity as great levellers and great enhancers. In reality individual sexual acts may be felt to be uncomfortable or unspeakable, but the myth suggests that all sexual acts are physically beneficial, morally sound, certainly more effective, and, here's the rub, more *normal* than no sexual acts.

Coition, copulation, concupiscence, debauchery, defloration, fornication, free love, flirting, philandering, lasciviousness, seduction, sexual intrigue, wenching, wife-swapping and voyeurism are all encouraged as a means to health and wellbeing.

Adultery, cuckolding, nymphomania, priapism, satyriasis, sodomy and whoring are accepted as either natural or reasonable. Even homosexuality, lesbianism, and sado-masochism, once defined as abnormal, are tolerated on the grounds that at least they involve genital activity.

The most insidious workings of the genital myth operate within and as an integral part of a culture where the seven billion dollar pornography industry (now the largest media category) trades innocently as erotica, and allows sexual harassment, gang bangs, incest, sexual assault and rape to be disguised as sex so that millions of women feel obliged to acquiesce in the consumption of these terrorist activities too.

As far as 'sex' goes, anything goes, except not going along with the notion at all. **Today it is celibacy rather than assault which is viewed as indecent.**

It is clear then that in this study, in dealing with celibacy, we are dealing with a loaded word. It is loaded against women who are unable to use it freely, with pride, or with the assurance that their motives for choosing celibacy, or indeed the fact that they *have* chosen it, will be accepted and understood. Women who decide to be celibate for positive reasons – the Passionate Celibates of this study – are generally accorded the same negative status as women who have unwillingly withdrawn from traditional sexual activity, such as those who have been thrown over by a lover, or widowed, or bereaved.

All women who do not participate in sex, whether by choice or by accident, are seen as women who have failed.

In today's sex-oriented society, where a mere clitoral orgasm is old-fashioned, where G-spots pinpoint perfect ejaculation, where vibrators form part of many women's wardrobes, there is an enormous onus on women to 'perform well' sexually, and a great deal of internalized anxiety and guilt if we do not.

This focus on sexual congress is matched by an onerous insistence on coupledom. Tax relief for married couples, restaurant tables automatically laid for two, single supplements slapped on hotel prices, a desire for solitude looked on as personal failure – these all tell the same story. Even a proposed new property tax assumes that two adults live in every house; those who prefer to live alone will have to apply for a discount. The idea of the media image of 'healthy attractive women' deliberately deciding on something other than men and intercourse (or occasionally in the more progressive media, than sexually active love with other women) is seen as ridiculous and incomprehensible. Although live-in partnerships are acceptable, marriage is still considered the norm. Single women are seen as a nuisance, an embarrassment, even as a species to be belittled by men or watched a trifle guardedly by other women. Being single and being celibate are seen as second best. Choosing to be in either of these situations appears unthinkable.

Fifty years ago it took courage for a single woman to admit that she was enjoying an active sexual life. Today it takes courage for her to admit that she is not. For a married or partnered woman to admit it often means that other people, openly or covertly, will intimate that there is something wrong with her partnership. Coming out as celibate means that you may be treated as a social leper. Overtly celibate women are often looked on with amusement, pity, disapproval, boredom, or as a suitable case for treatment by women and men alike. Few people perceive it as a reasoned or reasonable choice.

Women's fears attached to celibacy are that they may lose out on closeness, touch, or affection. Sex and love have been so intricately tied together in recent years that it is difficult to contemplate that rejecting one may not force you to miss out on the other. Many women say they could give up genital activity and not miss it at all, but few of us wish to deny ourselves an opportunity for loving. Will someone really love me if I decide not to go to bed with him or her, or can someone really love me if he or she does not want to go to bed with me?

These are the questions women ask, questions which stand in the way of choosing celibacy with ease. These are the questions which advertising and much of the male-dominated media instigate and promote as part of the insidious genital myth which sustains women's anxieties whilst firmly keeping women in line. Willingness to co-operate in heterosexual activity is as much a part of today's carefully constructed feminine image as highlighted hair and polished nails. The genital trap, into which those who try to avoid the genital myth inevitably fall, is that choosing celibacy on those terms is choosing to be unfeminine. Choosing celibacy is choosing to be different, but it is not yet a difference that is celebrated. Women are asked simultaneously to believe that they have achieved sexual liberation and to accept that such liberation depends on consistent, regular sexual congress. Liberation, it seems, does not include the possibility of choosing not to have sex at all.

Society today offers women a very restricted number of ways by which to gain self-respect or esteem. One way that has been presented to women is to offer our bodies up for male admiration and desire. Many women believe that not to desire other people, or not to be desired by them, leads to feelings of low self-worth, rejection, or insecurity. The fact that today women who choose to be celibate are finding that it may bring them more affection and friendship not less, that it may allow them to relate to men as whole human beings rather than merely as lovers or as enemies, that it offers them more autonomy, and busier, contented lives, is ignored. This interesting series of possibilities is too threatening to be acknowledged openly. Women could gain a certain power, a certain freedom, from such a situation. Men might panic. Their penises might droop. Men depend on women to reflect them at twice their natural size, and part of that reflection is through sex.[11] Thus the fact that women's self-chosen celibacy can be both emotionally fulfilling and spiritually satisfying, is a fact that is diminished, distorted or invisibilized.

Yet many women today *are* choosing to become celibate with a passionate conviction, almost a revolutionary fervour. They are women who believe that celibacy offers them the strength, the sense of personal identity and independence, the creative time and energy for their own growth and work, which conventional sexual activity has not allowed them.

In this book I have tried to explore what celibacy as a word means, what it meant yesterday, what it means today, and in what ways the meaning has shifted. I have investigated how celibacy differs from chastity and virginity, and discovered in which ways they are linked. Some of the explorations look at how women used the word in previous centuries and how it was used against them. I have ranged from the early Christian centuries through to the suffragettes in Britain and to the Shakers and Sanctificationists in nineteenth century America. Some of the explorations look at what celibacy means to contemporary women in both North America and Great Britain.

During the last two years I have listened to many of these women both in Great Britain and North America. Some of the interviews were conducted specifically for this study, some were taped as part of the research for a proposed series of radio documentaries on celibacy for the Canadian Broadcasting Corporation and were then incorporated as part of the material for this book.

I wanted to learn from a variety of women what celibate experiences feel like in this society at this time. I wanted to discover what difficulties there are in not adhering to the genital myth. I talked to women in North America and Great Britain, of different ages, religions, sexual orientation, marital status, and social backgrounds.

Some women were mothers, some were divorced or separated, some were widowed. These situations inevitably changed the way celibacy operated in their lives, as did the fact of illness or disability.

Many women who had suffered from a debilitating physical or mental illness or from an emotional trauma became celibate either because they had no energy available at that time for sexual activity, or as a defence mechanism against being in a vulnerable situation. Initially many saw celibacy as something that was imposed upon them for negative reasons – a very different experience (and often a painful one) from voluntary celibacy undertaken as a way of gaining space or developing strength. However, many involuntary celibates discovered, as their illness or trauma receded, that it was perfectly possible for a woman to live a fulfilling and creative life with affection but without sexual activity.

My own first experience of celibacy came three years ago, after I had been suddenly hospitalized for heart disease and was back at home recovering from the shock. For the first time in my adult life, sex was not merely low on my personal agenda, it was simply not relevant. I had only one concern: to regain my health, my confidence, and the feeling that I was 'like everybody else'. The fact that in one significant way I was no longer behaving 'like everybody else' (or rather like I had always assumed other people behaved) almost went unnoticed, until one day I realized that I had been sexually inactive for several months. Now that I was becoming physically healthier, I found to my great surprise that I did not immediately want to rush back into a sexually active life.

Up to that point, I had regarded myself as 'sexually inactive' but not as 'celibate', as I had neither chosen my situation, nor at that stage did I identify with it. As I emerged from the illness I became more self-conscious and intentional. Slowly, as I discovered there were many advantages that I had never guessed, I began to perceive myself as 'celibate'.

Becoming celibate, though not initially through a conscious choice, brought about a substantial change in the way I viewed myself and the world. I had an extraordinary, somewhat alarming, sense of personal space. As I was living alone, also for the first time in my life, this feeling was intensified. I missed being part of a family, I missed not having teenagers around, but I became aware of entirely new and delightful experiences. I was not servicing anyone. I was not compromising my sense of self in order to sustain a partnership. I was able to do what I wanted when I wanted. I could fit meals in around my work; I could even have them on a tray in front of the television, rather than at the familiar family dining-room table. I was able to devote more time than in the past to my friendships with other women. From the age of twenty, I had lived for years at a time with one sexual (and domestic) partner after another, always being seen and seeing myself as part of a sexually active couple. This had the advantage of making me feel emotionally secure, but the disadvantage of increasing my dependence both on that kind of domestic unit, and on sex itself. Suddenly I felt more independent, more able to use my own resources. I had a new kind of energy. Where might it lead? I had no idea. All I knew was that I no longer lived partly through someone else, nor did I constantly need the approval of the person with whom I was in a sexual relationship.

I was lucky in one respect. At the time of my illness and for some considerable time afterwards my current lover totally understood the new needs my ill-health imposed. At first I was worried, even embarrassed, about saying that I had no energy or couldn't cope with making love. However, with only the most undemanding of discussions, we set about translating our relationship from a sexually active one into an affectionate celibate intimacy that made me feel constantly supported.

Many women who are in sexual relationships are not as fortunate as this when they decide to make such a transition. They often feel guilty or distressed about the effect their newly chosen celibacy will have on their lovers, who in turn may feel rejected or disturbed or may become actively hostile. This was only one of the many difficulties I explored with the women who were making celibate choices. I recorded their reasons for this choice, their understandings and their definitions of celibacy, and their descriptions and the meanings they fixed to what many called their 'celibate sexual practice'.

In this book I am trying to work with categories defined by women for women. The book makes every attempt to encourage women to examine socially conditioned beliefs and feelings about 'what is feminine' or 'what is sexual', with a view to rejecting what fosters dependency, and restricts maturity, and considering new ideas that may promote autonomy.

I am working within parameters where women are still socialized to view only certain attitudes or feelings (both sexual and social) as appropriate. We are still educated towards roles that are labelled 'separate but equal', but in practice are separate and subordinate. This double-bluff cultural system is another function of the genital myth, which uses dominant-subordinate bedroom politics to maintain inequality even at the most intimate level.

Because my own personal socialization, through a variety of experiences such as marriage, separation, divorce, motherhood, single parenting and co-parenting, has been, at various times and stages, Jewish, lesbian, feminist, middle class, Western and white, this inevitably offers me a limited (and in some ways contradictory) perspective on the issues that I raise. Therefore I do not claim that this book offers resources for black women's growth in the sexual or political area, but I hope there will be something of interest they might wish to take up. When I use the word 'women' in the book, it predominantly reflects the experience of white, working-class and white, middle-class Western women.

I talked at length both to women who had made a positive choice to become celibate and to the large category of women who did not see celibacy as a choice at all. Widows and divorcees for instance found themselves forced into a sexually inactive situation, often for years. Some who found this sad or hard, looked quickly for sexually active replacements. Often it was companionship they sought. Someone to tell the day's news to. But they were accustomed to thinking that sex was a necessary part of the companionship package. Others who fell into a celibate state quite by accident blossomed within it, and very gradually came to decide that this was to be their preferred lifestyle. Some women who were feminist, formerly heterosexual or formerly lesbian, now felt celibacy was the way forward for political progress.

Some women were celibate because they were interested in emotional growth. Others were celibate out of spite. Some women wanted autonomy. Others wanted to get back at men. Some women were lyrical about celibacy. Others had a deep hatred of sex. One woman felt celibacy had literally saved her soul. Another woman felt she had been drowning in a world corrupted by sexual need, sinking under the demands made upon her exhausted body.

Several women used an analogy of witchcraft to explain their relationship to sex or celibacy. One woman felt sex had turned her into a witch:

'I felt like an old crone. I felt like I'd had it. I kept babbling these words. I didn't want to do it. He kept making me do it. But it's like I was a witch with a useless broomstick. It was kept in the cupboard. All I used it for was sweeping leaves from the garden or the children's toys off the kitchen floor. When I'd done that it was time for sex again. In the end I had to get it out and fly away.'

Two women felt that it was celibacy which gave them witch-like powers. One woman said: 'When I was married and doing it all the time, I never had any power at all. Now I'm like a white witch with all my power inside me ready to spring out.'

The other woman said: 'I'm celibate and I live in a community of women, and we have this magic, like good witches have, no matter what people say about us, we have this power between us to strike back.'

Germaine Greer suggests that if the world has dubbed you a crone, you might as well be one. Witches are descended from the sibyls and female saints, their lineage is noble and no woman need be ashamed to call herself a witch. She stresses that there is no point in growing old unless you can be a witch and accumulate spiritual power in place of the political and economic power that has been denied you as a woman.[12]

Spiritual power was indeed what many celibate witches were attempting to find within themselves.

Whatever their reasons for taking on celibacy, none of the women felt any need to carry on as consumers of sex. By kicking against the politics of purchase, all of them knew they were out on a limb. Most accepted that they risked punishment and stigma. So why were they doing it? Why were they running that risk? There were high-minded reasons and low-minded reasons. This book explores them all. It traces women's moves from heterosexual activity to celibacy, or from celibacy to lesbianism, or from lesbianism back to celibacy. It records women's feelings about passion, the nature of desire, friendship and intimacy, as well as looking at history and literature to provide alternative meanings for celibacy and a context for contemporary women's disorderly celibate behaviour.

Many of my ideas have grown out of and have been changed by what women have told me. One group of women to whom I have been listening during the two and a half years' research, are single and live alone. These are the women who see as central to the idea of celibacy the critical notion of singleness, of not being in any kind of sexual relationship.

A second group, who also adhere to this idea that celibacy implies not living in a couple, choose to live with friends, former female or male lovers, or with relatives. A third group, who have decided to opt for celibacy whilst staying within the structure of a relationship, live with husbands or long-term partners and conduct a celibate lifestyle within these partnerships.

The fact that these women consider that their celibacy is part of their sexuality, and is not antipathetical to it, nor outside of it; the fact that most of the women whilst explaining why they have chosen, or why they may choose, not to be sexually active, emphatically insist that they are 'sexual', invites us to reassess the way we perceive and label women's sexuality.

Those outside, who ardently subscribe to the genital myth, have long labelled celibate women 'asexual'. Today many 'insiders' who have taken on the identity of 'a celibate woman' are redefining their behaviour as essentially sexual. Although there are differences between the women who fall into a group I have termed Ascetic Celibates, who eschew absolutely and totally any form of genital intimacy and most physical sensual expressions, and those I have termed Sensual Celibates, for whom touch is not taboo, masturbation is enjoyed, hugging, embracing and affectionate intimacy are prioritized, nevertheless, both groups see their celibacy as part of their sexuality, and see themselves as sexual beings who do not need sexual activity with men or other women to feel that way. These women are attempting to forge new definitions, outside the genital myth, of what 'being sexual' means to women.

If celibacy can be seen and talked about as a form of sexuality even when what celibate women 'do' can in no way be described as *sexual activity* (in the current terms in which that phrase is used), then a philosophical change has occurred in women's understanding of the word 'celibacy'. That it can include masturbation, intimate touching, and a high degree of physical affection, but that it is not about relating to other people, and that it focuses on women's personal development, illustrates a cultural shift in the way celibacy is perceived. In the area of sexuality, women are breaking new ground, linguistically, philosophically and practically.

It is not easy to come up with new definitions. The genital myth ensures that sexual pressure on women affects all areas of their lives. Women have been socialized to expect that the knowledge that someone is having or not having sex or making love with someone else will affect the value placed on the relationship. Many women find it difficult to combat the subtle way that higher values are set on relationships defined as genitally active. Several women outline the problem:

'Acknowledging you are having sex with someone makes it a formal relationship. People start to pay attention. There's higher status.' (Susannah, forty. Scientist.)

'When I've been to bed with a man, friends talk about him in a different way. I'll say "John is my friend." Someone will correct me and say "He's not only your friend now, he's your lover." ' (Marian, thirty-five. Computer operator.)

'Sexual twosomes give you more security. You're more accepted. People treat it more seriously. It's seen as more positive than a non-sexual relationship. When you're describing someone you aren't going to bed with you can fall into the trap of saying "Oh she or he is *just* my friend." So even if the relationship is important, you've diminished it.' (Carol, thirty-two. Shoemaker.)

'It's sex that gives it legitimacy. Turn up at school with a sexual partner and you'll both be listened to. More if the partner is a guy of course. If you turn up with just a buddy, she won't be taken seriously. I'm a single parent and I share my apartment with my best buddy who takes a real interest in my kids and comes to school meetings. I'd like her to participate genuinely but largely they ignore what she says.' (Bessie-Jo, forty-two. Researcher.)

One way the genital myth functions to imprison women is through linking ideas of jealousy and love with genital activity. Several women in their twenties showed how this works:

'Just because you slept with a boy you feel you ought to matter more. Jealousy creeps in. If I'd met a new boy and spent six hours talking to him, even if I'd fancied him wildly, Teddy my boyfriend wouldn't be jealous. But if we'd made love for just ten minutes, even if it was bad and boring, even if I didn't care anything for him, Teddy would go mad. It's naff how we set this value on what we do when we take off our clothes.' (Victoria, twenty-one. Student.)

'If you aren't sleeping with someone you think "Oh they don't fancy me." Then you think "They don't love me." ' (Marie, twenty. Secretary.)

'Me and my best mate Annie decided even though we fancied each other we wouldn't sleep together. She thought sex might spoil our friendship. So we had this celibate thing going but I still worried about whether she really loved me. Not to show love in the usual way by going to bed is hard. It's like sex gets this stamp of approval.' (Caro, twenty-four. Veterinary assistant.)

Relationships defined as genital, in Carol's words 'are more accepted', are 'seen as more positive', are given Susannah's 'higher status', have Victoria's 'value' set upon them, and receive Caro's 'stamp of approval'. As Bessie-Jo summed up: 'It's sex that gives it *legitimacy*.' This is the key word.

I know from my own experience how much one can *want* that legitimacy, how hard it is to think outside our sexual framework in order to set a significant value on celibate associations. It is often difficult to believe that someone 'really loves you', as Marie says, if the two of you are not making love as part of that relationship.

There was a time, some years ago, when my closest and most important relationship was with my friend Jordan. We had made a mutual decision not to become lovers for a variety of seemingly sane and rational reasons. At that stage four other people were important in Jordan's life. I knew that over the years, at some time or another, every one of the four had been Jordan's lover. I had not been. Irrationally, stupidly, intermittently, I was jealous. Sometimes Jordan and I would be out drinking, or sharing a meal, and I would hear the words: 'You are unbelievably important to me, I need you in my life. I do love you, you know.' Sanely and rationally I did know. But there were moments, in the middle of the night, when I would lie awake, worrying and agonizing: How *can* I be that important, how can I know I am loved, if we are not making love? My mind would struggle with the question, over and over as the hours dragged by. It was all I could do not to voice it out loud. My thinking was operating within the mental set of the genital myth. Even today, in the face of outside pressures that insist that genitally active lover-relationships are more valuable than non-genital ones, I have to keep reminding myself that within a newly developing feminist sexual-celibate framework, women can love and be loved, value and be valued, as much as or more than in traditional genitally focused relationships.

However, as I have discovered, celibate women today have a more complex rendering of the term celibate, than merely 'non-genital'. For Ascetic Celibate women, the term celibacy does not include genital intimacy, however for some Sensual Celibate women, as we can see from the interviews, it may occasionally do so, without, in their viewpoint, distorting or destroying the ideal of celibacy.

If the issue of celibacy is timely because a reassessment of women's sexuality is crucial, it is also timely for a more disturbing reason. In what has become popularly and disturbingly known as the era of AIDS, when this medical condition whose results are a range of illnesses is regarded as a single disease of 'epidemic proportions', is frequently described as a 'plague' or an 'invasion' so that the stigmatized reputation of the illness adds to the suffering of those who have it, we might expect celibacy to be increasingly on the agenda for both women and men. That the consequences of the AIDS prevention propaganda in terms of women's sexual behaviour are as contradictory and complex as the propaganda itself, is one of the interesting paradoxes this study explores.

Against this background we find ourselves faced with another series of controversial questions: is good sex necessary for good health? (This has been one of the most pervasive dogmas attached to the genital myth of recent times.) Or have the increasing variety and frequency of sexually transmitted diseases, culminating in AIDS in the eighties and nineties, acted as a bitter climax to the obligatory orgasm era which preceded those years?

Today the Genital Geniuses of the medical profession, in sex therapy, and in the media, unequivocally assert that it is normal, and above all healthy, for people to enjoy sex. Some of us excitedly endorse this at the points in our lives when we are engaged in a glowing sexual relationship. For that (often short) period of time nothing could seem more magical, nothing could make us feel fitter. But times change; everyday life suddenly has a singular lack of rainbows. We gaze at the object of our sexual frenzy with total bewilderment and a dreadful clarity. Can that wonderful man or woman with whom we made wild love so passionately only five months ago, be the same slob who now leaves dirty underwear in a trail through the bedroom and never has time to wash up?

In any case not everyone receives fervent and lyrical gratification, or any gratification at all, from a sexual experience. The opinion-formers, however, make no allowances for this. As far as they are concerned, the lack of such gratification and pleasure is a symptom of a sexual disorder. Messages on teatowels may assure us that celibacy is not hereditary, but we need that assurance because we are socialized to believe that not enjoying sexual activity is an indication of disease. This socialization is the primary function of the genital myth. The 'patient', possibly suffering from no more than a well-balanced inclination towards a calming measure of celibacy, is told that her malady can be relieved and her deeper self suitably restored to a healthy (i.e. sexual) life, by appropriate medical intervention, by sex therapy, or by psychiatric counselling. Even more prescriptively, the holders of this viewpoint go on to insist that people who are not interested in sex *ought* to be treated by such means. Means which in many cases are actually abusive and inconsistent with a genuinely healthy stress-free condition.

The pervasiveness of this notion, that interest in sex and men illustrates good health on the part of women, was unexpectedly illustrated for me by one of my conversations with some Canadian nuns. Two of them, working in the community as nurses, to some extent had both internalized this idea.

Sister Anne: 'I was discouraged by my family from entering a convent. I was too alive. I was not the right type for a nun. They thought the right type would be quieter, less interested in going to parties, less interested in going out with guys. You can see I was a really ordinary *healthy* young girl. I wasn't too noisy but I enjoyed life. I went out with guys. I was a healthy young woman.'

Sister Mary: 'In the past, nuns have tried to transform themselves into something they're not. I think we cannot deny our humanity, our womanhood, or that physical expressions of our sexuality are *healthy*. But for the good health of my spirit I have had to work at focusing my love and sexual energy on a lot of people rather than on one person.'

Clearly the genital myth, that promotes the 'good sex equals good health' notion, is alive and well even in convents.

To balance it, here is Sister Claire's view:

> I see sexual desires as both healthy and unhealthy. Sometimes I have felt I have had to examine the feelings that rush up inside me, to see to what extent giving in to a desire is making me grow. I have always recognized and accepted that I do feel sexual desires and I do not want to negate that because I see it as energizing, but what I do with it becomes the issue. How will it affect others particularly in my community? Could it have harmful consequences? These are the issues I struggle with. I never repress the desires I feel, but sometimes I just stay with them, and let them be, and do not act them out if I see that as the healthier way forward.

In a paradigm in which sexual activity, particularly with men, is seen as equalling good health, not acting out sexual desires is rarely seen as 'healthy' – it is perceived, rather, as repressive, which is why purposeful female celibacy suffers from being viewed and treated as a disease.

Several women, whose stories will be heard in a later chapter, reported being treated as 'sick' or 'disturbed' by boyfriends or family when they revealed their decision to become celibate. Women choose to give up sex to improve their psychological well-being. Men find a celibate choice so threatening that they bring in verdicts of mental disturbance. When it comes to the notion of 'good health', looked at through the lens of the genital myth, it is obvious that women themselves are seen by men as incapable of making valid judgements about themselves if celibacy is the issue.

There is another curious paradox. The current creed is that regular continuous satisfaction of the sex urge is a significant sign of fitness, and loss of libido (or abstinence) must be treated as a medical problem. But recent scientific evidence regarding the nature of arousal hormones and their affect on the body, suggests that sexual activity can in fact be stressful to the emotions and harmful to the physical constitution.[13] It could be that celibacy, which creates in the body a condition of calmness, peace and well-being, both physically and psychically, is less of a health hazard than sexual activity. This, however, is a possible line of inquiry heavily suppressed by the genital mythmakers.

Certainly the customary terms in which celibacy is viewed, as frigidity, disability, and abnormality, allow the medical profession and sex educators systematically to misrepresent moral prescriptions and cultural conventions as health facts.

If good sex is posed as salubrious, and a desire for celibacy seen as sick or aberrant, so too is living with someone seen as reasonable and 'healthy' while the desire to live alone is more often seen as the reverse. There are several reasons for this. Most of us spend large portions of our lives linked to someone else, trusting in others for our validation, our self-worth, our emotional stability. That someone else, those significant others, are very often sexual partners. It is hard for women to throw off the notion that we are completed by being attached to another human being. But those women who choose celibacy are doing just that, throwing off, throwing over that very idea. For some women celibacy is literally about *being single*. Living alone. For most women who choose celibacy, it is in some critical sense about *feeling* single. About being able to make decisions for oneself without reference to somebody else; to travel light without sexual encumbrances; to learn a self-sufficiency and to face what may sometimes be a frightening aloneness by trusting in oneself to find the path that one needs.

These are unusual attitudes for women to hold, and may be difficult for people to accept because they are attitudes that threaten the validity of the lives most people choose. Ours is a society where intense emotional dependency on other human beings is encouraged. The dominant viewpoint is that intimate interpersonal relations are the primary source of happiness. People, but more especially women, whose lives and choices run counter to this assumption are viewed with suspicion. Anthony Storr and other psychiatrists have pointed to the two basic drives in humans: one is the drive towards love, intimate connection, and emotional relationships with other people. The second is an opposing one: the drive towards autonomy, independence and separation.[14] Purposefully celibate women do not deny the first drive, but many prioritize the second. Passionate Celibates, in particular women who have creative jobs or who work in professions which demand a high level of dedication, also attach as much fervour and passion to the second drive as most women attach to the first, and appear to gain a great deal from a solitary, autonomous living condition.

If the pleasures of solitude through celibacy are one area to explore, there are other equally critical areas with which celibacy is associated. Indeed it is as a series of linked explorations that I envisage this book. Interesting issues give rise to further questions: Does the power dimension between any two people diminish or change when sexual activity is absent? If women's widely broadcast quest for sexual self-discovery has altered neither society's views nor male privileges, can celibacy alter women's position by changing cultural attitudes rooted in the genital myth? Certainly nineteenth and early twentieth century Utopian American societies, such as the Shakers, the Koreshans, and the Sanctificationists, which used celibacy rather than heterosexuality as their key symbol, saw celibacy as a catalyst for redefining gender identity, for achieving greater social status for women, and for establishing unity and equality between the sexes.

In a later chapter I shall explore whether celibacy is, as these nineteenth century groups believed, a possible means to equal social status for both sexes. This will raise several questions: Firstly, is the goal of 'equality' ultimately one that is productive for women's interests today? Secondly, can celibacy be a relevant response, either symbolically or actually, to some of the key problems twentieth century feminism faces? I see the term 'equality' as it was used in the late nineteenth century, and as it is most commonly used today – that is meaning the equality of women with men rather than autonomy and independence for women – as a problematic notion because it starts from a male-centred universe, in which men are perceived (by both sexes) as the ultimate mediators of social reality, who tell women what is 'normal' and what is not, and who set up a male-defined standard of equality, just as they set up a genital standard of female sexuality. I see it as more useful to start from a woman-centred viewpoint, to discover the ways in which celibacy, for short or long periods, could help women become 'equal' to their authentic autonomous selves.

I shall look at how these new styles of independence, which appear to be by-products of a celibate viewpoint, affect and change the relationships between women and men, and in what ways they contribute to women's creative enterprises or spiritual growth. The exploration starts with the obstacles to celibacy which women are forced to confront, which I have termed genital messages and manipulations, it moves on to the reasons why women should wish to become celibate, looks at varying responses celibate women receive from family and friends, and analyses the relationship between celibacy, chastity, virginity and passion.

Hostile and explosive reactions have been stirred up whenever women have chosen celibacy. Passionate celibates have always been women who disturbed the social order, but there are differences in the nature of the disturbances, differences in the way women in the past defined celibacy from the way women today are defining it, which I shall attempt to extrapolate.

As a working definition of what passionate celibacy means today, I suggest this:

> Passionate Celibacy is a form of female sexuality. It is the choice to be without a sexual partner for positive reasons of personal, political, or spiritual growth, freedom and independence. Passionate Celibacy is a sexual singlehood which allows women to define themselves autonomously, whilst still retaining a network of connections, rather than in terms of another person and his or her needs. It is a form of sexual practice without the power struggles of a sexually active relationship, which is neither maintained by nor supports the genital myth.

In a context of mandatory sexual consumption, in an era of obligatory orgasm, where pressure is put upon all women today not merely to be genitally sexually active, but if possible to be so with men, it is a revolutionary ideal to suggest that women might celebrate celibacy as a genuine sexual freedom, that they might see it as one of their 'rights' to be chosen and enjoyed without justification and without guilt.

Over the last twenty years, through the energy and success of both the second wave of the feminist movement and the gay rights movement, lesbianism has emerged as an allowable option for women, but in the sexual hierarchy which men have created, it is still not seen as a socially desirable choice. Female celibacy is even further down the hierarchical ladder. From the dominant viewpoint it is seen and treated within the same pathology as lesbianism, as something no 'normal' woman would voluntarily choose, as something in need of a cure.

Self-chosen celibacy on the part of women is either ignored as inconsequential or is regarded as a sexual dysfunction instead of, as Thomas S. Szasz describes other sexual acts labelled as illnesses; 'the solution of certain life tasks . . . that is, as the expression of an individual's lifestyle. Or, I would add, of her politics.'[15]

The basic theme of this book, then, is that despite the functioning of the genital myth it is possible for women to have a passion for celibacy, a fact either overlooked or contradicted in our sexually satiated society, whose current orthodoxy is that life without sex and life without men is no life at all.

The basic assertion of this book is that passionate celibacy, currently treated as the impossible possibility, should be viewed in a new light; women who opt for celibacy should have their positive choice in the direction of personal independence and political empowerment validated and approved. If celibacy becomes an approved option for women it will re-interpret what we mean by female sexuality and could also be used effectively in women's struggle against male power.

A second contention is that the negative male definition of celibacy as 'frigidity' or 'puritanism' should be positively redefined, and that this renaming should be extended and enlarged to include the controversial idea that celibacy is a part of female sexuality rather than antipathetical to it, and that celibacy for women is *not* primarily determined by abstention from genital sex.

If self-chosen celibacy for women, which I have termed 'passionate celibacy', becomes incorporated into our ideology as an authenticated option it could expand and change the cultural meaning of female sexuality. It is therefore a third contention of this book that a new understanding and affirmation of passionate celibacy could revise what it means to be female.

CHAPTER ONE

Genital Messages

I sat down at my desk to write the next two chapters. I planned to call this one 'Sexual Messages' and the following one 'Sexual Manipulations'.

In my mind was the recent television version of *The Men's Room*, a serious satirical fable by Ann Oakley about the sexual-social problems of Charity, an eighties' feminist. Nothing serious, but a great deal sexual about the television exploration.

Do I mean 'sexual'? What we got was nothing more and nothing less than *genital*.

For five weeks Harriet Walter as Charity and Bill Nighy as her academic lover rubbed each other's erogenous zones, displaying dangling boobs and erect penis. For five weeks the screen sparkled with the wicked wobbling of bare bums romping, as actors gave out gargantuan gasps and mighty moans. For five weeks audiences were riveted by prime-time porn posing as culture. For five weeks everyone I know watched it fervently.

A serious sexual-social message from one of today's finest feminists? Or a transmission (and distortion) from today's media genital mindset?

Somewhat rattled, I typed the title 'Sexual Messages'.

On my desk is *Cosmopolitan* magazine. The front cover offers in bold red print: 'The new sexual fantasies: domination, control, 15 male slaves and an excited Alsatian.' This is not a yellowing leftover magazine from the decades before feminism revealed what men were up to. This is November 1991, purporting to tell us what women would like to be up to. Inside, Nancy Friday, fantasy queen, tells readers that sexual guilt hasn't disappeared, nor has the rape fantasy, but today women are just as likely to rape men as men are to rape women. (In fantasy of course, not in life. In life they still know what's what.) Fantasy themes include servants and housekeepers, penetrative sex with four men at a time, mixed lesbian-het sex in threes, the roping of ankles and wrists, and a huge dog licking a woman's anus while she straddles her husband and deepthroats the dog's master. Nancy Friday sees these sexual fantasies as a step forward.

A serious British sociological-sexual exploration or a genital media manipulation?

Across the water in France, erotic novelist Alina Reyes, who believes taboos are bad and that women should be able to write about anything, has written about the fantasy copulation of a blood-stained butcher with his 'butcher woman' hanging from the metal hooks in his shop like the other carcasses, and the actual seduction of a girl student apprentice whom he woos by telling her the thrills she can have by being skewered, mauled, chopped and eaten, nothing more or less than a piece of meat under his hands.[1] The book presents sex as depersonalized, lustful, alienating, focused on genitals. The book is billed as a poetic journey of exploration into the mystery of sexuality.

Mystery? Not a lot I am afraid. Most of it is hanging out, blood, guts and all. Sexuality? I leave you to judge . . .

The telephone rings. It is my oldest-friend-in-the-world, Hollywood film maker Davina Belling, producer of such films as *Breaking Glass*, *Gregory's Girl* and the recent smash hit *Other People's Money*, starring ancient sex idol Gregory Peck.

'Hi Sal,' she says enthusiastically. 'What are you up to? What are you writing now?'

I tell her I am working on a book on celibacy. There is a long silence. I ask her what she is up to. She tells me about ancient sex idol Gregory Peck giving this powerful performance in *Other People's Money*. She says warmly: 'Tell me what your book is about.'

I tell her it's all about celibacy. Indeed it's about a passion for celibacy. 'Hmm,' she says. Then she goes into another silence. Finally, in the kind of helpful voice that oldest-friends-in-the-world use, she says, 'Sal, have you forgotten it's SEX that sells, not celibacy?'

I stop wondering whether I'll ever write a book she can turn into a film that will make me the recipient of other people's money, and I type a new title for this chapter: 'Genital Messages' and a new title for the next chapter: 'Genital Manipulations'.

We appear to live in a sexual society, but it is not genuinely sexual, because a truly sexual society offering free choices for both women and men would be threatening to the power elite. What we live in is a genitally-fixated society which communicates messages to women that change with the times to serve the social order. These are what I call 'genital messages'. Men's prescriptions of what is feminine, what is sexy, dictate women's sexual behaviour. At different times women are said to be hot mamas, swinging chicks, or frigid bitches. At no time can a woman freely choose to be celibate as a form of sexual behaviour, because at no time has a woman freely been allowed to choose her own mode of sexual activity. Men have always outlined what is proper, decided what is desirable. Despite the changes from place to place, time to time, there appear to be two constants: firstly women's sexuality is seen either as dangerous to men or as demeaning and trivial; secondly a competitive dualism has been attached to women's sexuality. Women have been portrayed either as mothers or virgins, with no desires, or as whores with overwhelming desires.

The role of culture leads us to choose some sexual acts (hetero-sexuality for example) by praise or reward, and to reject others (homosexuality) by scorn, or condemnation. So individual sexual acts like kissing or oral sex have to be understood in terms of the prevailing codes of meaning. This means there is often a gap between women's lived sexual experience (what women do and like doing) and constructed social reality (what women are told we *should* do and *should* like).

Women's sexual options are transmitted through a series of genital messages via advertising, films, videos, television, radio, pop songs, magazines, newspapers and confessional literature; but women's sexual choices are constrained and controlled by a set of geni-tal manipulations. The manipulations are manifestations of power constricting the lives of women. They include the power of language, the power of access (which includes control of the media), the power of violence (which regulates women's sexual and social behaviour), the power of labelling (depicting sex as healthy, celibacy as mental illness, women as prudes), the power of definition which allows geni-tal mythmakers to construct heterosexuality as normative, orgasm as obligatory, penetration as popular, and to set up intercourse as the most important sexual activity. All these genital manipulations occur within and as a legitimate part of a pornographic culture.

In the past, genital manipulations persuaded people to look on sex as a disease; today a new set of genital manipulations means we look on sex as a cure or a treatment.

In the Victorian era genital manipulation set up the double standard by which men were allowed to be unfaithful whilst women were
constrained to be chaste. Genital messages said that masturbation
caused mental disorder, sexual activity in 'good' women was a disease, good women who did not have sexual feelings suffered sex for
the sake of their marriages, whilst 'bad' women who had tumbled
from pedestals of purity to the impure pit of prostitution kept good
marriages intact. Dutiful 'ladies' did not have or at least did not
admit to having sexual fantasies; gentlewomen were expected to be
passionless and modest; romantic friendships between women were
approved often because their sexual possibilities were denied; sex for
women was about lying back and receiving the vigorous embraces of
those whom Charlotte Brontë called 'the highly uninteresting, narrow
and unattractive specimens of the coarser sex'.[2]

In the late twentieth century new genital manipulations have
turned these ideas upside down. A consumer society is better
served by women who are sexually available, sexually adventurous
(within prescribed limits) and sexually insecure. Genital messages
do not merely suggest that sex is good, healthy and fulfilling, they
indicate it is healthier if it is with men, and they persuade us it is
compulsory. Passionate friendships between women for example,
no matter what their basis, can be labelled 'lesbian' and run the
risk of stigma. The genital message about celibate relationships is
one of loneliness, oddity, and error. Celibacy in our society speaks
of failure. As a sexual state it is trivialized.

The pressure towards compulsory genital sex began to accelerate
in the sixties, during what is usually called the Sexual Revolution or
the Era of Sexual Liberation. It was the time when the pill provided
more reliable contraception, when the social effect was felt, first of
the Kinsey report, later of Masters and Johnson's studies, and when
Alex Comfort's The Joy of Sex was top of the bestseller list.[3]

The sexual liberationist philosophy that said sex was a drive
requiring constant expression for healthy living, and celibacy was
symptomatic of sexual repression, caught on and spread rapidly.
Women were encouraged to turn out and turn on in the wildest
positions and with the weirdest partners. Wife swapping, orgasm
improvers, and sex games at parties became the norm.

The era brought, of course, some benefits but not necessarily the
ones commonly claimed. By 1966 ten million women in different
countries were estimated to be on the pill, which at least promised
if it did not instantly provide an important separation between sex

and reproduction.[4] Women could have intercourse without the threat of unwanted pregnancies. Kinsey's research, based on what eighteen thousand women and men said about their sex lives, showed that there were such variations in sexual behaviour that many sexual practices previously believed to be abnormal were now regarded as ordinary. Masters and Johnson, who studied the physiology of orgasm using measuring equipment and film, discovered that contrary to traditional beliefs that men's arousal differed from women's and that women's orgasms had to be achieved vaginally, the facts were that fundamental theories of sexual arousal and orgasm were the same for women and men, but that it was a woman's clitoris not her vagina which was the source of her arousal and the transmitter of her orgasm.[5]

There were however less liberating matters relating to this genitally fixated period. A big disadvantage of reliable contraception was that women no longer had a justifiable excuse to refuse unwanted sexual advances. The removal of the threat of pregnancy meant coercive sex became more frequent. There were also problems with the pill itself as escalating evidence demonstrated dangerous side effects. The mania for multiple relationships began to produce a new array of sexually transmitted diseases whose full impact did not surface until the eighties with AIDS, which may perhaps in these difficult sexual years persuade men to explore 'safe sex' and intimacies other than penetration which are an essential and enjoyable part of women's sexuality.

Masters and Johnson's second study *Human Sexual Inadequacy* suggested that many partnerships and marriages were severely sexually dysfunctional and were in need of correction. Women who could not or did not orgasm were offered a two-week rapid sex therapy course by Masters and Johnson with the use of replacement partners if the woman's own partner was diffident about accompanying her.[6]

When a certain kind of sexual behaviour is designated a disease and another kind of sexual behaviour is looked upon as a correction or cure, we are no longer in the realm of sexual freedom, we are in the arena of sexual oppression.

Masters of manipulation have managed successfully to portray the sixties as a time of freedom for women, when in fact it was not freedom as such but freedom to have more sex more often provided it was pointedly directed towards male pleasure, relentlessly supported male domination and kept women in submissive roles. It gave men more access to women's bodies, it justified male promiscuity and power, and it encouraged a separation between body and emotion, or sexual behaviour and loving feelings. It may have been male sexual liberation, but for women it must more aptly be named Genital Appropriation.

That era had two significant characteristics: firstly women were encouraged to find their eroticized subordination exciting, and secondly there was no freedom for women to withdraw from sex. Those are the genital messages that have stayed with us until the nineties.

Much of modern Western literature offers sexually active experience, and subsequent frank confession, as the ultimate goal of women's lives. Male genital mythologists like Norman Mailer, Harold Robbins, Henry Miller, and female imitators like Erica Jong portray women as sexual objects ripe for exploitation. More radical modern novelists offer autobiographical sexual disclosures which, despite recent changes in women's social and political lives, still show women primarily in relation to their sexual history. Initially it was male writers who depicted women in this way in relation to men. More recently lesbian and feminist writers have shown women relating in a similar sexually confessional mode to other women. In much of this body of revelatory literature, women are seen as sexual types who are not considered 'real' or 'fulfilled' until they 'come out' sexually. A major theme is that women must depend on someone else for their happiness. Sexual activity becomes the means by which women are further imprisoned in non-autonomous roles.

On a practical and pragmatic level, restrictive sexual dependence on men means that the two sexes do not see each other as people but merely as sexual partners or enemies. Two women in a similarly circumscribed sexual situation may be equally blinded to each other's full human potential. At present women can be coerced into sex by the unjust workings of the law, by custom or other people's attitudes. Where women do not have the freedom of choice to engage in sex, a distressing degree of emotional alienation may result. The consequences of sexual activity under coercive conditions can be feelings of grief, rejection or anger. For these women celibacy could be a positive option, but it is not one that is freely offered. For women to give up sexual activity in favour of celibacy is a mighty decision by which they risk stigma and disapproval.

This then is the background for our current compulsory sexual climate in which several significant genital messages are transmitted:

Sex as Genitally Fixated
Sex as Compulsory
Sex as a Commodity
Sex as Power
Sex as Violence
Sex as Conversation
Orgasms as Obligatory
Intercourse as 'Normal' and as the correct form of sexual expression
Masturbation as good, but as a mere substitute for penetrative sex
Sexual partners as more valuable than friends
Youth as Sexy. Middle and old age as 'past it'
Sex as Performance, Technique, Method
Fantasies as Vital

The idea that sex is a commodity is central to the genital myth. Women are sold the idea that we can all buy into it if we are the right shape and weight. This has the consequence of making women see sex in material and consumerist terms, which omit the spiritual or emotional facets to sexual expression which are of great importance to many women. It has created anxiety about our bodies and the artificial construction of eating disorders such as bulimia and anorexia which are literally killing off young women and maiming the self-esteem of women of every age.

Advertising and the communications industry support and maintain the existing sexual orthodoxy of sex as consumerism. Marketing requires sexually obvious areas of women's bodies to be accessible. Images of women who appear to be available for sexual activity are used to sell products. In this way sexuality is heavily constructed to work efficiently for consumerism and industry. Celibacy inevitably has less marketing value. Women's behaviour, once directly controlled by state, church and family, is now indirectly controlled by the media through organized visual ideals of womanhood disseminated by photography, film and television.

The notion of sex as performance comes from viewing sex through a male lens that restricts sexual pleasure to a narrow focus on genitals, and leaves women's minds and emotions alienated. The ethos of obligatory orgasms has offered the media an opportunity to create another kind of sexual nervousness. 'Am I doing it right?' 'Am I doing it enough?' have become depressing refrains. The predominance of orgasm is seen as crucial to heterosexual sex and important in some

kinds of lesbian sex, so that the phrase 'Did you come?' is enough to
jolt many women into a state of anxiety. The tyranny of the orgasm
has had especially serious implications for lesbians because lesbian
sexual desire is not the same as heterosexual desire and where this
particular pattern *has* been mirrored it has generated feelings of
failure and rejection where none need have occurred. For celibates,
a society with an emphasis on intercourse and orgasm means that
cuddles and hugs, the areas of affection open to celibate women,
are rarely represented in female images, unless they are locked into
motherhood.

Sex as violence, where an act of power such as rape is portrayed
as an act of sex, and sex as power, where because of the power
dimension constructed within every sexual relationship, there is an
inherent inequality, are two genital messages that affect all of us.

Regardless whom we make love to, all sexual activity (bisexual,
lesbian, heterosexual) takes place in the context of an inevitable
power relation in which men are perceived as dominant and women
as submissive. This perception colours how we all behave sexually
even when we do not want it to. Against that context we make
love, and we discover a second power dimension, fed and nurtured
by the vulnerability we feel when we are skin to skin, not always
and not necessarily heart to heart or mind to mind. It is as if lying
naked, skin to skin, is enough to make us feel vulnerable. Whether
we enact our wildest fantasies or dare to admit our most dangerous
dreams, we open ourselves up, we cry, we scream, we explore our
own and someone else's body, we break down barriers. Such ways
of behaving ought to make us feel equal in each other's eyes; ought
to make us interdependent, even independent. But sex strangely does
none of these things. It drives some of us back under the duvet when
the outrageous or mindblowing acts are over. Some of us withdraw,
hostile and aloof, from those we said we loved. Some of us fall
into an addictive situation of emotional dependency or frightening
sexual need. We feel able to make claims, to assert rights; we do
not generally feel equal. What we cannot help but do is absorb the
messages of our genital culture.

To examine how this message of Sex as Power works in practice,
and to illustrate why celibate women are trying to find a different
way, I have chosen three passages, one describing lovemaking
between a man and a woman, one between two women and one
between two men. The first is from novelist Jenny Diski's *Nothing
Natural*.

Rachel, thirty-one, a realist, independent, lives alone, prefers to keep sex and emotions apart. She meets Joshua at a supper party, and is warned by friends of his preference for one night stands. She invites him to supper. The meal is ready as he arrives.

" 'We can eat in a few minutes,' she said.

'I'm not very hungry. It'll keep won't it?' "

Rachel feels cross, her schedule for the evening was being disrupted by this male stranger. 'Were they then going to fuck before dinner?' she wonders? She had planned a leisurely meal and then perhaps . . . Joshua has other ideas. He starts asking her about her fantasies as she finishes the preparations. For some reason she feels impelled to tell him the truth.

" '. . . someone, a man comes through my window while I'm asleep in bed. He, well, he ties me to the bed, he's very strong, and he rapes me . . . Something like that.' "

Joshua looks at her then ask quietly:

" 'Has anyone ever tied you up in real life?' "

Rachel tries to laugh off the situation and says:

" 'Shall we eat? I'll make the dressing for the salad.' "

As she mixes the salad dressing he comes into the kitchen and says:

" 'What a conventional girl you are. I didn't come for dinner and I couldn't care less about eating.' "

He comes up behind her and lifts her dress, his fingers stroking her bare thigh and moving up to feel her crotch.

> Rachel worked on at the already well-amalgamated dressing . . .
> Joshua said, 'Bend over the table.'
> His voice was calm but firm, he was giving an order . . . He delicately edged her knickers down using the tips of his thumb and forefinger . . . He stroked each buttock gently then slipped his finger between her legs and stroked her clitoris until it was wet. Suddenly he began to smack her, short, sharp slaps, pausing for a second between each. Six, eight smacks, hard enough to make her draw in her breath.

Rachel asks herself why she is letting something happen that is straight out of the pages of a smutty magazine.

> But the part of her that wasn't watching was arching her back, lifting her buttocks to receive each smack as it came.
> 'That's right. That's a good girl' . . . 'Now arch your back

more. Lift your arse.' . . . Another series of smacks, this time
very hard, Rachel crying out a little with each one. Then he
opened his zip and pushed his erect penis against the cleavage of
her buttocks.
  'Where do you want it?' he demanded . . .

Rachel refuses to say though she knows what he wants.

  'Where?' he repeated angrily.
  'Do what you want.' She wanted him to just take her. She
wanted him.
  'I said where? Do you want my cock in your cunt or your arse?'
Very angry, icy cold.
  'Oh, please . . . in my arse . . . in my arse.'
  He . . . began to push into her. She cried out in pain, it hurt,
really hurt as he probed deeper and deeper. She felt a sudden urge
to shit and cried against it and then he was fully inside her and she
felt her muscles relax . . . She groaned from somewhere in the back
of her throat . . . She felt everything: violated, released, hugely and
darkly excited . . . She was angry and rendered helpless, wanting
this more than anything . . . it was as though he had got home, and
was where finally, he belonged . . . he touched her clitoris and she
came in long broken moans, on and on until suddenly she hissed
explosively through clenched teeth,
  'Bastard!'
  And again,
  'Bastard!'

Joshua orgasms then pulls out of Rachel who is lying over the
kitchen table.
  " 'Let's eat,' Joshua said, quite composed, his voice cool and
amused, a small, ironic smile playing around his mouth."[7]

Rachel's rape fantasy is women's characteristic internalization not
merely of male fantasies in this culture but of the acted-out male
reality. Violence is an everyday part of sex, as she finds out before
dinner. Joshua's lack of interest in Rachel's supper plans is as casually
overbearing as his dismissal of Rachel as a person. It is not enough
for him for this woman to act submissively, he needs her to tell him.
'Where?' he repeated angrily. Only when she says, 'Oh, please . . . in
my arse . . . in my arse.' is he satisfied. Rachel's feelings of violation,
of being 'rendered helpless' could as easily come after being sexually
abused, as after what is termed a piece of lovemaking. Sex as power

is rendered in literary terms as 'darkly excited'. Rachel is right: this scene is straight out of the pages of a smutty magazine but written in painful, energetic prose it was hailed as a brave exploration, as impressively insightful, as courageous and compelling. The story of one woman's collaboration with her own sado-masochistic degradation is certainly troubling. Perhaps the most troubling part of it is the extent to which as a book about relationships between women and men it leaves us respect for neither.

The power dimension in sexual relationships does not necessarily disappear with relationships between people of the same sex. How we rewrite our sexual histories is another way we illustrate that play of power. Take for example a scene from Kate Millett's fine autobiographical novel *Sita* about her love affair with the woman of that name.

Kate leaves her loft in New York to rejoin Sita, her ex-lover, a woman older than herself, in Sita's house where they had once lived and loved, a house now taken over by Sita and her grown-up children. Kate, her marriage broken, an attempted suicide behind her, leaves her solitary writer's life for a woman who patently is no longer interested in a sexual relationship with her. Sita is making a highly successful life without her. Sita does not ask her to come, 'was punctillious about that, keeps reminding me how she never insisted I come'. Kate goes anyway, an addict for the pain that is to follow, masochistic with unfulfilled desire, living on memories of yesterday's love.

'Came to her now in January, knowing that I was helpless . . . couldn't get away.' Kate, no fool, recognizes immediately 'already it was wrong'. Their first weekend together, even before they reach the house, is 'a downer'. She acknowledges 'making love was not what it had been in New York . . . We had even been afraid to start . . . Rushed out and bought a bottle of champagne, postponing it . . . And the thing perfunctory almost when it happened.' They who 'had once been such lovers, so hot, so intemperate'. Poor Kate had wanted to make love all afternoon in that hotel which had once been the scene of their most ardent lovemakings. Now in this 'disappointing little room' where Sita hurries, anxious to be away, anxious to get back to her new life, Kate appalled by the 'dismaying absence of romance this weekend' knowing she is no longer the passionate idol of Sita's life, chooses to remember one curious occasion in that hotel in the past. It had been when Sita, the arrogant, powerful, competent, University administrator who had always held the purse and the power strings, had, for once, broken down. She had been frightened and anxious at the thought of a job interview the following day. Kate recalls 'how she wept and shivered before the fire . . . lovely in the naked brown skin of her body . . . crying . . . afraid they'd hire her, afraid they wouldn't . . . Her body shaking in my arms.' Kate admits that there were a 'thousand Sitas' all of them assured, all of them poised, all of them powerful, whom she might have remembered. But she chose to dwell on the memory of this 'lost and terrified woman rocking naked before a fire'. Kate, now at Sita's mercy, comforts herself by recalling 'I comforted her, I listened, I reassured.' On that occasion Kate had been in charge; Kate had been the one with power. It is necessary for her to know that on the day she recognizes she has now lost it. As Kate thinks back, and wishes Sita would come back to bed for a 'leisurely exploration' in the two hours before check-out time, Sita says exasperatedly: ' "Why did you wait till now to suggest it? I've long since lost interest. I'm ready to go." '

Many of us will find this scene painfully reminiscent. Did we act like Kate? Try to restore the balance of power by rewriting sexual history, or putting an emphasis on some events rather than others? There is nothing quite like a bitter re-run of the past, when present love is indisputably waning, to bring out the power dimension in a sexual relationship, and Kate Millett writes it to perfection.[8]

The third episode of 'love' between two men, comes from Alan Hollinghurst's *The Swimming Pool Library*. Our man of passion is William, a young white aristocrat who leads a life of privilege and promiscuity. Among his privileges is the attainment of seventeen-year-old pigtailed Arthur, his eager black lover, whom he had met on a dance floor the night before. William was part of that 'tiny proportion of the populace that indeed owns almost everything.' Unemployed Arthur comes from Stratford East where he has just killed his brother's mate, after which brother Harold unsurprisingly attacks him with a knife. These two very different and unequal social worlds serve to increase William's secret sexual pleasures. He keeps the boy a secret from his peers and assures readers he was 'certainly sentimental with Arthur, deeply sentimental and lightly brutal, at one moment carelessly attentive, the next glutting him with sex, mindlessly – thoughtlessly. It was the most beautiful thing I could imagine – all the more so for our knowledge that we could never make a go of it together.'

So sentimental is he about Arthur, that when bored he slips away and spots 'a lone Arab boy wandering along', and decides he must have him. 'I felt a delicious surplus of lust and satisfaction at the idea of fucking him while another boy waited for me at home.'

When he discusses Arthur with his doctor friend James, first it is his lover's mind he condemns: 'He's no Einstein, I grant you . . . We have a kind of baby talk – except all the words are rude . . .' Then it is Arthur's member he dismembers. When James asks what Arthur's penis is like, William says, 'Not your kind of thing, perhaps – short, stocky, ruthlessly circumcised, and incredibly resilient and characterful.'

His patronizing appraisal of his lover leads him to admit he couldn't be in love with him because 'We couldn't sit down and listen to *Idomeneo* and feel a deep spiritual bond. It must just be an infatuation.'

The quality and inequality of this infatuation becomes more blatant and focused when Arthur, having committed murder, retreats to William's house to hide. 'As soon as the new terms were forced upon us . . . he must have felt as much as I did a sinking of the heart at our incompatibility,' says William.

Yet there they are, a young black man on the run, a white aristocratic protector, uneasily trying to find a unity through sex. What they discover is that William has 'spells of repugnance, both at him and at my own susceptibility. Sex took on an almost purgative quality . . . Sex came to justify his presence there, to confirm that we were not just two strangers trapped together by a fateful mistake.'

Yet that is indeed what they are, strangers in an unequal power relationship, becoming more trapped into roles of master and slave. Inevitably the sex begins to mirror this. William says: 'I saw him becoming more and more my slave and my toy, in a barely conscious abasement which excited me even as it pulled me down.' Predictably in self hatred and arrogance William finally goes for him. With brutality and pain he 'fucked him cruelly'. Arthur the willing victim 'let out little compacted shouts of pain, but I snarled at him to shut up and with fine submission he bit them back.' Then pink with excitement, horror and pleasure, William admits he is both disgusted by Arthur's need of him and moved by the sexual power it gives him.'

The book hailed as a cross between pastoral romance and sulphurous confession, said to be erotic, erudite and accurate about the sexual rapture of male gay life, gives a credible rendering of the way men eroticize feelings and activities in which one partner is powerful and the other powerless. If men believe there is splendour and erudition in this sadistic coupling between themselves, when the power and powerlessness is only partially institutionalized (between black and white, working and middle class), how much more easily can they believe it and act on it when they have as partners women over whom their dominance is in every respect publicly legitimized.

It is genital messages, such as these sex-as-power transmissions which affect us all every day, from which celibate women are attempting to withdraw. However to do so they need to be conscious of, and find ways to withstand, the genital manipulations which underpin these messages, which are the subject of the next chapter.

CHAPTER TWO

Genital Manipulations

I F genital messages keep celibacy off the sexual agenda and tell women how to behave sexually, it is genital manipulations which underlie and control them. To see how they work I want to look at three of the most significant: the construction of sexual activity, the power of language, and the labelling of mental illness. Then I shall look at the pornographic culture within which genital messages and genital manipulations meet.

Sexual activity

The way in which sexual activity with men, whilst appearing to offer the chance of a passionate and desirable equality at least in the bedroom, actually maintains women's subordinate social position is a particularly cunning manipulation. Through sex with men, a woman can be persuaded to reflect her man, to boost his ego, to believe that her 'beauty' is her sexuality, to compete with other women for male attention. Through sex a woman can be encouraged to become compliant, to be taken care of, to starve herself to a Belsen thinness, to enjoy appearing immature, to seem more helpless than she is on her own or with other women, to accept her low status or to pretend it is not that low. Through sex a woman can be magnetized to believe that love includes force, that rape is not what it seems, that the violent and power-riven context of the world outside in which her individual lovemaking takes place, is somehow separate from her man's sexual behaviour and her own response.[1]

The high success rate of this particularly persuasive genital manipulation can be seen in the low reporting of 'date rape', the deathly intrusion of pornographic images into women's fashion magazines, the near-starvation and terrible side effects suffered through weight loss by more than one tenth of all young American women, and the frightening rise in cosmetic surgery for reasons of 'sexual attractiveness'.[2]

These consequences of the genital myth, which appal us when we stop to think about them, rest solidly on another manipulative foundation: the idea that intercourse leading to orgasm is the most correct and most satisfying sexual activity *for both sexes*.

The manipulation works by romanticizing the act of intercourse as a pursuit which involves women and men equally. Certainly women have always wanted intercourse to be an experience of mutual passion, of equality of pleasure, we have wanted it to be a sensitive or stirring act that fuses two people's bodies and emotions in a sensual or rapturous way. Unfortunately it is rarely like this. Female arousal and female fulfilment may occur from time to time during intercourse, but they are not necessary constituents of a sexual congress based largely on masculine needs and desires. Some women *do* derive happiness from it, often through the knowledge that they are giving their men pleasure. Other women find it a duty. For still more it is an event from which to escape.

What lies at the heart of the manipulation is that no matter what our feelings are during intercourse, acting our part correctly means acting out the subservient female role, for passivity and masochism are symbolically central to it.

Our language mirrors the contradiction between the mutuality set up by the genital myth, and the reality experienced by women. Linguists Cheris Kramarae and Paula A. Treichler observe that, grammatically, polite expressions for what is designated as 'the Act' tend to be symmetrical, giving the impression that what a man does to a woman, a woman likewise does to a man. But their definitions give a different picture. 'Although both male and female genitals are mentioned, the activity is characterized solely in terms of the male responses that constitute it.'[3] Webster's dictionary tells us that coitus is 'the act of conveying the male semen to the female reproductive tract involving insertion of the penis in the vaginal orifice followed by ejaculation.'[4] Our language does not suggest that it is the woman's vagina which actively encloses and contains the man's penis. The act might appear very differently if it did. As it is, there is thrust in one direction only.

As our children used to say when they were teenagers, somewhat more succinctly than Webster's, but making exactly the same point: 'He did it to her!'

When 'orgasm' is similarly defined as 'the climax of sexual excitement typically occurring toward the end of coitus', the language again illustrates that it is only the *male* orgasm that is a necessary condition for sexual intercourse. Women's own experiences sadly confirm this. For most women, seven out of ten according to Shere Hite's studies, intercourse does not cause orgasm.[5] Language, like lived experience, illustrates that 'sexual activity' in its restrictive meaning of intercourse, is an act largely pursued by both parties for the primary pleasure of men. Women who do not achieve orgasmic heights or fulfilment in other ways from it may end up in a state of sexual anxiety, guilt, or distress. Mythmakers have constructed this mode of sexual behaviour to work efficiently for men, but to appear to work beautifully for both sexes. When it does not, it is women who feel they have failed.

The genital myth which insists firstly that orgasms are central to a satisfying life for both sexes, and secondly that women should have orgasms during intercourse, forces women into a situation where their bodies are inadequately stimulated and their minds are coerced. This results in sexual situations of frequent failure, which breeds in women feelings of insecurity, resentment and distress. As Anne Koedt said in her paper *The Myth of the Vaginal Orgasm*:

'Perhaps one of the most infuriating and damaging results of this whole charade has been that women who were perfectly healthy sexually were taught that they were not. So in addition to being sexually deprived, these women were told to blame themselves when they deserved no blame. Looking for a cure to a problem that has none can lead a woman on an endless path of self-hatred and insecurity.'[6]

Anne Koedt's brilliant exposition of the myth about where orgasms were at encouraged hundreds of women to feel less insecure when they received orgasms clitorally but not through intercourse. So far though, nothing has encouraged women who do not want to orgasm at all, who do not want to partake in intercourse, who do not want to involve themselves in any kind of genital expression, who want to try a celibate sexuality, to feel good about themselves.

The manipulative mechanism which establishes orgasm-oriented sexual activity with men as 'normal' and renders non-orgasmic sexual activity, with women, with oneself, *or with no one at all*, as 'abnormal', puts a high value on the sexual behaviour in which men have the most interest.

Twentieth century literature has helped to maintain this manipulation. Within the range of possible heterosexual expressions, an enthusiasm for penetration, which has been explored in full frontal confessional writings by such literary sperm salesmen as Miller, Mailer, Robbins, and both Amises, has ensured that it is intercourse and intercourse alone which is designated as THE sexual activity.

This has the effect of reducing or minimizing the importance of all other forms of sexual behaviour, so for example, non-penetrative heterosexual activity, which may please a lot of women, but perhaps not a lot of men, is regarded as a considerably inferior mode of sexual expression. Lesbian sexual activity which pleases a lot of women and no men is not merely deemed inferior, but deviant. Yet, in the ludicrous genital ranking system assigned to our society, both achieve 'higher grades' than celibacy.

Celibacy challenges the manipulative device of intercourse. Through intercourse a woman learns to be a 'girl', to please a man, to be dependent, to want approval, to expect her happiness to come through a sexual relationship with someone else. Through celibacy a woman learns to control her own life, to take risks, to grow up, to make decisions, to live on her own, to value other women, to see men as possible friends and potential equals not as merely lovers or enemies.

Language

The second significant manipulation is language which we saw playing a critical part in manipulating intercourse. This is skilfully achieved because language is not a neutral means of communication; it transmits values, attitudes, and models of behaviour to all who use it. It is instrumental in maintaining male power within our particular social organization. A word that is female-specific and descriptively destructive such as 'slut' may tell us more about what men think of women than it does about what the word means to women, just as 'fuck' tells us more about men's part in intercourse than it does about women's experience of it.

Excellent research has already demonstrated that man-made language in general operates to exclude, disparage and trivialize women through such mechanisms as universal male pronouns, misogynistic insults (bitch, whore, tart, etc.) and the use of 'girl' instead of 'woman' (in contexts where 'boy' instead of 'man' is never used).[7]

There are however particular linguistic manipulations through which the genital myth works to shackle and reshape women's sexuality in ways that exclude or stigmatize celibacy.

A significant manipulation is the use of *conversation* to reveal and discuss what is deemed important and to conceal and suppress what is constructed as trivial. The genital power elite therefore ensures that everyone talks about sex but nobody talks about celibacy. With the advent of AIDS, people who are slightly more cautious about casual or promiscuous sex, are using as a substitute casually audacious sex-filled conversation. A description of two social occasions at which I was present shows how this operates.

The first social occasion was a birthday party taking place in an Indian restaurant in Cambridge, England, on which I eavesdropped from my seat at the next table. The conversational fare at this particular restaurant usually revolves sedately around the drop in house prices or who is reading what for the Cambridge tripos. This time however it took a decided turn for the raunchy.

As the ten birthday guests got progressively merrier, the revelations became more sexually explicit. Outrage followed outrage. With the starters, the guests counted on their fingers, and each other's, how many people they had slept with, and exactly which positions had been the most fun. Trevor, being the birthday boy, naturally won with a score of thirty-seven, of which, if he was to be believed, twenty-seven encounters seemed to have taken place suspended from garden hammocks, moving punts, and even a wall light.

'Some of you girls couldn't get enough!' he enthused, ogling his female guests. It *was* his birthday so none of the generous-spirited women at the table denied it, though two of them did look up at the ceiling in incredulity.

With the main course, the group moved on to erogenous areas. Bums and assholes (these were the areas not the people) were more popular than nipples and ears. Trevor's girlfriend revealed that she loved nothing better than sliding a hairbrush between Trevor's buttocks, but preferred peaches and cream inside her vagina. When a girl with plaits the others called Boozie Suzie said she had started to braid her pubic hair to match the hair on her head, and that she'd once done it with someone keen on coprophilia I decided to call for the bill. I felt as if I had taken a time trip back to the sixties. I thought by now everyone had given up on peaches and cream as a cliché!

If the noses of the genital mythmakers have been slightly put out of joint by the caution surrounding sexually transmitted diseases, they have retaliated smartly by manipulating an exchange of social promiscuity for sexual promiscuity. Sleeping around may be on the wane in some circles, but conversational orgies, and cerebral fucks appear to have taken their place.

The second gathering was one I attended recently in North America, where the company was middle-aged and mixed. After an excellent dinner, when we were all lounging about in chairs glancing at papers and magazines, I raised the issue of celibacy. People were uneasy with the topic. They shifted about. A married couple asked me discreetly whether the 'disease' only affected single people, glancing covertly at each other as they spoke. Most people ignored the subject. Then a stylish 36-year-old woman revealed loudly that she was celibate. She said she hadn't felt so happy for years. Several older men held newspapers before their eyes as they glanced warily at her. If she had remarked that she had just started simultaneous affairs with the teenage husband and wife team who are her seventeen-year-old daughter's ex-schoolfriends, the whole room would have been alight with curiosity. But confessing to celibacy? Implying she was happy without a man and without sex? Sounding proud? It was nothing less than a social faux pas.

At the time no one responded to her remark, several women smiled nervously, and the hostess, a television executive's wife, adroitly changed the subject. Later, when the self-acknowledged celibate woman had left the gathering, my host, the television executive, said:

'Maisie was always kinda odd you know. Likeable of course. Oh sure, great to have around if you were one short for a supper party, and still quite attractive. But kinda odd.'

'Still' attractive and already thirty-six! Now 'out' as a celibate, and already the label of 'oddness'. Language manipulation is working well. The more *positive* and autonomous the state of celibacy seems, the less space will be found for it on the conversational agenda. What is striking is how frequently we stumble across the *negative* words connected to celibacy, such as 'frigidity' or 'prudery'. These occur in conversations, on radio or TV, they are the subject of lighthearted gossip or serious discourse, they abound in glossy magazines, in literary texts, in reference books, in dictionaries. Celibacy (as applied to women) is noticeably absent.

Women wheeling trolleys in supermarkets or talking to their stylists in hair salons, who can be heard discussing intimate details of hysterectomies, miscarriages and sexual adventures simply do not chat about chastity. I was having my hair cut recently when I overheard the woman in the next chair 'confidentially' telling her assistant about a racy girlfriend who went to a director's dinner with no knickers on and got felt up under the table-cloth between the starter and the soup. But in hairdressing salons or laundrettes (both highly popular places for intimate dis-closures) as indeed everywhere else, celibacy is kept severely under wraps.

Even in Jane Mill's fascinating and scholarly feminist dictionary called *Womanwords* which offers readers three hundred women-related key words, all the derogatory words such as frigidity, prudery etc. are there pinned to the pages in canny and complex detail, but celibacy is not to be found.[8]

In order to explore what it meant in the past and what it means today to be a woman in a patriarchal society, Jane Mills selected a number of key words in a vocabulary to reveal how through the cen-turies radical change and conflict as well as continuity and acceptance have affected women's lives. She explains that she chose those words that best enabled her to explore the history both of changing and relentlessly unchanging attitudes towards women. Yet she left out 'celibacy'.

Celibacy has a rich semantic history which as we see provides some shocking clues to the way the patriarchs view women's sexuality. Celibacy, more than many words, suffers from an un-changing perjorative male interpretation, and yet is currently, even as I write, having its meaning transformed, opened up, and radically overturned by women who are using it positively, and acting it out with courage.

Did Jane Mills think that celibacy was not then a 'womanword'? Or did she unwittingly fall into the next trap set by the genital myth-makers: that in books, as in conversation, female celibacy is to be traced only as a lack, a blank, as something invisible.

In Shere Hite's mammoth report on women in love, although she informs us that celibacy was chosen by 33 per cent of the single women in her study for a period of at least six months after they had been sexually active earlier in their lives; although she hastens to reassure us that almost all the women praised it for the chance it gave them *not* to have intercourse, to take an emotional break, to focus their energy and attention elsewhere, the actual space celibacy warrants in her tome of 922 pages is just three pages.[9]

If allocation of conversational and literary space is one problem, *naming* is another. The genital myth manipulates women's sexuality through language by portraying sexual congress in particular as fulfilling and setting it against celibacy which it names as lacking. Men's constant portrayal of celibacy as a lack is based on their refusal to recognize women's decision to become celibate as anything other than either sexual failure (because the women are not sufficiently 'sexy' to get a man), or as a situation in which the women are waiting and hoping to be penetrated by the next available male.

Let us listen to the men:

'Your sister has decided not to do it anymore? You must be joking! What she *lacks* is a bloke who knows how to fuck her properly.' (Husband to his wife about her newly celibate sister.)

'Mary calling herself "celibate"? Don't make me laugh. We all know what she *lacks* and we all know why. I know she's your friend, love, but no one could call her exactly sexy. She's not going to get any by calling herself fancy words.' (Husband about his wife's friend Mary.)

Many women have internalized this interpretation of celibacy as a lack. Betsy, a literacy campaigner who spends her teaching life looking at word usage, said:

> I do not like using the noun 'celibacy'. I feel the word means a kind of *lack* of something so I never feel good saying it. It would make me feel like I was blaming myself, or that I was deficient. I guess it is because I've heard men use it in that way, so I am left with that impression. However I do use the word 'celibate' as it has an active positive feel. When I say to someone 'I am celibate' the sentence has a calm, confident ring. It is not at all like saying: 'Oh God I'm horny', or 'Oh God I haven't had sex for a week', which are all frustrated, discontented statements. The kind of things men think celibacy means.

Katie, a researcher, said:

> The way men use the word celibacy when they're talking about women, is to set it up against genital sex, probably penetration,

which becomes the standard of what we are all supposed to do and to like doing. I don't like doing it. After a lot of thought, I decided I would stop doing it, and that I would be open about it and tell people. But as soon as I said out loud to my men friends that I'd become celibate, they made me feel I was *lacking* something. Lacking them, lacking their pricks. I hadn't wanted penetration for over ten years. As I couldn't find boyfriends who would be content to make love without penetration, I became celibate. With a few small sexual happenings (a one night stand with a very old boyfriend, a brief sexual romance with a guy my brother knew), just minor interruptions, I stayed celibate that whole decade, and kept my head together, and felt more independent. But I never stopped wondering what was *lacking* in me. Why didn't I feel what I was supposed to feel, what I presumed all my women friends felt?

Years later I found out that lots of them didn't feel like penetration either, and many were utterly uninterested in sex. They just bought it for the companionship. Several times I almost went to a counsellor or a therapist. Thank goodness I didn't. I just stuck it out. The Women's Movement here in Canada helped me to recognize that there is nothing lacking in me. If celibacy could be added to the spectrum of what women can opt for sexually, none of us would feel it as a lack.

Katie's account depicts the general view of celibacy as a lack, but by describing her move into celibacy not only for reasons of dislike of penetration, but also as a need for independence, she reveals that celibacy is about more than genital behaviour. When she says 'I stayed celibate that whole decade and *kept my head together*' we see that celibacy is as much a mental attitude as it is genital abstention. Attached to that is the notion that her 'few small sexual happenings' were seen only as 'minor interruptions' to her celibate state. These sexual encounters in no way caused her to re-evaluate her celibacy.

As well as depicting celibacy as a lack, genital manipulative control of language operates to describe it as a blank, as something that is invisible, or as negative, cold withdrawal.

Again, let us listen to the men:

'Celibate? What do you mean Marjorie has decided to be celibate? What you mean is Marjorie is practically *invisible*. People just don't notice her. That's all that's the matter with her.' (Husband to wife about her newly celibate friend.)

Young girl: 'Becca says she *chose* not to do it with Tom.'

Tom's mate: 'Don't be stupid. Girls can't choose. Becca's just a *blank*. Who'd choose to do it with her anyway?'

'It is no wonder men don't find her attractive, she has such an *icy* stare. I should think even the older boys she teaches find her *frosty*.' (Male comment about a schoolteacher who lived alone and was rumoured to be celibate.)

These examples, characteristic of many that I heard, show some of the ways men perceive a mode of sexuality that is not in their interest. For there to be a change in the asymmetrical classification of the sexes women must begin to reclaim the power of naming. Betsy, the literacy organizer who disliked the word 'celibacy' because it implied a lack, felt that renaming the word out loud would be useful.

'Women are not seen as having choices around sexuality so to say on television or radio loud and bold: "I'm celibate. I love it!" would be a dramatic act of self-determination. I've never heard a woman do it yet.'

What is heard by both sexes are men's voices and male messages. The message is deficiency. The manipulative device is invisibilization.

Prudery

If celibacy as a positive word is invisibilized or rendered deficient through genital manipulatory language, other words connected to celibacy (such as frigidity and prudery) have suffered a distortion, so that their originally strong or even celebratory connotations have become negative or dismissive.

Prude, a label all too often applied to celibate women, is a word that has been drastically and perjoratively reinterpreted from its original meaning. It is a word which has the same origins as 'proud' derived from the eighteenth century French 'prudefemme', meaning an excellent or respectable woman, someone worthy of esteem. Like the English word 'proud' it originated in the Latin 'prodesse' meaning to be of value. Yet historically it has frequently been used in conjunction with the word 'puritanical' which at certain times has had negative overtones.

Unfortunately, when 'prude' first entered English in 1704 (as a direct adoption from the French) it had none of the strong valuable ring of respectability or excellence. Jane Mills points out that it was applied adversely to women who appeared excessively modest or showed an over-propriety of behaviour or speech; women in other words who held themselves back, away from male advances.[10] There were strong implications that such women were affected or prim. Although the word was meant to describe a person of either sex who behaved over-modestly with regard to relations between the sexes, it was more often used negatively to describe women's behaviour. Although in the eighteenth century the ideal of femininity insisted on such characteristics as demureness and decorum, nevertheless the way the word 'prude' was administered, left the woman to whom it was applied looking unappealing and sounding extreme. Rather the way a celibate woman called 'prude' today is made to feel.

In the nineteenth century, genital mythmasters of that era used the concept of the female prude as a key weapon with which to attack feminists and their controversial opinions about men's abusive sexual behaviour. In *The Spinster and Her Enemies*, writer Sheila Jeffreys points out that the word prude was consistently used to threaten and undermine female reformers who savagely criticized men's brutal behaviour.[11]

In the late Victorian period almost one in three of all adult women were single and one in four were unlikely to marry.[12] By 1851 the census showed that there were 405,000 more women than men in the population, which the press chose to describe as 'the problem of surplus women'. This problem caused consternation amongst male commentators who saw celibate spinsters who did not service men as so superfluous to society's needs that they suggested the women should emigrate. While men at that time wanted to get rid of celibate single women because they did not adhere to the genital male values of the day, feminists between 1850 and 1860 aimed at dealing with the fact of 'surplus' women in quite different ways which would focus on and support celibate women's needs. Many of these spinsters made a positive choice not to marry, either because they wanted to pursue a career, or because they regarded marriage, its consequences of dependence, and the sex attendant upon it, as abusive, humiliating, or in extreme cases as a mode of slavery. Other feminists of the time decided not to have sexual relations with men at all. Some of them were shocked at the ways in which women were oppressed by men, others asserted that the status and situation of all women could only improve if society had at its centre a large group of celibate women.

In men's eyes these ideas were nothing short of revolutionary. With feminists suggesting that female celibacy could be a positive measure for women until such time as men's animal nature was transformed, it is hardly surprising that men hit back at such women by terming them prudes.

One women's rights campaigner, Elizabeth Wolstenholme Elmy (who worked alongside Christabel Pankhurst and Josephine Butler to campaign for women's suffrage, higher education for women and the abolition of the Contagious Diseases Acts) came under particular attack. Angered by men's sexual abuse of women and outraged at the way women were reduced to mere bodies by men's obsession with genital sex, she wrote several books and articles suggesting that the ideal form of sexual relations between women and men should exclude intercourse except for brief periods set aside solely for the purposes of reproduction. Men, she said, should exert self-control. 'Psychic love' should replace genital lust.[13] Apart from temporary reproductive periods, Elmy suggested that for the rest of the time a contented fulfilling life for married women, which would be beneficial to both sexes, would be one that was celibate. Male response at the time to Elmy and to the growing band of women who were choosing to live independently and genitally free from men, was to label these political thinkers as prudes in order to dismiss and discount their radical ideology.

Militant writer Francis Swiney, who began to write and publish with prolific passion and rage from the 1890s, believed as did Wolstenholme Elmy, that women's sexual subjection by men lay at the root of women's oppression. She saw women's constant submission to sexual intercourse whenever men wanted it, even at those periods which should be most sacrosanct, such as during pregnancy and immediately after childbirth, as the greatest burden of their subordinate status.[14] Swiney and other radical women saw intercourse as undermining to women's self-respect or to any chance of an equal relationship with men. Like Elmy, Swiney suggested that men should exert self-control over their lustful desires and that, where at all possible, genital sexual activity should be eliminated between women and men. Her considerable influence on the militant wing of the women's movement of her time meant that in her own day she was fiercely denounced by male critics as prudish and extreme. Like Elmy, she has subsequently suffered exactly the same perjorative labelling by contemporary male reviewers who have dismissed her as a crank and a prude.

Modern historians, whose writing and theorizing has taken place during or after the sixties' Genital Appropriation (née Sexual Revolution) are of course subject to modern genital mythology which means they have no familiarity with the notion that a loving and satisfying relationship between men and women *could* exclude sexual

intercourse. Inevitably, therefore, contemporary critics have characterized all those feminists who wrote and campaigned as did Swiney,
Elmy and others, as puritanical prudes, i.e. unfeminine women who
were anti-genital sex, and therefore in male eyes anti-love, even
anti-life.

By the 1920s sexologists and psychoanalysts felt so threatened
by the spinster suffragettes, bluestockings and purposefully celibate
women who were not merely taking to the streets to demand the vote,
but were resisting men's advances back in the bedrooms, that they
widened their manipulative use of the word prude to condemn any
women who spurned heterosexual relationships or who challenged
the nineteenth century stereotype of the feminine angel in the house.

According to influential sexologist Walter Gallichen, author of
The Poison of Prudery (1929), prudes were not merely dangerous
they were also 'diseased', afflicted by severe mental illness.

'The erotically impotent women have an enormous influence
upon the young, the conventions and regulations of society, and
even upon sex legislation. These degenerate women are a menace
to civilization. They provoke sex misunderstanding and antagonism;
they wreck conjugal happiness, and pose as superior moral beings
when they are really victims of disease.'[15]

Prudery here is designated neither as a positive choice nor as
a reasonable reluctance but as impotence, degeneracy, and most
significantly as psychological disease. As we shall see, using mental
illness as a way to deal with the challenge of women's celibacy is
another genital manipulation still in use today. We do not yet live
in a society where women may say 'no' and have their responses
automatically regarded as reasonable and legitimate.

For many men, a woman's 'no' is a stage in a sexual power
game, whose outcome is scheduled, one way or another, to be 'yes'.
If being a prude is to opt for positive choices in the area of sexuality,
then Mary Daly's use of the word 'prude' to mean a woman who is
wise, good, capable and brave, should be taken as a model.[16]

Frigidity

If celibacy-as-prudery is not a sufficiently successful weapon of
control, genital mythmakers can always draw 'frigidity' from their
linguistic armoury.

Like the word 'prudery', the word 'frigidity' too has been negatively manipulated to destroy women's sexual and social confidence.

Genital manipulation is clever in the way it can denigrate whatever women do sexually that is not in men's interests at any particular time. Thus too much sexual response towards too many men, if threatening, can be labelled nymphomania. Too little sexual response to one or more men can on the other hand be labelled frigidity. Neither label is out to boost women's egos. Both are systematically constraining.

The word 'frigid' which comes from the Latin 'frigus' meaning frost, entered English in the late fifteenth century. From the seventeenth century, according to several dictionaries, the term frigid had a primary meaning that was neutral and genderless and could be applied equally to men or women. The Oxford English Dictionary suggests it means merely 'destitute of ardour or warmth of feeling, lacking enthusiasm or zeal, cold, indifferent, apathetic, formal, stiff'.[17] Collins too follows this seemingly neutral line and offers as the primary meaning: 'formal or stiff in behaviour or temperament, or lacking in affection or warmth'.[18]

There is no reason why 'frigid' in this sense could not be applied equally to both sexes. Indeed in 1700 lukewarm, weak or impotent husbands were being defined as frigid.[19] Not any more. Today it is a word rarely applied to men, rarely used with an unproblematic connotation. It has long been used as a term to castigate women who failed at whatever was the shifting feminine standard of the day. By the early twentieth century 'frigid' was not only undeniably female-specific, but also intricately connected to penetrative sex.

Collins dictionary itself points out when offering its secondary meaning that it is used 'especially of women' who are seen to be a) lacking sexual (i.e. heterosexual) responsiveness or b) averse to sexual intercourse, or unable to achieve orgasm during intercourse. Webster's dictionary follows suit by defining it as 'abnormally averse to sexual intercourse – used esp. of women.'[20]

In other words women 'especially' are not performing in ways designated by the genital power elite as 'normal'. When they behave 'abnormally' these apparently 'frigid' women are exhibiting signs of mental disturbance or disease; the same manipulation we saw at work with the word 'prude'.

The invention of the 'frigid woman' which today does not have an equally disagreeable counterpart in the idea of the 'frigid man' (some would say the juxtaposition of 'man' and 'frigid' is laughable) was based on the idea that lack of interest in or lack of pleasure in heterosexual activity could be seen in terms of disease for one sex but not for the other.

As Thomas Szasz points out in his book *Sex: Facts, Frauds and Follies*, 'Failure of the heart, the lung or the liver to perform its function is always considered a disease, in men as well as women. This is not always true for failure of the sexual organs to perform theirs: some such nonfunctions do not count as disease at all, while others may count as disease for one sex but not the other.'

His brief review of 'coital disorders', in which women as well as sexual organs fail to perform properly, includes both female engagement with coitus but without satisfaction, and women's deliberate non-engagement with coitus (i.e. celibacy), the second situation possibly but not necessarily resulting from the first.

[Where] 'the sexual performance is *normal*, but the performer experiences no pleasure: in women this is called *frigidity* . . . in men this was, until recently, not considered to be an illness' . . . [Where] 'sexual acts are deliberately avoided and the subject regards his or her non-performance as meritorious: this is called chastity in both men and women (and it may or may not be considered an illness)'.[21] (Emphasis mine.)

Szasz's second point is that chastity where considered meritorious by the subject may sometimes but not always be thought of as an illness. The fact is that when *men* consider their chaste state worthy of merit it is not considered a disease. Indeed in many religious traditions at different times and places it has been elevated as a loftier, purer state than marriage with its attendant fleshy, sinful lusts. For women, however, throughout history, as long as their self-chosen celibacy was linked to religion or mysticism it was largely (though not entirely and not always) seen as virtuous, but when it was linked to politics (it is interesting how quickly individual domestic 'withdrawal' becomes labelled 'politics') it was looked on with fear, displeasure, and contempt. 'Frigid' or 'sick' then became popular perjorative dismissals for a chastity that was part of a celibate line.

The genital manipulation of categorizing withdrawal from heterosexual relations as sickness and the use of frigidity as a taunt was as common in Great Britain in the 1920s as was the put-down 'prude'. For years feminists waged vociferous campaigns against men's violent sexual behaviour in the areas of prostitution, sexual abuse of girls, marital rape and other sexual excesses. For years any women who refused to partake in sexual activity with men were stigmatized as 'frigid'. For years any women who showed 'reluctance to adjust' to men's sexual behaviour were attacked as 'frigid man-haters'. The concept of female frigidity became the main weapon which sexologists used to undermine the feminist critique of male sexuality and to pressurize women away from celibacy.[22]

From the 1920s when changes in sexual ideology saw a massive campaign by sexologists to conscript women into marriage and more significantly into a cheerful, contented participation in sexual intercourse, women who resisted were not merely classified as 'frigid', but *ill*. Sheila Jeffreys suggests that 'the frigide' who has marched through pages of sociological and sex-advice literature was actually invented in the 1920s to explain the phenomenon of some women rejecting marriage and other women finding sexual response within marriage impossible.[23] Such 'abnormal' women were regarded by genital mythmakers who included psychologists, psychoanalysts, and sex-reformers as pathologically hysterical. By 1926 psychoanalyst William Stekel estimated that between 40 per cent and 50 per cent of all women were frigid. In his book *Frigidity in Women in Relation to her Love Life* Stekel suggested that: 'To be roused by a man means acknowledging oneself as conquered.'[24] In other words a woman's ability to feel pleasure from penetration depended on the extent to which she was able to accept with enthusiasm her inferior status.

Andrea Dworkin suggests something similar today. She poses the idea that there is a relationship between intercourse and the low status of women.[25] She asks whether an occupied people, women, physically occupied inside, internally invaded, can be free? Or does pleasure in intercourse depend on acceptance of nothing less than a twentieth century slavery?[26] In a more passionate voice than William Stekel (she is after all, unlike him, not only on the side of the powerless, but also on the powerless side), Dworkin asks us to recognize that intercourse occurs in a context of a power relation that is incontrovertible and pervasive. Whatever the meaning of the act of penetration, in and of itself, that act takes place in a context in which men have social, economic, political and physical power over women. Obviously certain men do not have all those kinds of control over all women, but they all have some kind of power over all women. As she says: 'Most men have controlling power over what they call *their* women – the women they fuck.'[27]

In the late nineteenth century and again in the late twentieth century, female frigidity can be seen as a form of resistance to male dominance. No matter what the motives are for a woman's celibacy, no matter how embryonic her politics, in a genitally-oriented world this establishes celibacy as a political act.

Although in the nineteenth and twentieth centuries the term frigidity so closely adheres to the notion of female celibacy that it is hard for women to separate them (which says much about the power of naming), it is by no means a term that genital myth manipulators have restricted to women who choose celibacy.

In the early twentieth century women who could not come to orgasm solely through penetration were categorized as immature, unbalanced and frigid. By the 1960s Genital Appropriation, (née Sexual Revolution) not having the 'right kind' of orgasms could just as easily earn women the barb 'frigid' as not wanting penetrative sex. When having a vaginal orgasm was the measure of a woman's mature and normal sexuality (this was the traditional Freudian notion) women who quite reasonably were unable to achieve this (for reasons shown by later research that clearly pointed out the clitoral nature of female orgasms) were accused of being coldly unresponsive at best, frigid bitches at worst.

Later, frigidity from such a cause was justified when sexologists Masters and Johnson successfully claimed the attention of the Women's Movement and the female nation by researching the tricky female orgasm and 'discovering', yes, it was after all clitoral in origin.[28]

By 1970 when Anne Koedt wrote her famous paper exploding the whole genital myth of the vaginal orgasm through penetration, female sexuality, which when unresponsive to penetration was categorized as frigid, had to be radically redefined.[29]

At present women who still do not meet the basic requirements of standard feminine sexual behaviour – i.e. behaviour that invites and welcomes sexual congress – still risk being labelled 'frigid'. Their behaviour is not frigid. Their behaviour is sexually autonomous. Women have not 'failed' in the matter of sexual behaviour. They are illustrating an independent sexual choice. Female celibacy today, like vaginal orgasms yesterday, must cease to be associated with frigidity if women are to feel free to make that sexual choice. When they can make it without pressure, a further re-assessment of the cultural meaning of female sexuality which is long overdue will be able to take place.

To look more closely at this idea of 'failure' we can gain some extremely interesting insights by seeing how differently the words 'frigidity' and 'impotence' are perceived. They are not, you see, parallel terms. As Dorothy Hage aptly points out: 'The female is seen to have "failed", while the male is simply "unable" . . . frequently women are also blamed for men's impotence.'[30]

The term 'frigid' used to attack celibate women masks an essential difference between non-participating females and non-participating males. Dale Spender suggests that while impotent males are physically prevented from engaging in intercourse, females termed 'frigid' who may wish to be celibate, can be forced to engage in intercourse.[31] From a female point of view frigidity could be more aptly named 'reluctance'; a reluctance to respond to male sexuality, not a reluctance to utilize one's own. Frigidity could then be redefined as an autonomous independent state, the consequence of women's well-reasoned debate and decision-making, *freely* arrived at in the face of possible alternatives. That kind of celibacy could be a form of power. It could be a form of passive resistance or a form of active passionate politics. I begin to suspect that men have greatly underrated women's desire, even loving heterosexual women's desire, to lead 'frigid' or purposefully celibate lives.

Mental illness
How does the genital manipulation work that underlies the message that celibacy equals some strange disorder? It uses the stigma of mental illness (for which 'condition' women can be calmed down, restrained, put into hospitals, drugged, 'treated' or mistreated) in order to combat the challenge of women's sexual choices that do not toe the genital line.

Viewing a desire for celibacy as a pathological symptom has been a masculine weapon of control through many decades. Evidence shows how lack of pleasure in heterosexual activity was manipulated to appear as a disease for one sex but not for the other at the beginning of this century. In the 1920s we saw women's active withdrawal from heterosexual sex being labelled sickness, and also feminist campaigners' and writers' theoretical and literary support for celibacy being dismissed as puritanical, eccentric, extreme and frigid.

What is the situation today?

Listen to four women's voices. They are all celibate for different reasons. One is bored after thirty years of marital sex. One is searching for spirituality. One finds more excitement and energy in a new job. One needs a short break from penetration. All of them need more space for themselves than they can find in a sexually active relationship.

Marjorie, thirty. Dental sales executive:

> I am quite an ordinary person. For years I led a very ordinary life. I was a saleswoman with a dental company. I spent a lot of time on the road, earning good money. After a while I felt I was always here, there, everywhere, but not getting anywhere. I knew there was somewhere I could go if I could just stop still. The money stopped being important because I couldn't buy whatever I was searching for. I had had a good sex relationship with Trevor, the man I lived with, for several years. But suddenly making love felt like a distraction, even annoying. I didn't know what was up.
>
> One day Trevor and I went to a talk given by a Buddhist woman about the way the planet is being destroyed. Other things like that. It made sense but it didn't have a great impact on Trevor. The woman talked a lot about what she called the meditation of attention, about how we are all interconnected with everything in the world. She called it a living web that we could use to act justly on behalf of everything. I wanted to find out more so I went off to another talk. This was about our subconscious despair at not being able to save the world, and about new directions within us.
>
> I felt fired with excitement. I started going regularly to meetings. Quite soon I decided I wanted to change my career to something more in line with my Buddhist thinking. I didn't want to sell dental products any more. I didn't want to buy things either. I even saw sex as a commodity. I wanted time on my own to think. I felt sex had become interruptive. I was still very fond of Trevor so I explained what was going on, why I didn't want to sleep with him all the time. I suggested that some days I slept downstairs.
>
> He said he didn't mind my going to Buddhist meetings but he didn't want any changes in our life. But I wanted to make changes. I hated upsetting him about sex, so often I would say I was tired or had stomach cramps. Finally I just came out with it and said that right now I had to be celibate. I would rather live in the same house, but if necessary I would be prepared to move out. I made it clear the choice had nothing to do with him. He didn't believe me and became very angry. He couldn't credit it was something just to do with me. He thought it had to be to do with him. I tried to be very gentle but he still saw it as an attack.
>
> He said I had become totally overwrought, that all this spiritual stuff was making me disturbed. He asked me to go and get a course of anti-depressants. I knew that was silly and I had reached the

point where I wouldn't change my mind. Then he said I needed help, that I was in a bad way, that I should see a psychiatrist. He started asking his friends about therapists. Of course I refused, but after that there was no choice but to move out.

Joanne, thirty. Public Relations Officer for hotel chain:

Why did I turn to celibacy? Partly it was my job. The excitement of my new job gave me the highs I used to get from sex with Dan. But I also needed more freedom than I got in my sexual relationship. I didn't want to get pregnant. There was always the hassle of having to use contraception. I still cared about him, no one better, but I didn't go a bundle on the sex any more. I didn't have the right kind of energy left over from my work. I had too much going on for myself. Sex was too demanding. Being lovers involved me in domestic chores, and socializing for Dan's job. No time for me. At first I didn't spell out the sex bit. Travelling for the hotel company meant I was away a great deal so he didn't suss for a while. But finally when I recognized I wanted to live alone, I had to say it. I didn't want to hurt him. I felt he was like my best friend.

What happened was terrible. He pounced on the phrase 'I've decided to be celibate' as if I'd said 'I've decided to commit suicide.' He said no woman in her right mind could decide any such thing. He rang up my Dad and had a long all-boys-together chat about how I'd been overworking and was obviously in a state of mental exhaustion, stress, and not to put too fine a point on it, mental breakdown. It was ludicrous. Okay, I was tired, but I had never felt calmer or more confident in my life. The problem was that once Dan had dragged my family in, my Dad got my Mum going, my sister started crying, my brother-in-law began to shout at me, until finally I lost my head and started yelling at everyone to mind their own business. Then I sobbed like a real idiot. I felt so guilty. As if I'd done something deliberately to hurt him which of course I hadn't. By the time they'd all gone, I was acting like a really unstable woman and Dan was calmly talking about 'treatment'.

Susan, fifty-three. Worker in her husband's timber business; mother of three sons:

I didn't want to do it any more. I was tired of pretending. Sex had never been good. We could have a much better life without it. We needed to say it out loud, then stop the whole charade and settle into separate rooms. I appreciated Will's companionship. I liked our family life. It was cozy. I didn't want to give that up. Of course we had our problems, but we understood each other's little ways, we put up with a lot because of being company for each other. As long as the boys were at home I thought it best to go on as if we enjoyed sex. Now that they have all moved away, I feel the time has come to be open. I'm at the end of my tether, so if we can't have separate rooms, and stop all that, I'll have to find some other way.

It wasn't easy for Will because we had lived together for thirty years, but he did take it badly. It was as if he had had a prize possession taken out of his grasp. It was stupid because sex at its best was boring and for me it was worse than that.

I couldn't believe how hard he took it. He kept telling me I was menopausal. He said I was lucky that I still had someone who wanted me, considering my flabby tum, and my big thighs. I was so hurt, because of course we'd joked about my flabby tum, lots of times (and anyway he had one too), but now it didn't sound like a joke. He asked me why I thought I could *choose* not to do it? Finally he calmed down and said what did I mean by saying I was deciding not to do it? No woman can decide that, certainly not his wife. I must be sick in the head. He said I needn't think I had any choice. He would soon see about that. I could hardly believe this was the man I was married to. We had had our ups and downs in all those years, but generally it had been quite comfy. We had always tackled the downs with a bit of a laugh. It was our way of getting through things.

The next thing he did was to go down to our family doctor. I didn't really know what he said, but when I went in to get my regular prescription, the GP said he'd like a little chat – he knew us both well you see – and he asked me about my menopause. He told me women did get mentally unstable at those times. He said he thought it was the menopause that had made me put on weight, but it was really quite easy to lose, and that always helps. He suggested that Will and I had a little holiday together to sort things out. He knew quite a few sunny spots on the coast not far away and he even had a brother with a caravan we could rent. He finished by saying surely I could see the sense of calming down, getting mentally well again, if I did that then things needn't go any further.

Of course not all married men or long term partners take such a strident and disturbing view of their partner's celibacy. Several men were said to be very supportive.

Sandra, thirty-one, a newly celibate wife, said:

My husband would rather have genital activity, but he is really trying hard to understand things from my point of view. I have told him I need a break from sex to sort myself out, but that doesn't mean I want to leave him. I want to be in separate beds for a bit. I need a bed to myself, but I don't want to stop being affectionate. He is trying very hard to see that we can be close and touch each other affectionately without it having to lead to those other things that have been getting me down. I actually hate those other things. I don't want him to put it inside me. I feel frightened even though I know he's doing it because he loves me. Of course I know secretly he thinks it's abnormal not to like those other things. He keeps saying he hopes in time I'll 'pull round' and 'get back to normal again'.

Several points are revealing in both the negative and positive accounts. In each case the men are apparently unable to accept that a woman has taken an independent decision in relation to her own well-being. They see it only in terms of harm to themselves. Marjorie said emphatically: 'I made it clear the choice had nothing to do with him. He didn't believe it and became angry. He couldn't credit it was something to do with me.' Men's egotism is enhanced by the way women reflect them at twice their natural size and part of that reflection comes through sex. Men become used to controlling their wives' sexual choices. Will felt sex with Susan was his 'prize possession' and resented its removal. He felt sufficiently proprietorial towards her body that he could talk aggressively about her 'flabby tum' and 'big thighs'. Trevor's method of control was to say he 'didn't mind' Marjorie going to Buddhist meetings but he did not want any changes in their life. He refused to see that a spiritual celibacy for Marjorie was intricately tied up with bigger changes on several fronts. Dan's method of control was to categorize Joanne's decision as mental stress, then to phone Joanne's Dad in a 'man to man' manner to discuss it.

Significantly consistent in the women's accounts is their acknowledgement that sex is such a big deal to their men that they must take care not to hurt them. Marjorie, the dental sales executive, said: 'I hated upsetting him about sex, so often I'd say I was tired or had stomach cramps.' Joanne, the PR worker, said: 'At first I didn't spell out the sex bit . . . I didn't want to hurt him.'

The women's accounts also show clearly that what the women value is companionship rather than sex. Joanne says Dan is 'like my best friend'. Marjorie by choice would 'rather live [with him] in the same house'. Susan stresses 'I appreciated Will's companionship.'

What is glaringly obvious from all four accounts is the equation made by men between a sexual withdrawal (not in their interests) and mental illness (not in the women's interests). Trevor describes Marjorie as overwrought and disturbed and suggests first anti-depressants then a visit to a psychiatrist. Dan's manipulative behaviour causes Joanne to behave like an 'unstable woman' at which point he can calmly suggest 'treatment'. Will decides Susan's problem is mental illness brought on by the menopause, and unethically visits the GP to discuss it. Even Sandra's so-called 'understanding' husband believes Sandra is 'abnormal' and given time may 'pull round'.

In these accounts there are also barely concealed threats, such as 'I need not think I had any choice' (Susan's husband), and 'Then things needn't go any further' (the GP).

Just as the women's motives illustrate that their proposed celibacy is as much about autonomy as it is about genital abstinence, so do the men's responses demonstrate how threatened both these situations make them feel. Their way of dealing with such a threat today is no different from the way men dealt with it at the turn of the century: they manipulate the label of mental illness as an attempt to keep women in line.

Pornographic culture

Genital messages and manipulations meet in the pornographic culture that is celibacy's most dangerous enemy. It is a society with elastic obscenity laws that say sexual violence against women is obscene, yet it promotes films and videos which show women being violently abused in the name of sexual love, such as *Blue Velvet*, *Dressed to Kill*, *Tightrope* and *Tie Me Up! Tie Me Down!* to name a few; and sadomasochistic images such as the Hermès perfume ad which shows a 'desirable' blonde woman, gagged and screaming as she hangs upside down, bound in harsh black leather, her hands chained at the wrists.

Pornography, once restricted to men's magazines, entered the female cultural marketplace in the early seventies at the same time as various laws enlarged women's sexual and social opportunities. The pill had been marketed and prescribed by 1961, the British Abortion Act became law in 1967, American women had the right to legal abortion following a supreme court ruling in 1973, United States censorship laws were relaxed in 1969 and by the seventies many women had entered the work force and had either joined or been influenced by the second wave of the Women's Movement.

By the eighties *Playboy*'s pornographic photography and other images of women's faces anticipating orgasm or recovering from it had become the hard sell for fashion and beauty products. Rochas Femme perfume shows the naked head, shoulders and part of the breasts of a woman sprawled sideways in post orgasmic exhaustion. Lancôme Rouge Absolu lipstick shows a woman's head and neck flung right back, red, moisturized, pouting lips very slightly open; the orgasm recovery position.

If the face had to register sexual ecstasy or shock, the so-called ideal body had to look razor-thin and adolescent. Starve to fit sexy clothes was the message; powerless equals attractive was the subtext, as the diet industry and killer starvation diseases flourished simultaneously.

Two genital manipulations from hard and soft core pornography pervaded women's culture and were used to sell products. The first manipulation is the objectifying of women's bodies in pornographic images to sell anything and everything. These bodies are usually shown in fragmented parts, and women assimilating this notion begin to see their bodies as 'my fat stomach' or 'my hefty thighs' or 'my drooping tits'. The Elbeo tights ad has a smart woman in a stylish black and white suit looking surprised as she hovers about a coffee table, her two legs missing. The caption reads: 'Jeepers I forgot my legs'. She should not have looked surprised – bits and pieces of women's bodies are missing on every page of every magazine.

The most explicit advert in terms of how genital mythmasters view women as bodies is the Christian Dior ad that shows only a fragment of a woman's pale pink face which features part of an eye with coarse black lashes, which is depicted in such an extraordinary way that several readers thought at first sight it was a woman's nude pink stomach leading to a naked open cunt sprouting coarse black hair.

Set against fragmented and unrealistic images like these it is not surprising that, for women, bodily self-hatred instead of bodily self-love became the norm. Women cannot become autonomous when they internalize these negative definitions of their own sexuality. Freedom depends on a holistic view of oneself, and the genital myth persuades women to see their bodies as sexual objects, fragmented and alienated from their minds.

If women feel alienated from their own bodies, this must be inten- sified when they watch men in heterosexual cultural representations appear alienated from sex with women and from women's bodies. In a characteristically bitter cult film called *Sex, Lies and Videotape* by Steven Soderberg, women watch Our Hero cut off from real love, dislocated and unable to make love to a real woman, listening to women's videotaped genital confessions while he unheroically masturbates. A mixed group of teenagers viewing this film came out of the cinema and reported to me that 'watching it was a better turn on than doing the real thing'. A double alienation for young girls and boys growing up in a sex-saturated, loveless culture.

The second manipulation taken from hard-core porn and sadomasochistic symbolism is women's supposed enjoyment of sexual violence. Rape is portrayed as glamorous and inviting, an act of sex instead of an act of power. Violence is now an intrinsic part of sex. Obsession ads for Calvin Klein perfume offer ecstasy in the age of the rope with a barefronted woman on a rope swing, back arched, head flung back, long hair drooping, as she hints at her passive intercourse with the assertive man swinging upright between the ropes. Another Obsession ad has a muscular male draping an even more lifeless naked woman's body over his shoulder. Beautiful but dead she won't be using much more perfume, but what a way to go. Is that the message or is it even more sinister than that? Bestiality and masochism are portrayed in the ad for Erno Laszlo skin products where a woman and her dog are tied together with a leather belt, and both animal and woman are sitting up and begging for it. In a range of other ads for cigarettes, cars, and shoes, the accessories are sadomasochistic symbols such as guns, hot iron rods, knives, and ropes, and the women represented are either screaming or appearing shocked or terrorized.

'Treatment' and cosmetic surgery
Murderous representations of women's sexuality that reshape women's behaviour into forms men may more easily control are sick. But the greater sickness lies in the way the genital power elite through the centuries has, as a political practice, 'treated' women's sexuality.

The idea that sexual organs ought to be surgically altered runs through history, and well before people rationalized sexual surgery on medical grounds they justified it on religious grounds. As symbolism is such an important part of our culture, and because genitals (like faces) have symbolic meaning, people easily become persuaded that in their natural state the sexual organs and their genital powers are not in their proper form. Thomas Szasz points out that this leads to decisions to enhance or diminish the organs by means of artefacts or surgical interventions.[32] It is because patriarchs in ancient religions feared the powers of what they saw as the 'insatiable cunt' that it is largely men who have made these decisions, and women's bodies into which the knives have entered. The promise of 'enhancement' – the ability to match up to an ideal of beauty or to a model of sexual attractiveness – has been the manipulative device used to control women. Diminishment or destruction of women's sexuality has been the result.

Other cultures have used ritualistic religious or barbaric medical 'treatments' to control women's sexual behaviour. Examples include the Sudanese vaginal shaft and shield, Egyptian clitoridectomy, or the terrifying chastity belts used consistently in Christian European countries in the middle ages which fastened together the woman's labia by means of a ring, a buckle or a padlock. Mary Daly reports that the ritualized African genital atrocities of excision and infibulation (by which the woman's entire clitoris, labia minora and parts of the labia majora are excised, and the two sides of the vulva sewn together) which were practised in many parts of the world in the past, are still inflicted upon women throughout Africa today.[33] Historian Rosalind Miles comments that such treatments are used to control *all* women through a technique which betrays a conscious determination to deal with what is seen as the 'problem' of female sexuality by destroying it wholesale.[34]

Lest we become complacent or feel safe and distanced from such sexual cruelties it is as well to remember that clitoridectomies and other mutilations have been systematically practised by modern American and British gynaecologists upon their female patients.

In the nineteenth century, doctors like William Acton (1814–1875) offered professional judgements on women's sexual and social behaviour. Their predominant approach was to minimize women's sexual desires, ignoring the possibility that women's own denial of their sexuality might have been a useful tactic for avoiding the discomforts and dangers of childbearing. A typical pronouncement of Acton's was: 'I am ready to maintain that there are many females who never feel any sexual excitement whatever . . . A modest woman seldom desires any sexual gratification for herself. She submits to her husband's embraces but principally to gratify him.'[35] This then was the characteristic genital message of the time, which authorized conventional medical wisdom to suggest that 'it was irrelevant to women's feelings whether she had sex organs or not'.[36] In the light of this attitude patients who had what was termed 'only' a clitoris and who used it for masturbatory purposes were surgically castrated for 'the sexual perversion of masturbation'.[37] It is curious how male doctors who never managed to convince themselves or their public that the proper treatment for male masturbation was the surgical removal of the penis, nevertheless were highly successful in convincing both themselves and a great many women that the proper treatment for female masturbation was clitoridectomy.

Isaac Baker Brown, an eminent genital mutilator, who later became president of London's Medical Society, was the first to introduce this operation in 1858. The reason he gave was that masturbation in women caused hysteria, convulsive diseases and epilepsy.[38] This wealthy gynaecologist who ran a fifty-bed private clinic claimed during the peak period of his genital activities (1866–1867) to have been overwhelmingly successful in curing not merely masturbation but all kinds of female anti-social behaviour by the surgical removal of the clitoris. His patients included single women whose symptoms included 'a great disposition for novelties – the patient desiring to escape from home, fond of becoming a nurse in hospitals – or other pursuits', and married women whose symptoms included a 'distaste for marital intercourse'. According to Baker Brown 'these physical evidences of derangement, if left unchecked, gradually lead to more serious consequences. The patient either becomes a confirmed invalid . . . or on the other hand, will become subject to catalepsy, epilepsy, idiocy or insanity.'[39] Another of his patients with an irritable clitoris was found to have a great distaste for her husband. Now obviously insane tendencies such as a desire for a nursing career, a dislike of sexual congress, or a wish for a marital separation could not be countenanced by the genital medical profession, so Baker Brown's policy was, in his own words, to pursue 'the usual surgical treatment' so that single women would remain passively at home, departing wives would return to the marital bed, and female careers would be abandoned. One can only be relieved that Baker Brown's own career finally came to an abrupt end when he was expelled from the Obstetrical Society for neglecting to inform his patients or their families of the exact nature of his 'usual operation'.

Although his disgrace rendered the coercive practices of other clitoridectomy practitioners less popular, their fundamental assumption that a woman's sexual physiology was potentially dangerous to her mental health shaped medical opinion on many women's issues for years to come. (A dramatic example was the later controversy over women's entry into higher education when genital mythmasters declared menstruation to be a disability which so affected those who suffered from it (i.e. women), that they could not possibly undertake higher education without severe risk of mental disorder.)

A century ago, genital mutilators claimed that masturbation was pathological, and proved it by torturing the masturbator and calling it treatment. Today, as Thomas Szasz points out, they 'insist that masturbation is healthful – and prove it by inventing the disease of masturbatory orgasmic inadequacy'.[40] Genital messages change through the centuries. Patriarchal punishments stay the same.

Though Western doctors no longer cut up a woman's clitoris to change her 'insane' approach to life, there are still surgeons who operate on the clitoris (by removing the hood, or reconstructing part of the vagina) to make it more accessible to penis stimulation during intercourse. Sheila Kitzinger reports that one American surgeon has performed this operation on more than four thousand women whom he claimed wanted to improve their sex lives. He used his own wife (on whom he had also operated) in a television demonstration to testify that whereas before the operation her orgasms during intercourse with him had been random, now she had them all the time.[41] Some husbands will go to frightening lengths . . .

Another operation regularly conducted today, episiotomy, the surgical incision of the perineum to enlarge the vagina during childbirth is often praised on the grounds that it ultimately makes a woman's vagina tighter, therefore making intercourse more exciting for her male partner. Doctors who knowingly sew women up smaller than before call this proudly 'the husband's stitch'. These operations, together with those cosmetic surgical shapings that trim off and tidy up the vagina because women have been persuaded that their vaginas are ugly, are manipulative mistreatments of women's bodies based on an ideology that it is reasonable to modify the female form surgically to meet male standards of attractiveness, or to mutilate it in order to increase male forms of pleasure.

Today sex therapy as 'treatment' for women who cannot or do not wish to orgasm or have intercourse is a similarly manipulative *mistreatment* this time affecting women's minds and emotional relationships. It leads inexorably towards the view that passionate celibates are women in dire need of a cure.

In this violent genital climate, celibacy as a calm and inviting sensual state is deemed disordered. The genital pathology of sex perverts the notion of non-genital passion, invisibilizes the possibility of equal relationships between women and men, which might come about through an intimate loving companionship based on an autonomous celibacy. Fully equal, fully human relationships between uncoerced women and men, would not suit the genital power elite. Fully human women and men who could love each other with tenderness and mutual respect, who could desire each other without the images of men's dominance and women's submission, who could honour each other's values, women's values no less than men's, would radically upset the thirty-three billion dollars a year diet industry, the twenty billion dollar cosmetics industry, the seven billion dollar pornography industry, and the three hundred million dollar cosmetic surgery industry.

Sadomasochistic culture is a costly business. It makes billions but it costs women their lives, thriving on hostile and violent depictions of sexual estrangement both between women and men and between women and their inner selves.

The market economy of sexual consumerism is founded on sexual discontent, and upon complementary male and female sexual insecurities. Its profit margins are enhanced by the destruction of women's pride in their natural beauty and innate sexuality, so that they turn to beauty counters for replacement products, or to cosmetic surgeons to undergo reconstruction at the point of a knife.

Celibacy which might reinstate female pride, which might restore women's self-esteem, which might see 'beauty' as intrinsic to a whole natural woman, which might offer equality and affection within male-female relationships, is definitely bad for business. As Naomi Wolf fiercely points out, the last thing the consumer index wants, is for women and men to figure out how to love one another. Even more threatening to consumerism, I would emphasize, is parity. Consumer culture depends on maintaining smashed lines of communication between the sexes and promoting male as well as female sexual anxieties. It is most successfully supported by markets made up of sexual clones, 'men who want objects and women who want to be objects, and the object desired – ever changing, disposable and dictated by the market'.[42] So pornography and advertising work to offer us beautiful objects (the fact that they are often severely mutilated beautiful objects does not seem to matter much), which have a built-in obsolescence. This ensures women's constant dissatisfaction with themselves and men's constant dissatisfaction with 'their' woman.

Why this stream of hostile images today? Why this sudden upsurge of brutal behaviour, cankerous with contempt for women?

It is not an accident. As women have been politically and publicly asserting themselves and challenging the structure of inequality, male violence against women in the home and on the streets has risen steadily and a proliferation of relentlessly corrupting representations has arisen to counterbalance women's public assertiveness. The social forces of a sadistic genital culture have put the shame and pain and dishonesty back into women's sexuality. Women see images that idealize an unrecognizable skinny plastic nudity termed 'beautiful' to which we are meant to aspire; women see images that eroticize our own degradation; women see images that turn our bodies into bruised and bleeding parts.

When those images are in your mind you are never the same again. And they are in all of our minds. Deadening our spirit, annihilating our thoughts. Some of us are more painfully aware of them than others. But at some level all of us register what we see in women's magazines, what we watch at the cinema, what we learn from even a not-so-nasty video.

The female body is merely something to be objectified. Used. Exploited. Objectified ornately. Used stylishly. Exploited elegantly. Inside the magazine's glossy pages or up there on the silver screen. That is the first message we learn from the pornography of a misogynistic society.

The female body is something to be harmed. Maimed. Numbed. Tortured on television where we can console ourselves it 'isn't real'. Dismembered in a snuff movie where the girl who was killed was 'only a prostitute'. Slit, spiked, ravaged and finally raped on the street our house is in. The woman was our next door neighbour. It could have been our daughter, our sister or ourself. That is the second message we learn from the sadomasochism of a misogynistic society.

These two conventions from hard and soft pornography have entered women's culture and infiltrated women's everyday lives. They cut across from life to art (are these Medusan media visions 'art'?) and back to life. The script diagrammatically looks like this:

Women see
Porn as Violence
Violence as Sex
Sex as Love
Love as Submission
to
Porn as Violence
Violence as Sex
Sex as Love
Love as Submission
to
Porn as violence . . .

To see how this works, and how it affects women, let us look at some writing by savage and satirical Kathy Acker, whose writing is born in pain of this invasive pornographic culture. Her literary landscapes cannot encompass the idea of sexuality without slaughter, or passion without blood, shit and masochism. Her subversive send-ups of what it feels like to be a woman ripped off and ripped apart inside this sadomasochistic society challenge us to see the sickness she sees, feel the horror she feels.

Yet at the same time, the way she writes cannot but suggest that she is soured and tainted by the violent and disgusting images she is compelled to use. I feel that what she indites has damaged her irrevocably, in the same way that looking at hundreds of pornographic images in order to understand what I was protesting against when I campaigned with the Women Against Violence Against Women group, once damaged me. Those images are in your mind. You are never the same again.

What Acker writes is disturbing. What she writes about is disturbed. Genital invasions have distorted our society so that mindless fucking and incest and a deep-seated contempt for women are intertwined and interchangeable. There is no equality for men and women in sex presented like this and Acker for one never pretends that there is.

In her novel *Empire of the Senseless* intercourse is what happens between men who have power and women, very young women, girl children, who do not. Listen first to the description of the young girl's view of love, then to the description of her father's 'love' for her. Abhor the daughter is fourteen.

At that age I didn't give a damn who I fucked cause any boy who
fucked me loved me. Fucking was love . . . I didn't know how my
parents felt about my fucking and yet I knew I was evil cause I was
fucking. So I knew daddy would kill me if he caught me fucking . . .
I was in the bathroom, fucking some boy. Daddy came home.
I threw on some clothes and ran up to daddy . . . 'Shall I get you
some Jack Daniels?'

Abhor knows her father will say yes, not that he is an alcoholic,
he merely drinks six martinis each night while her Mommy the
moralist tells him he is an alky. Mommy the moralist is away at this
point in the story. So Abhor sneaks the boy out but daddy finds the
boy's tie in the bathroom. Not for a moment does daddy believe his
daughter's lies.
'My daddy was almost crying.'
Being a bright daddy he has worked out what Abhor and the
boy have been up to. No greater love hath any father than to feel
his daughter has been wronged at the age of fourteen. Any caring
father will now put this right.

'Abhor.'
My lips were frozen with tension.
'Abhor, I know what you've been doing.' . . . 'These men
don't respect you, Abhor.'
How could I explain that I cared neither if they respected
me nor who they were.
'Abhor,' daddy explained, 'I'm the only man who'll ever take
care of you properly.' His hands were reaching for my breasts
while tears were coming out of his eyes.
'Why don't you do it with mommy, daddy?'
'We're too old. We don't do it any more.' His right hand
was rubbing my breast.
'I'm going to phone mommy.' Over the phone I told her that
her husband was trying to do something to me. I didn't use the
word 'fuck'.
She said 'Let me speak to him.'
'Daddy, mommy wants to speak to you.'
I don't remember if his hand left my nipple. I don't know
what they said to each other.
After he put the phone receiver down on the table, he put
his cock up me. There was no more blood than in a period.
Part of me wanted him and part of me wanted to kill him.[43]

What this young fourteen-year-old girl has learnt from this genitally trapped culture is the tragically confused message that 'fucking was love' and that 'I was evil cause I was fucking.' Violence is sex, sex is love.

Innocence is something this child (for fourteen is still childhood) is not allowed. She knew 'daddy would kill me if he caught me fucking', and in the deepest sense, if not with literal application, that is what he does. He kills off her sexual spirit. He kills off her young girlhood. The image of the hubristic father casually collaring his daughter's nipple while conversing with his wife on the telephone is one of utter contempt, a despicable disdain for both women involved.

Abhor's own dislocation from the act, her alienation from her own emotions, are shown when she says, 'I told her that *her husband* was trying to do something to me.' (My italics.) She does not use the phrase of attachment, the phrase 'my father'. The genital myth works to separate woman friend from woman friend, sister from sister, *mother from daughter*. The genital message that women of a certain age are 'past it' reverberates loud and clear when Daddy tells Abhor that he and Mommy don't do it because 'we're too old', meaning that Mommy, the middle-aged woman, is too old.

The sardonic oversimplicity of putting the phone down on the table and the cock up the young girl's vagina lays bare the meaning of the sexual act in a context of paternal 'love'. Significantly I made a typing error and typed 'contest' for 'context'. Either word will do. They are as brutally interchangeable as the father's actions. He might just as well have put his cock on the table and the phone up his daughter.

Behind the rage and the ferocious energy of this contemporary orgiastic tale is something reminiscent of the mechanical dissoci-ated adventures of cock and cunt that pervaded and perambulated through the genital mind-set of Henry Miller's *Tropic of Cancer* which came out in 1939.

In this passage, written by a woman, what we see reflected with blood, guts and accuracy is today's edition of yesterday's pornographic climate with penis as machine, sex as technology, and the genital message that fucking is about not giving a damn. Certainly not giving a damn about women.

That some women who can no longer breathe in this air wish to create a celibate climate is a healthy sign. That they should encounter ugly opposition, that they should be damned as *unhealthy*, is integral to a struggle which is taking place in a social world which has at its heart genital messages and genital manipulations. If we want a genuinely sexual society to exist it seems we must make space also for celibate messages.

CHAPTER THREE

Celibacy Begins in the Mind

'I REMEMBER hearing, years ago, an old priest say that celibacy begins in the mind. We can be completely non-physical and yet so possessed and unfree that we are uncelibate. Or we can be physical while being free and still celibate.'[1]

Sister Hana Zarinah, who has been a nun since 1963, wrote those words in an article called 'The Gift of Sexuality in the Spirit of Celibacy'. Several of the ideas she expresses are a challenge to the received messages of a genital culture. Firstly, the notion that for women, celibacy begins in the mind; secondly, the suggestion that non-possession is a more critical determinant than genital behaviour for assessing celibacy; thirdly, the idea that within the celibate spirit is the gift of sexuality. These are in direct contrast to the genital messages which we have just considered, predominant amongst which is the message that celibacy, a foolish abstention from the wonders of genital activity, is an asexual state.

Women today, both nuns and lay women, are saying something different. The genital myth may tell us that what we do with our genitals is what we consider 'sexual', but the fact is that for women *it is not.*

Even though sexuality is the wild card in our pack, even though we can rarely tie it down to a particular ideology, even though adventurous women are timid about pleasuring themselves, or right-on feminists suddenly find they are lusting for chauvinist pigs, nevertheless for most women erotic needs are connected to emotional needs. What women consider 'sexual' is rarely restricted to specific bodily organs. Being sexual comprises a whole range of experiences, it infuses our emotions as much as our bodies. Making love takes place as much in our minds as in our bodies. Our heads are a more erogenous zone than our genitals.

The way women think about celibacy is similarly not restricted to genital behaviour or genital abstention. What goes on in our minds is at least as important.

Listen to how women define their starting point for celibacy:

> For me, there are two aspects to being celibate. There's a sort of intellectual celibacy as well as a physical celibacy. The intellectual celibacy is a celibacy of non-involvement. You can have that even though you are in a sexual relationship because you are not giving up yourself. Whereas a mere physical celibacy is just not participating in intercourse. So a total celibacy would have both aspects.
>
> (Canadian nurse, thirty-six years. Celibate three years.)

> Celibacy is a conscious decision. You have to be comfortable with it in your head for it to have a good meaning. Being celibate doesn't mean necessarily not having a sexual relationship, because I have one with myself, which might sound bizarre. You stay feeling a sexual person but it is a way of living with yourself. It is keeping myself free for myself.
>
> (Canadian boat builder, thirty-eight years. Celibate two years.)

> I think it's a state of mind. It's something that goes on in your head and doesn't go on in the rest of your body. Physically you might even want to have sex but mentally you are just not there. You have already become celibate.
>
> (British law student, thirty-two years. Celibate two years.)

> Celibacy is a state of mind, something that is a conscious act rather than the act of not having sex. Your genitals aren't where it starts. I could give up sex but if my head wasn't in the right place I wouldn't be celibate.
>
> (British gardener, thirty-one years. Celibate five years.)

For these women, whose remarks were characteristic of many more, as for Sister Hana, celibacy begins with a mental process. The boat builder bears out Sister Hana's notion of the gift of sexuality when she says 'You stay feeling a sexual person.' She confirms the nun's view of the importance of non-possession when she says 'It's keeping myself free for myself.' For all of them the decision to become celibate is so much more than a physical retreat from genital sex.

I talked to a group of women who had decided to opt for celibacy whilst staying within the structure of a marriage or a long-term partnership. Many of them said that the way outsiders viewed their relationships had a decisive effect on how they themselves viewed their partnerships.

Bunty, a first grade teacher, was a woman who had married twice, and after a genitally focused first marriage, had now remained celibate for eleven of the thirteen years of her second marriage to Ross, a lawyer. During several interviews she emphasized this problem of other people's attitude towards celibate marriages. The couple worried that if people knew they did not have intercourse and did not express themselves genitally more than perhaps twice in a decade, they would no longer perceive them as the loving affectionate couple which is their public image.

'We don't say too much about it. After all other couples keep quiet about their sex lives so we keep our life quiet,' said Bunty.

Although Bunty and Ross felt somewhat apprehensive at the disclosure of the celibate orientation of their partnership, Bunty felt it was important for women to feel there are alternatives to the conventional heterosexual marriage, so she agreed to being interviewed and Ross appeared to be tolerant of her decision.

At the outset both of them were keen to emphasize they were a 'highly sexual couple', even though they had not practised intercourse for over a decade. 'I think of myself as a very sensual, very sexual person,' Bunty said.

> I think of Ross that way too. I don't like to use the word celibate in the anti-sex way other people use it. I don't like to put a name to how we are because the name has been clouded with negative associations. For me it has to do with making a conscious decision to live in a certain way, without genital sex, and that does not alter whether or not I am a sexual person. It has become my way of expressing being sexual at a certain time. Lots of physical contact, stroking – but not sexually, cuddling and hugging. We have passion without sex. We feel excitement in every cell, we are totally engaged in a world that is usually only half engaged. This morning was a good example. We were cuddling in bed before work, and I was stroking Ross, nothing genital. Later in the day he phoned me and said 'I feel good all over, I've been tingling from head to foot with that lovely cuddle we had this morning.' I think we are trying to re-invent our sexuality but when everyone else is on the genital path it isn't easy.

During her first marriage, Bunty had adopted the genital sexual path. At our first meeting she talked about it.

> I certainly did not enjoy sex in my first marriage, yet I was
> incredibly sexually active. It's what you did. But I never liked
> it. It felt wrong. Not wrong in the moral sense but just not
> comfortable. It was not the way I really am. It was always like
> some kind of act, something you were supposed to do. I remem-
> ber once saying to my first husband, half joking but half serious:
> 'Are we ready for the performance?' He became really angry
> with me.
>
> I remember reading this article by a woman who said she'd
> decided not to have her husband penetrate her any more because
> she felt this was symbolic. At the time I felt this was absolutely
> crazy, stupid, ludicrous, but I couldn't stop thinking about
> it. I just thought and thought and realized that one thing the
> Women's Movement has done is to give us the gift of decision
> making. So we could be free now to say I decide not to be
> penetrated. But of course lots of women don't think it is their
> decision. They're afraid − there is so much to lose. If you
> said you didn't want penetration you might lose your husband
> or your respectability. So you might trade sex for a washing
> machine.

I asked Bunty what she felt she had traded sex for in her first
marriage. At our second interview she told me.

'Affection I suppose. Affection is always a prime motive when
I settle for a mate. I need it badly.'

During the period between her two marriages, Bunty looked
for it everywhere. 'I was what you call promiscuous. I would
have slept with anybody. I would often go to bars just to pick
up guys to sleep with. I was looking for something, I was wanting
to be appealing, attractive, desirable. I wanted someone to care for
me and I tried to get that through sex. Thankfully Ross came
along.'

When Bunty married Ross, she felt stable for the first time in
her life. 'It was my first secure relationship. I was accepted for
who I was. I felt very safe in the relationship so I put up with the
sex. Suddenly I decided that I would like a child. Just at that point
I heard I had to have a hysterectomy.'

The shock, followed by the operation, was the beginning of
Bunty's slow but steady decision to lead a celibate married life.

I felt violated and out of control even before the operation.
And I felt worse after. Sex for me has always been tied up
with having a baby. When someone says you can't have children,
when they decide to cut you open to make that come true, that is
an incredible thing to learn. It is as if you have no control over
your own life. Sex had never been enjoyable – now it almost
seemed irrelevant. Then when I went back to the surgeon for
a check-up, nothing had healed, and they discovered he had
not gotten all the right bits out. So I had to have a second
hysterectomy. After another three months I went back for a
check-up and the surgeon said: 'Are you having any problems?'
I said: 'Well yes I am. I can't get away from nightmares or from
feeling I've been violated.' He said: 'Oh no problem, I'll give you
a prescription.'

After that I couldn't stand to have anybody touch me. I told
Ross that when the pain went I'd probably go back to being
comfortable with sex again. That was easy for Ross to understand. If sex is painful you don't have it. So we didn't. But
then I realized that not having sex was liberating. I really liked
it. We cuddled, we were intimate. That was the important thing
for me. Eventually the pain went away but by then we had a
new pattern of no genital sex. Well, we might have it once in
a very long while, but it's always by my choice. The process
has gone on for eleven years now, and I am very happy in my
relationship.

During the eleven years Ross has not been quite as content as
Bunty. 'When we talk about it he always says that he would prefer
it if we were more sexually active. But he has to be understanding
if he is married to me,' Bunty said firmly.

After our third conversation, Ross's understanding appeared to
be on the wane. Bunty suddenly reported: 'You know we had
that long period of celibacy, all those years. Well we have just
had sex. Recently. Between the last time I talked to you and
today.'

It was it seems not entirely Bunty's choice, nor her idea.

'I think Ross felt a little threatened,' she said. 'All this discussion
of celibacy and so on.'

We know from previous studies that men need women to reflect
them and their values and to bolster their frail egos, and this is often
done through intercourse.[2] Bunty had chosen not to do this but as
long as her decision was kept discreet there would be no obvious
repercussions. However 'coming out' as a celibate was perhaps

breaking an unwritten code, even though both partners had seemed happy with her decision to do so.

The case of Bunty and Ross highlights a particular problem identified by married or partnered women. Because outsiders generally consider couples who live together as genitally active no matter what the two people actually do in private, this notion of partnerships as necessarily 'sexual' is internalized by the couples themselves. So women who by their own definitions of celibacy were acting in a celibate manner, found it hard firstly to say they were celibate, and secondly not to see themselves as part of a sexually active couple. Married or partnered women found it significantly more difficult than did single women to use the term 'celibate' to describe their situation without also feeling guilty or frightened. Part of their guilt was about letting their partner down by 'admitting' or 'confessing' that they were not a sexually active couple. Part of their fear concerned being regarded as socially odd. We may speculate that Bunty later felt she might have let Ross (and his manhood) down by confessing to celibacy, no matter how satisfactory that particular celibate relationship was to both parties. We may speculate further that Ross the lawyer with a professional image to keep up certainly did not want people to think he was quirky or strange. Both guilt and fear grow out of a genital society's cultural edict which categorizes sexual activity as normative and fulfilling and celibate behaviour as deviant.

Take the case of Trudie and Peter. They are in their early forties, and have been married for twelve years. I asked Trudie for her definition of celibacy.

'That's easy,' she said. 'It means when you don't have intercourse, in fact it is more than that, it is when you don't have sex of any sort with anyone.'

This seemed simple enough. I asked her if she and Peter had a sexual relationship.

'No not any more. We haven't had intercourse for over five years; in fact we haven't fucked or done anything genitally in any way for perhaps longer than that.'

Peter, in a separate conversation with me, confirmed that this was so. Neither of them, it seemed, had had sexual affairs with other people during this time. Trudie said she was very happy and content with the level of affectionate intimacy and companionship they had reached.

'Do you see yourself as a celibate wife?' I asked her. 'Oh no!' she said in horror. 'Oh goodness, absolutely not.'

When I asked her why not, she said slowly, obviously thinking about the reasons:

> Everyone knows us as a couple. We have always been a couple. So obviously everyone sees us as sexual, so of course *we* do. Well, I do. I mean you don't want to say you're not doing it today in case you do it tomorrow. I think I'd feel guilty towards Peter if I said openly that I was celibate. That's one reason why I don't. But another reason is because we never *chose* to stop having sex, not out aloud. Though a few years after we had stopped, we gave up the double bed and went out and bought two comfy singles. We told ourselves, and our friends, it was because of Peter's bad back and my snoring. I suppose being in a couple you always pretend that one day you might have sex again, even when you know secretly that you won't. But we never said it to each other, so we can't call it anything. Everyone thinks sex is important. They would wonder about us, about whether we still meant something to each other. I think it is that lack of decision, that lack of openness, not being able to confront our changed way of life that makes it seem not a celibate way of life. Anyway if we called ourselves celibate, we might not feel so good about it.

There are some useful notions revealed in Trudie's account. Seeing yourself as celibate comes as a shock to a married or partnered woman. Being a 'celibate wife' is almost a contradiction in terms. Accidentally drifting towards sexual abstinence does not carry the same weight as choosing to become celibate. Trudie's reading of it is that if celibacy does not begin in the mind with that mental choice, then celibacy has not happened. Finally there is the problem of naming. When partners have not 'said it to each other' they cannot 'call it anything'. Without a label the state cannot exist. There is the further problem of the name being stigmatized. 'If we called ourselves celibate we might not feel so good about it,' Trudie said, because 'celibate' is not yet a good label. Decisions about what does and does not constitute celibacy are taking place in the couple's minds, and are affected by what other people think and how other people view their partnership. As Trudie said, sex is so important in this society that if a couple admits to celibacy, people will wonder whether they really care about each other.

Trudie's initial simple definition of celibacy was repaired and widened during the course of her account, and in its conclusion it incorporated several features which occurred in most of the interviews.

The case of Mandy and Claire, another couple, shows some similar characteristics, confirms the notion that celibacy begins in the mind, extends the definition of celibacy, and illustrates a further problem in the way couples view celibacy differently when having to apply the term to themselves.

Mandy, a potter, and Claire, a receptionist in a health centre, are both in their late thirties, have known each other since college when they were eighteen, live in the same street but in different houses. In their words they have been 'together as a couple' for eight years. Initially friends, they became lovers for two or three years but have not been as Claire put it 'technical lovers' for 'a very very long time'. Claire said that (like Trudie and Peter) they used to make love, 'but we have not done so for over five years. Perhaps once or twice, but that isn't what our relationship is about.'

Mandy the potter defined celibacy as 'no sexual involvement, no sexual relationship, no relationship with anyone where there was more than social hugging. No genital stuff. You have to have a sense of being alone.'

Mandy told me it was her work, 'my pots, that are important. My passion goes into that, and of course being with Claire is very important. Genital stuff is not.'

Claire said that they were very affectionate, sometimes slept together but more often slept apart, had separate housekeeping and financial accounts, though usually ate and shopped together, loved each other without having any pressure to make love. 'Often,' she said, echoing Mandy's phrase in her definition of celibacy, 'we do no more than a lot of social hugging.'

Did they feel they were a celibate couple? I asked.

'Absolutely not,' said Mandy firmly. 'I don't think you can be a "couple" in a deep sense, like we are, and see yourself as celibate.'

Claire, mirroring Trudie's words, said: 'For a start, once people think you are a couple you are automatically defined as sexually active. If they felt you weren't they'd think you were weird. That gets into our heads too.'

Mandy said she had been thinking about what celibacy meant to her and that her definition was too limited.

It can't only be about sexual abstention because if it was, I might think we were celibate. But perhaps we do not have the freedom to think we can be both partners and celibate. I used to think of myself as celibate when I lived alone and was sexually inactive, but now I have Claire in my life I don't even think about it, even though sex plays hardly any part. It is because we are in a longterm committed relationship. That means we try and find time to focus on ourselves but we have to balance that by focusing on each other. If you were truly celibate you wouldn't have to do that balancing act. Also people see us as a sexual couple. It's hard to get out from under that.

Claire pointed out that if you measured their relationship in terms of genital activity 'it would measure celibate, but that isn't a full measure. You can't feel celibate when you have a partner, or perhaps you are afraid to. Would it hurt them?'

'Feeling celibate' is something that happens in the head, another instance of the idea that celibacy takes place or at least begins in the mind. Mandy carries this idea further when she explains that for her the pivot is emotional focus and possession.

If you have an emotional focus sufficiently directed towards someone else you are not celibate. The emotional as well as the sexual focus has to be on yourself. It is about possession and non-possession. We try in our relationship not to be possessive in any way, to leave space and time for our own individual lives, but once you are a unit, you are made to feel that unit is a sexual one. When I was single and celibate I never felt possessed.

Claire said she thought they might be 'trying to reach towards a celibate partnership but we do not have the framework. Outsiders are not kind to women who say they are celibate. They think there is something odd about them.'

Trudie started with a simple definition of celibacy as a lack of sexual activity. Mandy's initial definition extended this by suggesting that sexual *relationships* and sexual *involvement* were equally inimical to celibacy. Like Trudie who began to enlarge her definition, so too did Mandy and Claire. Into it they incorporated ideas of solitude ('You have to have a sense of being alone') independent interests, and non-possession.

Both Mandy and Claire were as convinced as Trudie and Peter that being a couple categorizes you in outsiders' eyes as genitally active, and disallows you the possibility of seeing yourself as celibate.

Both couples mentioned the internalization of normative attitudes to sexuality and coupledom. Mandy and Claire however were clearer about society's 'framework' being so genitally pressurizing that it did not offer women a context against which they could act freely. 'Everywhere you turn – magazines, pop songs – there are messages about doing it, or how to do it better. It gets worse if you're in long term couples, then the messages say sex has gone stale, and offers you remedies. There is no freedom to think we can be both partners and celibates.'

Other people's choices, when they are made from conviction and when they are proclaimed publicly, challenge all of us to look again at our own. This can be a threatening experience, which is why women who are still locked into sexual relationships with men or other women find celibacy somewhat discomfiting if not downright disturbing. It also helps to explain why men's response to women's celibacy is either openly hostile or quietly contemptuous.

Several women substantiated both these points:

'I've always accepted the idea that lasting satisfaction comes from a sexual relationship with your husband, or live-in lover, so it's been very off-putting to see several of my women friends who have decided to have neither, looking so damn calm and contented.'

'My husband thinks my celibate women friends who are all single, and a pretty calm lot compared to me, stir me up. He's always getting at them in a jokey way of course. I think he feels sorry for them. My brother agrees with him and says it's obvious my friends are not doing it because they're not the types men want to do it with.'

'Not doing it' with men, is often the initial clichéd shorthand description of celibacy used by people who have not reflected on what it may actually mean to the women concerned. For as we can see from these women's accounts, this is a familiar but nevertheless merely a male version of a largely undocumented form of female sexual behaviour.

My own first encounter with the term 'celibacy', which came in the seventies in Liverpool, bears some of the hallmarks of this same ill-considered approach. It, too, shows just how intimidating a woman's choice of celibacy can appear. It is a story of a friend's celibacy, which I, at that time, like some of the women I interviewed recently, found extremely disconcerting.

Christine, one of my woman friends, was engaged in a passionate love affair with a man who was married to Emmy, another woman friend. Emmy in turn was excitedly involved in her first lesbian relationship with another woman in our social circle. As you see, the sexually swinging sixties had come a decade late to Liverpool, but come it had, swing it did, and exhausting it certainly was. Everyone I knew at that time was involved in the complex 'permissive' merry-go-round characteristic of the sexually frenetic society of the sixties and seventies in Great Britain.

Suddenly Christine announced that she was going to transform her life, give up John, her male lover, give up all sexual activity.

'I want to feel independent,' she said. 'I need to have a sense of autonomy. I want to make some creative changes in my life so I have made the decision to become celibate.'

Few friends took her seriously. She looked to me for support in what was at the time (and perhaps even now) a brave and non-conformist decision. It was seventeen years ago, and at that point, although a feminist, I had never heard any woman use the term celibacy with serious intent, apart from the nun with whom I taught at Walton Jail. My overriding feeling at hearing Christine's proposal was one of shock. I also recall feeling a certain discomfort. The traditionally ascribed relationship of celibacy to religion made the reality of a friend's decision which did not appear to have that spiritual commitment less comprehensible.

How did I respond? I have to admit that my reply was singularly lacking in support. What I said was something like: 'Oh Christine, poor you! That's awful. And I've always thought of you as such a sexual person. Why don't you think about it?'

What I did next was to rush out and buy her a thin handbook on masturbation. I inscribed it: 'To Christine, in case things get difficult, love Sal.'

When Christine says she is making a 'decision' to become celibate and that what she needs is a 'sense of autonomy', once again we see that celibacy is both more than and different from mere genital abstention, and that it is a process which begins in the mind. What we learn from my verbal responses to Christine's controversial statement is that three narrow notions: that celibacy must be an asexual state, ('I've always thought of you as such a sexual person'), that the celibate woman is somehow a failure, ('poor you! That's awful') and that masturbation must be integral to the state of celibacy, are implicit in my reaction to Christine's decision to *choose* celibacy, just as they would have been had she told me that her sexual partner had deserted her, and that she was therefore unwillingly in a state of sexual inactivity.

I am not calling the *unwilling* disengagement from sexual relations by the term 'celibacy', as I have reserved that label for a situation which includes the element of choice. I use the term 'passionate celibacy' for the form of behaviour where a highly conscious and thought-out decision has been taken for positive reasons. As one interviewee said: 'Celibacy is about *your* choice. You aren't celibate when someone else chooses that for you. Not having a sexual relationship but wanting one is *not* celibacy. It is circumstances and usually miserable circumstances at that.'

Today there is a much more flexible and open attitude towards forms of sexual activity adopted by women, but there is still a rigid resistance to the idea that women might want to choose to be celibate.

Corrine Beaver, an Australian youth and community worker, who has systematically and humorously fought male resistance to her decision to be celibate at different stages in her life, told me how she dealt with the problem.

> I have been celibate for several long periods. Each time the men who knew me insisted that I was only celibate because I couldn't get any, or they said that there was something wrong with me. Several men suggested 'Your last experience must have been a bad one dear!'
>
> I could have written them off as irritating bastards, but I didn't. I decided I wanted to continue to relate to them as friends if that was possible. I enjoy male company, so I decided to educate them in the hope that eventually as the friendships developed they would come to see my celibate choice as a choice.

Making choices is a key concept to Corrine Beaver as it was to all the women I interviewed in this study. At twenty-eight, Corrine believes in empowering the young people she works with, especially the young women, so that they can speak for themselves and make their own choices rather than have other people speak for them and restrict their lives with limited options:

> This world does not allow or want women to make choices. Let alone a choice which says no bonking. I believe that though

an option like celibacy is difficult for young girls, at many times in their lives it may be essential for their development into independent productive people. I want young girls to go for it, to be able to say 'men and sex are standing in my way just now. I won't dump them but I'll do what's best for me.' It is the way I've learnt to act in my own life.

Part of Corrine's work with adolescents is to teach sex education to thirteen to seventeen-year-olds. Her classes become forums for discussions on abortion, contraception, differing life options such as how to choose lesbianism or homosexuality, how to decide to be a nun, or how to opt for celibacy.

At first the kids think it is a bit of a joke. Certainly the concept of a girl deliberately deciding to be celibate isn't exactly widespread. At the beginning the boys, almost without exception, define celibacy as 'can't get any'. The girls don't go for that and look mad as hell but a lot of them stay quiet. Then a couple of brave ones will say it is not 'can't get any' it is 'choose not to'. That is when the discussion really gets going. As we look at all sides of the issue, which certainly interests them as well as getting some backs up, more and more girls recognize that celibacy is not merely an abstention from sex, it can be a decision in favour of a form of self-sexuality. I try to show them that a woman who is celibate is still sexual because our sexuality is a total part of ourselves. The way we walk, the way we talk, the way we give out certain expressions with our eyes, all this is sexual. Being celibate is being sexual: sexually active with ourselves and affectionate with other people. It is just another sexual option like being gay.

Corrine said that the girls were much more aware of what a total sexuality meant than the boys were. 'They had a holistic idea. They didn't cut themselves off, or cut up love from sex from affection. The boys had a very cut off view. When they said "sex" they all had images of their penises.'

By the end of her classes most of the students had come up with ideas about the usefulness of not having a sexual relationship when you needed to focus your energies on something else. 'Studies or sports were the favourites. They all felt celibacy could be useful in that way. Several girls felt it might give them time to develop a new part of themselves. But many were afraid the boys would still laugh at them.'

The significance of the two phrases used by Corrine's class: 'can't get any' and 'choose not to' is that not only do they point to the overwhelming prioritization of genital expression in our culture, but both phrases also point to the way in which sexual activity *with men* is used as the norm for all sexual expression. In other words, the boys decided that celibate girls 'can't get any sex with men' and the girls retaliated by saying they could 'choose not to have sex with men'. Only later in the discussion was Corrine able to lead her students away from this view of celibacy that is male-defined as deficient and negative (because it does not relate to men) and towards a view of celibacy that is woman-defined as a form of autonomous female sexuality.

In this society we seem unable to hold in our heads at the same time the twin concepts of a woman being sexual but not genitally available to men. We still evaluate celibacy according to three narrow notions: failure, asexuality and the legitimacy or otherwise of masturbation.

A very large number of Sensual Celibates, when interviewed, chose to point out that they masturbated regularly and said that they saw masturbation as part of an autonomous sexuality for women. Here are some speaking:

> I used to think being sexual meant falling in love or making it with men. When I first told people I was celibate I knew they all saw me as asexual. It hurt at first, but then as that was the way I used to think, I became comfy with it. But after moving away from sex with men two years ago, slowly I began to realize that celibacy didn't mean I wasn't still a sexual being. I still masturbate a great deal. Masturbation keeps me aware of my body and in control of it. So does expressing physical affection. I no longer want to express genital feelings with other adults, I am perfectly happy to express those with myself.
>
> (Forty-year-old British sociologist)

> I am a single parent, and I work long hours. There's just Becky my six year old and me. We are a team. I became celibate partly to make sure she had enough of my time. I masturbate a lot. That is important as a way of expressing my sexuality. But Becky is my main outlet for loving. With her and my friends for support I am content.
>
> (34-year-old British technician)

For some women however, masturbation was taboo. Even some Sensual Celibates who enjoyed hugging and kissing and 'the kind of touching that comes when you are intimate with someone' ruled out masturbation if they saw it as part of a genitally fixated behaviour which men impose on women. Their deep-seated fear and abhorrence of the violent culture within which women live and to which we are all exposed daily, as much through advertising and pornography as through the traumas of rape, incest, battering and other sexual abuses, had made several married women decide to give up all genital activity with their husbands.

One woman, characteristic of many, was Kit.

'Mike and I have been married for eight years with less and less genitally based sex, almost none at all for the last six years. We have a wonderfully intimate and affectionate companionship.'

She explained where she saw masturbation fitting into this picture:

> I see masturbation as mixed up with the rest of that kind of genital sexuality which men go on about . . . I don't like the images, they are violent about women; I don't want my sexuality to be expressed in that way. Or shown on billboards. And masturbation, well, no, that isn't violent, but it's a similar kind of focusing on one area of the body. Men go on about that bit of the body all the time. Male sexuality centres on women's genitals as if that's what it's about. Well it isn't. I'm sexual all the time, but I don't want the violent pictures and I don't want that stuff centred around my genitals.

Kit sees herself as a highly political person, and believes the problem is a matter of power.

> It's about being submissive as a woman, all that connection between penises, knives, guns and sexuality. I don't want men eroticizing my subordination or acting out their domination on my body. It makes it difficult for me in an individual relationship with a man to separate that out and say 'Well this man and this lovemaking is different from all that.' I can't separate those images and the fact that for years I responded to them, from what I now want in my life. I don't want violence in any part of it. I don't want to participate in that kind of sexuality. So I have asked Mike to accept a relationship that is celibate.

Although Kit did not share Mandy and Claire's view that being a couple in some sense ruled out the possibility of being a celibate partnership, she did share with them (and with Ross and Bunty) the knowledge that other people would either assume partners were sexually active, or would adopt discriminatory views about the couple if they chose to be openly celibate.

'Mike, much more than me, thinks people will get negative ideas about us as a couple when they know we are celibate. For me there's a different sense – I live in my head a lot.'

These negative attitudes applied to celibacy by outsiders are not merely held by men and women who are sexually active, who perceive celibacy as a threat to their way of life, but are often internalized by consciously celibate women themselves.

Part of an account given by a celibate woman called Polly Blue (for an anthology of varieties of women's religious experiences) shows how both positive and negative attitudes to celibacy can be simultaneously internalized.[3]

Polly Blue, the 33-year-old daughter of a rural dean, is a poet with a job as office manager in a Methodist Church, who after twelve years in the women's movement, spent the next seven years in what she describes as '(mostly) self-chosen celibacy'.[4] Although she describes her life as one in which 'I do (usually) feel good, sharing my life with friends, spending a lot of time alone, generally being sexual with nobody but me', she finds herself both highly confident about her celibate choice but at the same time almost unconsciously prey to disquieting negative feelings.[5]

'I must confess at the outset that yes, yes, I blossom and grow all over the place like a briar rose, I learn new hobbies, I have energy to spread around like jam, I am the solitary magic huntress in the forest, *the wise spinster*, the renewed virgin that meets the last unicorn, but damn it, *I still feel like a failure*.'[6] (My emphasis.)

She goes on to say: 'I don't feel terrible on my own – far from it, I live with friends in a noisy open household and hoard my moments of privacy, *I don't feel asexual* (yes, since you asked, and **everybody** confronted with the word celibacy does ask, *I do masturbate a lot*), I don't feel unsupported or unloved ... Nowadays with my feminist rage unimpaired, and my clarity, I hope undiminished, I still sometimes feel like – well *a spinster in my thirties* ...'[7] (My emphasis.)

Polly Blue knows that men use the word 'spinster' to show contempt for women who have chosen to become sexually unavailable to them. When she reminds herself and us of Mary Daly's heartening reclamation of the term 'spinster' ('She who has chosen her Self, who defines her Self, by choice neither in relation to children nor to men, who is Self identified – a whirling dervish, spinning in a new time space'), we know that she recognizes how important it is for celibate women in particular to use the word in a positive way. Yet in her account she is unable to do that consistently.[8]

She starts optimistically by calling herself 'the wise spinster', using the word in its most positive sense, using it as Mary Daly does, in celebration. Then she admits that sometimes she still feels 'like a failure'. Or worse 'like – well a spinster in my thirties'. In this second use of the term we hear the perjorative male put-down.

Polly Blue made the decision to live such a life after a solitary country childhood, and several tormented adult years in which as a vicar's 'difficult' daughter, a 'stroppily independent' radical feminist, a tall freckle-faced lesbian poet, she tried exhaustingly to reconcile Christianity with feminism, but found she never quite fitted into either category.[9] Then her lover was killed.

Bereavement, which cast longer shadows than she had ever imagined, sent her into a black hole where she 'poked hopelessly around in the rubble in an unchosen aloneness'.[10]

Initially what happened to her in sexual terms was part of her grief, and could not be separated from it. Celibacy was not a choice, it was, in the circumstances, the only option. At that point, and for a very long time afterwards, she had no wish for another sexual relationship. During the next stage of her grief, she alternated between disastrous minor sexual skirmishes and strengthening periods of celibacy. She felt there was a choice: either to search for reassurance, comfort, and distraction by becoming sexually involved or alternatively to rethink, reshape, and rebuild her life on quite different lines. She decided on the latter course.

On her own, with no sexual involvements, she felt a self-control and a new spirituality which she had never previously experienced. In the article she wrote later she reported: 'I feel strong now ... though I don't remember deciding to live this way, I must on some level have meant to and mean to still.'[11]

Despite her doubts, anxiety, lack of clarity and social oddness, she found there was growth in aloneness, growth in integrity, privacy and pride.

This development of integrity, this ability to live alone but not feel lonely, and this increase in pride, all felt by Polly Blue, were the same three most highly regarded benefits of their celibacy mentioned by most of the women to whom I talked.

Polly Blue said that she put those attributes to work in a new engagement with the women's peace movement, and in doing so came to a different understanding of the meaning of 'passion' in her life. She said that when working for peace, 'the threat to life sometimes seems too urgent for us to find the distractions of [sexual] passion anything but irritating.'[12] It was the political passion which empowered her. She wrote in an article: 'It is our passion, the political possibilities of our loving, that we are inspired by and fight with.' These became for her possibilities that were 'personal, political, sexual and most definitely spiritual'.[13]

Other celibate women consistently report that celibacy brings with it a new understanding of the word 'passion' that is wider than and different from sexual passion and is often linked to spirituality or to politics.

For nuns like Sister Hana Zarinah whose words were quoted at the beginning of the chapter, a non-possessive passion lies at the heart of any spiritual engagement.

Sister Hana herself entered a pre-Vatican semi-cloistered order in 1963 and in 1985 gave an interview to two former nuns Rosemary Curb and Nancy Manahan, in which she emphasized that celibacy was rooted in non-possession, that its origins are in the mind, and that it is one of women's strongest ways of being sexual.[14]

Sister Hana has battled with its implications during her twenty-five years of being a nun, particularly in the most recent period when she has also become a lesbian without feeling the need to stop being a nun, or to redefine her celibate life based on her vow of chastity.

'I love the vows I have taken, and I believe in their spirit. The vows are meant to set us free, not to shackle us. My vows of poverty, chastity, and obedience set me free from undue attachments to material goods, people and power. I vowed freely to give, freely to love, and freely to listen . . . Celibacy begins in the mind . . . This has proven true for me. During the periods of my life when I was very emotionally involved with a woman, I gave up all freedom.'[15]

The woman with whom Sister Hana fell in love was another sister in the convent.

'Although I felt OK about our relationship, it was a struggle for the sister I loved. She decided we would not be sexual. I agreed because I wanted her friendship . . . But she couldn't be close and not be sexual, so she finally broke it off completely. I was heartbroken.'[16]

Sister Hana's view is that when she was so possessively tied to her friend that she was 'heartbroken' when the friendship ended, then she was not celibate even though she was not being sexually active.

'I gave up all freedom. I was completely attached, either wanting to be possessed or to possess. Because I was unfree to be myself or to love others, I would call myself during those times, uncelibate. During my life now, when at times I express my love sexually, I feel free. I neither possess nor feel possessed. I live my vow of celibacy: my vow to love all.'

The importance of autonomy and a self-focus which enables women to look outward and love others well, identified by Sister Hana as a key part of a celibate woman's sexual feeling was confirmed by most women I talked to. Most felt that with the intimate caring and support of women friends and a loving relationship with offspring, genital sex is not missed.

Corrine Beaver, who was determined to open up young schoolchildren's minds to the idea that being celibate was a positive sexual option like being gay, rooted her teaching in the belief that everything we are and do is part of our sexuality. To be celibate is to be sexual in a woman's way. For her, and for many celibate women, the key lay in not having *relationships* that were sexual rather than not having occasional sexual *activities*. What you did or did not do in bed was less important to their definitions of celibacy than having or not having sexual relationships. Their focus was on freedom. Critical to contemporary women's notion of celibacy is something that starts in the mind, something rooted in the oldest historical definitions of celibacy: the idea of autonomy, of not possessing another human being within an emotional-physical relationship and not being possessed by one. Non-possession was seen as more significant than occasional 'sexual flings' within an avowed celibate life.

For Sister Hana there were occasional 'sexual happenings', but if the mind is fixed on celibacy and unfettered by possessiveness, then the label celibacy can be claimed. 'During my life now, when at times I express my love sexually, I feel free. I neither possess nor feel possessed. I live my vow of celibacy: my vow to love all.'

If celibacy, as Sister Hana thought, begins in the mind, then we have already come some distance from Corrine Beaver's class who thought female celibacy was 'a choice which says no bonking'. While schoolboys (and grown men) still say that female celibacy means 'can't get any', young girls (and grown women) are saying not only 'choose not to', but also more significantly, choose *to* have a mental and physical life of our own, free from male demands, free from sexual pressures, free to redefine our sexuality in a new way.

CHAPTER FOUR

Spirituality? A Simple Life?
Or Just Sheer Spite?

Down among the women, there are whispers. Certain phrases occur and recur. Certain sentences start to haunt me. Women are whispering their needs. Women's words become refrains in my mind . . .

I wanted a simple life . . . I've had it with men . . . No more sexual anxiety . . . I was frightened of AIDS . . . I wanted a simple life . . . I did it out of spite . . . He was a tight bastard . . . I was a widow, I didn't have any choice . . . Sex was boring . . . I wanted more time for my women friends . . . I was searching for passion . . . Sex was boring . . . I liked living alone . . . I needed more freedom – a space to create . . . No more sexual anxiety . . . I needed that break before I loved women . . . I did it out of spite . . . My job exhausted me . . . I was frightened of AIDS . . . I was searching for passion . . . Give me companionship not sex . . . My soul was suffering . . . Coupledom stifled me . . . I needed to grow spiritually . . . Sex was boring . . . Give me companionship . . . I needed more freedom – more time for my work . . . I was scared of the violence . . . I liked living alone . . . My soul was suffering . . . I was a widow . . . I was searching for passion . . .

On both sides of the Atlantic, women's voices told me their tales. Told me which needs celibacy fulfilled. For some it was simplicity:

'I wanted a simple life . . . you don't get that with sex . . .'

'I told friends I intended to stay off men for a few years. Lots of them said they were jealous of my simple life.'

'Other women, who are still having sex, expect me to become

available to them as a counsellor for their men problems. Their lives aren't simple, mine is. That's what I value.'

Women's idea of simplicity was often bound up with the feeling that they no longer had to 'perform well' sexually, or with freedom from anxiety about their bodies:

> I used to be caught in the fat thigh syndrome. My thighs are much bigger than yours. They're bigger than everyone's. I felt men looked at them first when we made love. I used to pull my tee-shirt down over them. I'd drape the sheet round them if I was naked. My fat thighs coloured all my sexual experiences. Even when I was having an orgasm I'd have this second when I'd wonder if he was going to comment about my fat thighs. One man was a hopeless lover and could never get it up. I used to think my fat thighs stopped him getting an erection! Now that I'm celibate, when I leave work I sigh with relief ... no one is at home waiting for the fat thighs to perform.

> I've got a hidden disability, motor neurone disease. Although you can't see it, it stops me from feeling beautiful in the way we are meant to. Partly through that, partly through inclination, I'm not an active lover. The women I sleep with haven't complained – at least not yet – but in the past I have felt inadequate. Being celibate means no more sexual anxiety.

When the tales were not about anxiety they were about dissatisfaction with sex:

> I had a series of poor sexual experiences. None of my boyfriends managed to give me orgasms. Sometimes I felt they did not even like me enough to spend time on me. I could be stroked to orgasm if someone wanted to take the time. Occasionally I could be sucked to orgasm, although that sometimes felt too powerful. But I couldn't have one by penetration.

> I was working two jobs, shifts in a factory and flexi-time in a catering place. I'd get home all hours, shattered. My husband hated me tired. He likes to call the tune about sex. When I was too tired to do it he moaned. If I got in late and fancied it, he sulked because he'd had to cook the tea. Sex got to be *the* issue. Then he got into these rages. I got worn down with the sulks and moaning and the bad tempers. It was sex,

sex all the time, so finally we split. I found I didn't miss the
sex at all. Looking back what I really gave up was the hassle.

'Sex was boring. Always the same old positions. Listening to the
same old words. I changed blokes but after a bit that got to be a
habit too. I'm better off masturbating!'
   'I used to find sex with lots of different partners wild. I thought
I was dead mature! Then the excitement wore off. Sex got boring.
Now I find a few real friendships more satisfying. Maybe I just grew
up!'
   Some women found sex empowering but needed a break. For
those who lived with men who believed in sharing all aspects of
the partnership equally, and there were many men like this, marital
celibacy became a test of whether male partners were merely paying
lip service to their women's needs or whether they genuinely understood them.

> I felt manic when we made love. It was our favourite pastime,
> but my partner always decided how we would do it. He always
> wanted to do it the back way. He would ride me and though it was
> exciting it also hurt. Sometimes I was afraid I'd shit so I couldn't
> let go. I had no idea what my own sexual needs were, except in
> fantasy. I had to have a temporary break to find out. He wasn't
> keen but he saw it as a test of his understanding so of course he
> went along with it.

Certain middle-class women fortunate enough to have 'careers'
rather than 'jobs' who enjoyed sex found it infringed their work
routines:
   'I'm crazy about sex . . . just crazy about it – but it started to
take up too much time. There were all these domestic obligations
that go with it. I couldn't concentrate properly on my law studies.
Now I've started my law practice I called a halt on sex and insisted
we have a break for my first six months.'
   Many women mentioned freedom to work, which is interesting
because in recent years genital mythmasters have put increasing
emphasis on sex and personal relations as a basic source of satisfaction for women. Without being over-cynical I suggest this is a
by-product of the lessening probability of most women finding fulfilment in work. Certainly for women in routine, boring or impersonal
jobs, sex could be used as a panacea to divert their attention from the
emptiness of their working lives. Under conditions of low pay and

unequal opportunities and prospects, the genital mythmasters have promoted sex as a surrogate for a more satisfying relationship with the larger world of work, or a more equal relationship with men. Nevertheless, despite these incontrovertible facts, women in all areas of employment appear to be finding some meaning in the work they do, and wishing for the space to do it efficiently. Women with high-powered, well-paid, rewarding jobs appear to need active sexuality less and may turn more easily to celibacy. For some, job fulfilment brought them the 'highs' which either they used to get from sex or they had been taught to expect from sex. For others, sheer exhaustion from a fulltime job, combined with homemaking and childcare, left them little energy and less inclination for sex even if the jobs themselves brought them few financial or psychological rewards.

> John didn't like it when I got a job in a community college. It meant less attention for him, sex and otherwise. I think he was jealous of my boss. He used to phone up to ask if I was going to cook that evening? He'd got something special arranged with his friends, he needed me to mind the children. He complained he wasn't getting enough sex. Now I please myself. I have friends from my office to go down the pub with, and if I need to work late, I can. Since we broke up and I took the kids, I've been promoted. I've gained confidence. Despite all my responsibilities I feel free.

> Janet and I had a lot of problems about styles of life. She liked eating Chinese on our laps while watching TV, then making love, usually rolling around bare in the sitting room, or trying fancy things up the stairs. At first that was fun. But I'm a quieter person. I like reading. I'd always gone to literature and drama classes before I met Janet. I loved going to bed on my own with some books and a glass of wine. After a bit I recognized the lovemaking wasn't a substitute for what I enjoy. There were so many more things for me to learn. I suggested a celibate period while I went back to college to study but she was devastated. We started to row; everything kept getting back to sex. I felt closed in. I wasn't free to say what I needed. Now I live alone – I like living alone – I needed more freedom ... I'm in my third year of a degree and very content.

Many women had no desire to exchange the comfort of a partnership for a life alone, but discovered that consistent *regular* breaks from sex could be useful in maintaining relationships:

> We've been happily married fifteen years. I need more time to myself than I used to. I'm changing more than he is. Once or twice a year both of us need to withdraw emotionally. Too much togetherness makes me feel shut in. We stop having sex, still hug a bit, but each of us goes off and attends to our own lives. I need a physical space so I leave him the bedroom and I sleep downstairs. These periods may last for two or three months. Fifteen years together is a long time. Habit takes over, boredom sets in. I think celibate breaks are a useful repair job.

For some women celibacy had long been the unspoken condition of their partnerships. Now the women wished to redefine their situation. Some wanted to acknowledge it openly and change its terms from 'accidental breaks' to fulltime celibate companionship. Others decided to stay celibate but separate from their partners. Sexual problems that occurred frequently were jealousy, feeling possessed, anxiety about being a 'good lover', feelings of inequality, dislike of penetration, over-emphasis on orgasm, double standards, physical or mental abuse. Some women were dissatisfied with certain men, or particular partnerships, especially those with financial or communication problems, other women's discontent was broader-based and focused on the male value system. Inequality was the theme.

'Why doesn't he understand what I'm saying? Communication is our biggest problem.'

'Whenever I want to talk, he is reading the Sundays. Even when it's Wednesday!'

'I am expected to do all the household chores, organize the kids, and do the weeding in the back garden. All the inside jobs or the ones I can't be seen doing. He mows the front lawn and washes the car. He feels really *visible*! That's not sharing jobs.'

'My guy is okay, he helps a lot, but the system supports him every time he wants to turn it around. For instance he gets to go on sailing holidays with the other guys. I get to camp with the kids. When we row it's always after we've made love.'

Often what appeared to be a problem about emotions was actually rooted in finance.

'I help him run his computer software business, but he never shows any interest in the history degree I am studying. I don't get the emotional support I need, and though he gives me plenty of money it is "his" money. I have never been able to equal his wages.'

'I work part time, for terrible wages. My money is counted as "our" money whereas his wages are "his" money. I often think of that when we are lying in bed.'

It is not surprising that money is a constant source of conflict when we recall that women constitute half the world's population, perform nearly two thirds of the world's work, receive one tenth of the world's income, and own less than one hundredth of the world's wealth.[1] As Hilda Scott points out, men are becoming so much richer while women become progressively poorer that by the year 2000 we shall see the feminization of poverty. In other words, poverty will be largely a female problem.[2]

These areas of dissatisfaction, battled over in the bedroom, often led to violence inside the home, or reminded women of the violence outside in the streets, or provoked bad memories of childhood abuse. Incest was mentioned frequently.

'I was abused as a kid by my father, it's left me frightened of sex. I keep trying it but these waves of memory come over me and I'm terrified. I have to have long breaks from sex, and I think I'm coming round to feeling I'd be better off celibate.'

> I was sexually abused by my grandfather when I was six. I've blocked a lot of it out, but I'm frightened of intercourse. I even have a hard time using tampons. I don't like the feeling of something in my vagina. Even when I masturbate I sob. Instantly I come I begin crying as if there's some experience too terrible to remember. I find myself lying curled up in a position in the bed like a child. I want to get rid of these negative thoughts around sex. I'm doing it by a chaste lifestyle where I'm exploring my own body and other people's in a kind of innocence. I have a gay man friend and we do body work naked together. I wouldn't have been able to have these experiences and work out their meaning if I wasn't celibate.

Incidents which provoke feelings like these are so common that the 1976 Home Office report that claimed 72 per cent of convicted incest offenders were fathers, is now a bitter underestimate. Judith Lewis Herman who examined five major American incest surveys in 1981 discovered that nearly one fifth of all women reported childhood sexual encounters with an adult male, that between 4 per cent and 12 per cent reported sexual experiences with a relative, and one woman in every hundred reported sexual experiences with fathers or stepfathers. When the abuser is not a father, he is usually found to be a trusted adult such as an uncle, grandfather or family friend. Today these figures are considerably higher, and still we only touch the tip of the iceberg as girls and women of all ages are reluctant to report such incidents.[3]

Women who escaped into celibacy and a life of their own from fear of violence, mentioned battering and rape almost as often as child sexual abuse.

> I was battered for five years. My face, my shoulders, across my back, and down there. It made sex a nightmare. If I didn't want it, he'd half kill me. Once he got a knife and sliced part of my ear off. He had already pulled most of my hair out for not wanting it when he did. That's when I'd had enough. I took the two oldest to Mum's and went with the baby to the public loos in the station, just to have a cry. It was there I saw an ad for a battered wives' place. I was terrified, but I couldn't go back so I rang them up. They took me in and I never went back to him.
>
> When I left the hostel, I thought well I'd better find another bloke. I had all those kids and Mum couldn't keep them. You felt you had to have another bloke. But it was funny, somewhere in me, I mustn't have wanted one, because I didn't look hard. The more I didn't have it, the more I didn't want it. What a bloody surprise. By the time I'd got us sorted I'd been without blokes so long I didn't miss it. I'm not looking for one now. I've got my kids and nobody owns me.

> I was raped when I was fourteen. It was my uncle; he tied my hands behind me with his leather belt (I've never been able to wear one of those belts in my jeans) and two of his friends held me down. It's affected me sexually all my life. To me, sex *is* being passive. But that isn't always good for my lovers so I become anxious. Now I'm celibate, being passive does not matter. I'm not letting anyone down sexually. I'm using my celibacy to recover myself in therapy.

The distress engendered by overt violence, as well as fear of other abuse perceived as 'routine', such as psychological violence at home or sexual harassment at work, is endemic in a society where US estimates, now said to be far too low, suggest that in a population of approximately 200 million, 1.8 million women living in heterosexual couples are beaten each year, whilst assaulted separated or divorced women bring the numbers up to six million women abused each year by male partners or men women know well.[4]

Rape cuts across all social classes, colours and ages. Education is certainly no barrier. A typical study in 1986 by UCLA researcher Neil Malamuth reported that 30 per cent of college men said they would commit rape if they could be sure of getting away with it. When the survey changed the word 'rape' into the phrase 'force a woman into having sex' 58 per cent of the college men said they would do so.

In 1988 *MS Magazine* commissioned a study, funded by the National Institute for Mental Health, of 6,100 male and female undergraduates on college campuses across the United States. One college man in every twelve had raped or tried to rape a woman since the age of fourteen. One in every four women in the survey had been raped. In the year previous to the *MS* survey 2971 college men had committed 187 rapes, 157 attempted rapes, 327 acts of sexual coercion and 854 attempts at unwanted sexual contact. Among the 3187 women surveyed, there had been 328 rapes, 534 attempted rapes, 837 acts of sexual coercion and 2024 acts of unwanted sexual contact. Of the women raped, 84 per cent knew their attacker. 57 per cent were raped on dates. For young women particularly, date rape, as it is misguidedly called, blurs the lines between sex and violence. More and more women, confused and distressed, are retreating from heterosexual contact.[5]

Of those women who felt physically safe within their home and partnerships, several abhorred the pornographic culture outside, from which they could not dissociate their particular man's behaviour. Some of these women saw their celibacy as a political stance, a means through which to challenge the genital mythmaker's power.

Not all the reasons for celibacy were good, political or 'worthy'. Bitterness or resentment led some women to become celibate out of *spite.*

> He kept me trapped in that marriage for fifteen years. Five children and no money. He always had other women, then he came back and wanted it from me. Every night was like that. I hated him and I hated my life. But he still made me. I stopped eating and got very ill. We had the doctor round and that worried him. Then I started to throw up. To spite him I didn't bother to go to the loo. Finally he agreed to separate beds, then when I got worse he said I could sleep with the youngest boy in the little room next to the bathroom. Once I was on my own I thought I'll show him, I'll spite him. I'll just stop doing it. Every time he came near me, I said I was going to vomit. I haven't had to do it for two years. Now I've got to plan how to get out.

*

There was no sex education at home. Dad was very strict and wouldn't allow any sex talk. One summer when I was eighteen, I wore this thin white cotton blouse over a bra and I leaned forward to take something off the table and a piece of skin showed. Dad threw a flakey and said: 'You're cheap! Sitting there without a vest on!'

He had me married off to Tom, whom I hated, five days before my twenty-first. Tom was more inexperienced than me and didn't know what to do to please a woman. He was quite brutal. He constantly demanded it as he thought he had every right to. Then in company he'd make me the butt of his jokes. He'd say 'My wife is like a fridge – when she opens her mouth a little light comes on.' He thought of down there as my mouth too. He never wanted the bloody light down there to be switched off! He was never affectionate, not once. And I'm forty-three now. After eight years I decided to spite him. I went down the doctor's and came back and said I'd been told my periods lasted longer than most women's. I said the doctor said I'd only have a week clear between them. He didn't know any better because his parents hadn't talked about sex either. He didn't know that a period doesn't last three weeks, and I didn't tell him. In the spare week I almost always got ill. So he couldn't do it. I'd spend a lot of that week on the toilet. He'd shout: 'It's been fifteen months since I've had my rights!' There was nothing he could do. He hated blood and mess. So I'd laugh to myself and think what a spiteful cow I was.

A number of women I talked to had come out of heterosexual partnerships and were deliberately using a celibate break as a 'breathing space' to consider the idea of relating sexually to other women.

I needed a break before I loved women. I'd always known it wasn't right with men, but I'd done what I had to and been a good wife and mother for twenty-three years. When my son went into the army and my daughter became apprenticed to a hairdresser, I was forty-four. I decided to leave the marriage and become celibate. In my four years of celibacy I got to know who I was. Then I fell in love with another middle-aged woman. The kids thought being celibate was weirder than coming out as gay!

I'm a single mother with three children. I have nothing in common with the men I meet. We inhabit different worlds. I tried short term affairs – useless. I've had it with men. I'm not sure if I've had it with sex. Celibacy feels good to me, but I am wondering if what I'll turn to will be relationships with women. At least they understand my situation. I feel drawn to women emotionally, I'm just not sure about sex. To start with I wouldn't have a clue what to do! But being celibate isn't just a transit station, it has given me a space to assess what I want for the future. I feel opened up.

Celibacy for many women was rooted in a retreat from coupledom. Women held strong feelings that the life which they had expected to find fulfilling had turned out to be too narrow:

'Lovemaking was magic but I felt my life with my lover became too intense. We did everything together. We were in the same badminton team, we went to the same peace group, we had the same friends down the pub, we went on cycle trips together, we were totally dependent upon each other. I needed more time alone.'

Illness, disability, fears about ageing, feelings of loss after a bereavement, an abortion, or a hysterectomy, left many women unable to cope with further genital activity. Some turned to celibacy initially in self-defence, but for several it became a long term strategy from which they could draw strength and make changes. Similarly, celibacy was sometimes used as self-protection after a woman had been emotionally damaged in a previous relationship.

Fear of sexually transmitted diseases, AIDS in particular, had begun to affect some women's sexual behaviour, though this was neither a consistent pattern nor did it cause as many women as I had expected to see celibacy as a positive option. Often when AIDS was mentioned as a grounds for celibacy it was linked to other reasons that were nothing to do with disease. Where some women already had a high level of sexual anxiety and were very relieved to give up sex, fear of AIDS was often mentioned as if to legitimize such a decision.

Young women under twenty-five appeared to be the group who were most knowledgeable about sexually transmitted diseases, and whose sexual behaviour had been open to change. They were nearly all aware that AIDS is caused by the Human Immunodeficiency Virus (HIV) that attacks the body's immune system, that it lives in the blood, semen and vaginal fluids of people already affected and can *only* be passed from one person to another if the virus gets into the bloodstream. Most young women I talked to understood that the virus can be transferred during unprotected vaginal or anal intercourse if a man catches it from infected vaginal fluids, or a woman catches it from infected semen getting into her vagina.

None of them were under the misapprehension that it was a gay disease, and most of them were practising safe sex with sustained celibate periods, or had become celibate with occasional genital forays but only with partners they knew well whose sexual history they trusted. Most young women had stopped using sex toys like vibrators, or if they still used them, no longer shared them. Several of them who were former drug users aware of the dangers of sharing needles or syringes, told me they were now trying to come off drugs, and were thinking about celibacy. Many of them chose to talk about the third main way that HIV can be transmitted, from an infected mother to her unborn child, as they saw this as the most traumatic consequence.

Young lesbians, interestingly, though a low risk group, all appeared well-informed about HIV. In the under twenty-five group, many had friends, both young men and women, who were HIV positive. This not only intensified their recognition of the dangers but also contributed to their realistic approach to methods of dealing with the disease. One young woman spoke for many:

> I am going out with a man who is HIV positive. We sleep together but we don't make love. We are constantly reminded that we may not have much time together. We never do anything genitally to put each other at risk. The heartbreaking thing is we'd been going out four years before this happened, and I'd always wanted us to have more of a spiritual celibate relationship, but God knows I never wanted it to come about because of this.

Unlike the under twenty-fives, in general the women over forty to whom I talked seemed to have a greater reluctance to discuss AIDS, less understanding of how the virus could be caught, and initially a more vehement disregard for any possible consequences or effects on their lifestyles. It was as if they preferred to shut such a repellent topic out of their minds and refuse to believe it could touch their lives.

Occasionally a woman in her first interview would deny making any changes because of fear of the virus, but in a second interview she might reconsider. This was a typical conversation:

'The idea of AIDS hasn't affected me in any way. It's disgusting. Of course I haven't changed the way I operate my sex life. Why should I? It has nothing to do with me. *That* sickness is nothing to do with the people I mix with.' (First interview.)

'I suppose if I'm honest I realize I'm very frightened of even the mention of the word. I admit after I secretly watched a lot of stuff on television about it, I went on to condoms. Then I got braver and started asking people about their sexual history. I certainly stopped sleeping with people I'd only met once or twice, which I used to do all the time. Then I began to fear they were all lying to me. In the end I gave up sex. AIDS had dirtied it all for me.' (Same woman, second interview.)

Some women in their middle years have reluctantly begun to change their sexual behaviour.

'Sex was my shorthand to intimacy. It was hard to get intimate with a man first and have sex second. Then I read more about HIV in the papers; now I wonder whether I should come off sex completely for a bit. I don't know what to believe, and I'm too shy to ask men I don't know well questions about their sexual past.'

Where AIDS had been the cause of death in a family, many women had understandably extreme reactions, though not always rational ones. I spoke to Hilary, a middle-aged woman whose homosexual son of twenty-eight had died of AIDS the previous year.

Celibate? *Of course I am.* I have been ever since the day of Martin's funeral. I believe I shall be until my own death. Some days I long for it. Martin was . . . well . . . you know . . . he went with . . . well . . . in the end he lived with another man. His father and I will never know where we went wrong, what we did to bring such an evil thing about. His father and I always had *normal* sex, now I can't even stand that. If anyone as much as touches my shoulder or tries to hug me I can't bear it, it makes me think of Martin and his life and those terrible things he did. I blame myself for his sickness. No, I don't mean that disease (his father thinks that was his punishment – but what had *we* done to merit that punishment?), I mean the sickness of how he lived. His . . . well . . . *that man*, his . . . that *person* came to the funeral as if he had a right. Gay rights they call it, what a stupid, stupid word to use about something so dreadful. He – that person – tried to talk to me, said something about 'We must comfort each other, we both loved Martin.' I thought I would scream aloud in the burial ground. My son, my son was dead because of all that stuff. What was it you were asking? Celibate? Oh yes, I think this whole sick world should be celibate.

Initially, I do not think celibacy offered Hilary any comfort in her suffering. Perhaps in time it might allow her the emotional space to come to terms with her great loss, or even to open her mind to another way of seeing her son's life.

Women like Hilary turned to celibacy as a safe place for emotional suffering. Other women felt it was their souls that suffered. They saw celibacy as part of a spiritual sanctuary. The missing ingredient in genitally fervent lives seemed to be spiritual growth. Was it irreconcilable with a materialist sexual culture they asked?

'My house was filled with things I'd bought that I didn't really need. After I became celibate, I grew spiritually. It has brought some magic into my humdrum life.'

> When my husband died he left me very well provided for. I have a lot of money. But not much meaning in my life. I see a lot of my family, I'd occasionally go out with someone; after a few weeks of friendship we might make love, but somehow it never made the right kind of sense to me. Even before Alan's death, I was searching for something. I started to read Eastern mystical texts, I went to a few meetings. I feel as if a light has been switched on somewhere inside me. I am very positive about being celibate now. It seems to allow me the space to concentrate on where this light will lead.

Several women said that a surfeit of sex, once seen as an exciting escape, now seemed like a trap. Initially the women were unsure of what they were looking for, but they were confident that they could not find it in the frenzied sexual activity which had become the pattern of their lives.

They used phrases like 'a search for meaning' or 'wanting rapture not just romance'. Some of them reported constantly 'feeling empty'. Others told me they had a 'longing of the soul'. Many were 'fed up with a life where you had everything money could buy, where sex was seen as the most important commodity'. In many instances the move 'to put my life in order' was difficult. Families were hostile.

'When I took up Taoism, my parents were frightened. They felt my head was in a place that was holy or deep that they couldn't fathom. I think the word "spiritual" scared them even more than the word "celibate".'

Women who used the phrase 'spiritual development' to explain their celibacy, used it in a wider ranging way than is popularly understood. Writer Joann Wolski Conn explains how the term spirituality can be problematic:

'When spirit is taken to mean "the opposite of matter" then spirituality is only associated with invisible thoughts or feelings. When spirit is defined as "what God is" then spirituality becomes a narrowly religious term.'[6] She feels that when spirituality is understood as a contemporary philosophical or psychological as well as religious term, in the way that I discovered celibate women are using it, then those distortions can be corrected.

When psychologists use the term 'spirituality', they mean that part of a person's essence that gives her energy, power or what Conn calls a 'motive force'. When philosophers use the term 'human spirituality', what they mean is a capacity to transcend the self by having the ability to know the truth, to relate lovingly to other people, and to commit oneself freely to people and to ideals. When religious people talk about spirituality they see it as making self-transcendence real through such methods as worship.

Specifically Christian spirituality is relevant because many women who have turned to celibacy for spiritual reasons were brought up within the Christian Church, or left it and then returned to redefine radically their relationship to it. Conn suggests that Christian spirituality involves this human capacity for self-transcending knowledge, love and commitment as it is made real through the experience of God in Jesus.[7] But because any religious spirit comes to us through experience and symbols that are inseparable from women and men's history and the kind of community we have built up, a Christian spirituality cannot help but be affected by the nature of that community. So a community that is sexist, misogynistic, or hostile to women's interests, obviously affects the nature of our spirituality. This may be why women are starting to look outside institutionalized religion and invent new models, and why many women are searching for spiritual growth within celibate communities.

There are two further reasons why women's spiritual development is puzzling or difficult. Firstly, the possibilities for women to adapt successfully to what is traditionally called 'mature spirituality' are restricted because women are socialized into conformity to subordinate roles that take place within a male-centred culture that eroticizes women's dependency, and treats as sexy women's passivity.

Secondly, women's spiritual growth within organized religions can be severely impeded by the fact that Judaeo-Christian tradition is undeniably sexist, and restricts women to dependent roles. This means that some strong women find it impossible to grow spiritually within it.

The story of 25-year-old Kim, the 'run-of-the-mill Christian', illustrates some of these themes.

'I had a typical Church of England background. I always thought of myself as a run-of-the-mill Christian. Someone who wasn't especially religious, who went to Church at Christmas and Easter and felt at home there. But nothing more.'

Kim taught Maths to children at a comprehensive school and to adults at night school.

> That made me feel secure. I knew I'd never be out of work. I was valued at work but I wasn't dedicated. I had plenty of money and plenty of boyfriends. I looked good, I dressed expensively, men treated me well. The whole sex bit was enjoyable. Lots of men wanted to go out with me. We went to films, pubs, theatres, racing, holidays abroad.
>
> But sometimes when I had spent a lot of money, or when the sex was over, I would suddenly think: well what was all that about? There must be more to life.
>
> I began to get this slight ache inside as if I was missing something. I wondered if it would go away if I had a steady? I had plenty to choose from, and I'd got close to Robert, an architect, very clever and attractive. He would do. He was very well off. No problems on that score. Other women envied me. He was kind and generous, offered to buy us an old house, and then redesign it just for me, to my specifications. He was very keen to marry me.
>
> I felt the walls closing in. Every time we made love or he bought me a huge present I felt emptier. He bought the house and began on the plans. I married him because I couldn't think of a good reason not to.
>
> I knew I was searching for something but I didn't know what. I couldn't find it at home, I couldn't find it at work. I became irritable with everyone. I began to drift back towards the Church. I spent a couple of Sundays with Mum and Dad, going to the old service in the village where I had been brought up. But the services

were awful. Truly misogynistic. The words were so sexist I could no longer relate to them. I got too mad to go again. I shouted my mouth off and upset Dad. Then to please him, and because I felt I was searching for something I went a few more times to Church with the family. Each time I felt alienated and sad. There seemed to be no place for a modern woman in that religion. For a few months I tried having fun, and forgetting about God or whatever it was. I went on making love with Robert and watching him plan this love nest. He got excited about all the plans but it left me cold. I felt discontented – no it was more than that – disconnected. I tried church again, and Dad was very happy. But I felt left out, no I felt let down. It couldn't reach me. I knew I wasn't going to find this great love, or whatever I called it then, either in the Church or in sex. So one day I just stopped both. Just like that.

I called up Dad and said I couldn't go back to Church with him again. Then it was Robert's turn. It was seven o'clock in the morning. The sun was beginning to stream in through the bedroom window onto the new brown and cream striped duvet which Robert and I had just bought for our new double bed. Suddenly I knew I was never going to sleep under it again. It was curious because we had never had a row. Hardly any cross words. I leant across the bed and woke him up. 'I don't want any of this. I am going. After work tonight. Straight after school. If you draft a divorce you can have everything. I don't want things.'

Robert was staring at me in shock. 'Coffee,' he said. 'Coffee.' Then he went and made us both some and sat propped up in bed staring at me. I said it all again slowly so that he would take it in. This time he heard me. He was so shocked that he spilt the coffee all over the duvet. There were all those dark brown stains soaking into the brown and cream stripes. Soon you couldn't see the cream for the coffee colour. It was funny. Really funny. I suddenly realized that I wouldn't be there that evening to put it in the washing machine. I started to cry and cry.

Despite her tears and Robert's deep distress, Kim moved out that night after school. Just as she had planned. She went to stay in a large communal house.

Everyone wanted to know what was up. Could I be serious? Had we had a major row? Would I go back? I told them I was getting divorced, that I was going to be celibate, possibly for a long long time. I intended to give up one of my jobs, I didn't need all that money. I said I needed to find spiritual peace and I couldn't find it when I was fucking. It went very quiet in the room. I was afraid they would laugh. But nobody did.

Kim has lived in that house, with no sexual involvements, for two years.

> I have spent my celibate time struggling with my spiritual feelings. Trying to come to terms with what mysticism means to an ordinary woman. It has become the most worthwhile part of my life. I have met other women and a few men on the same path. Sometimes I look to the East for my path and sometimes to the West. We do guided meditations together and sometimes we sit in worship. It is as if I am trying to find the spiritual area where I am most comfortable. I haven't found it yet and I don't feel it can be in the straightforward Christian church, yet I am held together sometimes by the acts of worship. Meditation being an act of attention brings one kind of peace but worship allows me to adore and perhaps I need that too. I expect in time I shall find my own way. The good thing is that I no longer feel separate from the rest of life.

Sexual activity had played a substantial part in Kim's life. Was it something she ever longed for?

'Sex? Making love? Do I miss it? No, not at all. Funny that. Sex used to take up so much time, it once seemed very important. I thought I would find that great love in sex. But it isn't there.'

This story of Kim, the ex-Christian, and her search for 'a great love' both through the conventional Christian Church (which she found misogynistic) and through conventional sexual activity (which ultimately she found sterile) is not uncharacteristic of women who have moved from life with a high sexual focus to life with none at all. Kim was patently a woman unable to envisage the growth of what was becoming to her a necessary spirituality simultaneously with the sexual-marital relationship she had previously appeared to enjoy. It was as if she had to leave both marriage and sex behind her before she could begin to develop in this new way.

Like many others, Kim had been brought up in a religious faith, and had vigorously moved away. In the next period of her life, she had substituted sexual activity for her religious creed. She is, however, by no means the only woman who has learnt to look at life through a sex-as-religion filter, and then found it wanting.

Many women brought up as Catholic felt it 'was urgent to sin', spent turbulent years filled with stormy sexual escapades in car lots, caravans, airplanes, 'anywhere we might get caught'. Often such adventures were followed by abortions, shotgun marriages to non-Catholics, or bizarre experiences in which the women said they walked around 'in a haze of sperm feeling carnal'. One woman used to wonder if Jesus was watching her. Then for many of them, at about thirty, fear set in. They became haunted by ideas of mortal sin, of the dangers of not being saved. They felt they had 'rebelled against the whole damn Church', but it had brought only emptiness. They needed something deeper in their lives. Most of them gave up sex, several returned to their faith on the grounds that 'you can never not be a Catholic', but others who had serious doubts about Catholicism, developed a new way of being with God.

'A mixture of prayer and meditation is as much a rebellion as all that sex was,' was a typical sentence.

This idea of celibacy as rebellion was held by several women who had been to 'repressive' schools which they felt incited them to revolt. Initially their rebellion had been through a defiant withdrawal from convent or church school, from a childhood faith, or from a strictly religious home life. The next stage was rebellion through 'sinful' sexual activity. Many women used this word 'sinful' smiling as they did so. Some apologized but said they had slid inside the skin of that idea many years ago, and could find no way out. For some women, a rebellion from traditional Christianity led them through celibacy to Buddhism. Lindy, a homeopath, explores the link between the two.

> It is passion which connects my celibate periods to my Buddhist beliefs. There are three components to my perception of spiritual passion: one occurs before the event, one during, one after. Before I became a Buddhist, I used to want something with a dreadful passion, then I got it and enjoyed it, then afterwards there was a huge let-down. An empty point. If I'd been attracted to someone I'd think if only I got that person into bed I'd be really happy. Luck had it and I did. Afterwards I always thought: 'Well it's still not enough. I'm not happy.'
>
> Then when I hit thirty a strange sensation occurred. I appeared to have everything I'd worked towards. I had just set up my homeopathic practice. I'd bought my own house. I had a good relationship. Suddenly I felt: 'Okay, so now what?' I had wanted

to do all those things, I'd done them, and I was deeply disturbed. I could have set myself more goals but that didn't seem to be the point. It was a real moment of crisis. That's when I began to meditate. Genital sex totally lost its importance. I did not stop my involvement with my partner but we rarely made love genitally; instead I became committed to Buddhism.

Some women's celibate spirituality does not have a label, it is neither Eastern like Lindy's nor Western like Kim's. These women, both sensual and ascetic celibates, go to no church, profess no creed. They recognize, though, that there is a life force in and around them. Through their celibacy they acknowledge that some expression is needed of the spiritual side to their lives.

Myra and Laura's story is typical.

Laura and I had lived together for six years and were very much in love. We had different interests and perhaps tried to compromise and please each other too much. I liked walking, bird-watching, spending time alone reflecting; Laura liked board games and TV. The sex was good though it began to feel too intense. It was as if that was our only way – we loaded everything on to making love.

I had this unease underneath as if my spirit was waiting for something. I joined a bird club, went to Scotland with the group. But still I did not feel I was growing. I was still waiting. I felt it most when we made love. Then I became very ill. I had a viral attack, then a second. Finally they diagnosed MS. I was ill for months and Laura was wonderful, but something inside me drove us apart. I knew that with the prospect of ending up in a wheelchair I had to learn to survive on my own. I wanted to break up the relationship so that I wouldn't become addicted to depending on Laura. I couldn't bear to drag her down, I loved her too much. Also this feeling of a search was still there. Laura was desperate at the idea of a split but she was wise and said she'd do anything to help me. She suggested I went away so I took off for the Highlands. One day as I was sitting by a lake I looked at the water and I could have sworn I heard a voice saying 'It is not sex and the world you need, it is peace of the spirit. I am with you.'

I didn't know if it was my illness or my overheated imagination. But I had known ever since I became ill that I no longer wanted to make love. I had to keep hold of my energy. I looked at the water with the trees reflected in it and knew quite clearly I would now search for the life of the spirit.

Today Laura and Myra still live together but they no longer make love. Myra goes regularly to meditation classes and has a spiritual teacher.

> Laura and I still love each other but the sexual dimension has quite gone. I need the calmness of a chaste life, but I did not want to give up the warmth we had as a couple. Laura is a very down to earth person and she is finding all this hard but she is trying to understand where I am going and stay with me. There is passion in my life but it is of a very different nature. Nothing to do with genital sex.

Connected autonomy
I want to be cautious about isolating one reason amongst many that may make up women's motives. Some women may have singled out a motive that struck them during the interview as the most significant but it may actually have been based on a series of intermingled causes. Because celibacy is a largely unacceptable or laughable choice, other women may have fixed on certain reasons because they seemed to them to be the most 'acceptable' either to their family or friends, or (as they believed) to me as the researcher on the project.

To understand the process by which women begin to see themselves as having a celibate identity, it is important that we do not see their 'reasons' as disparate determinants but as interconnected. Each motive follows on from or merges into another. Celibacy as an interim stage, for instance, leads out of and back into the need for a break from sexual activity. Dissatisfaction with men and male values leads on to fear and hatred of male violence or marital problems. Spirituality is linked both to the need for a break from sexual activity and to the search for a non-genital passion. Reasons entwine or are embedded in each other, so that it is more useful to see them as a *web* of motives rather than a list.

Of course there are differences between the positive feelings women have about spiritual development, increasing their independence, or focusing on their work, and the negative feelings they hold about male violence or economic dependence. Nevertheless, even these positive-negative causes are more closely associated than I perceived at first sight.

I found links between women who desired a celibate solitude, and women who needed close female friendships. I found connections between women who were dissatisfied with a value system that isolates single people, and women who were retreating from coupledom.

An interesting discovery was that women's motives were not as straightforward as they made them appear. In almost every case, the apparent motive was most often grounded in a woman's desire to develop her sense of self.

All the reasons women give for celibacy are in some way related to a central notion of autonomy. 'Autonomy' and 'independence' were the words I heard most frequently. What do women mean by autonomy? Do they use it in the same way that men do?

To test out how women and men understand the word, I asked several couples what they thought it meant. Here are their responses:

Lindsay: It is not being dependent, emotionally, physically or financially, it is being able to support myself. (Long pause) Wait a minute, while I think. The way I have just described independence could make one feel lonely. I don't think that is true independence. You need some connections as well. I believe you can be connected and independent at the same time.

Michael, her husband: It is an ability to make decisions that affect me without having to refer to other people. It is being able to support myself. It's a freedom from external rules and restraints.

Jean: I don't have it so it is not a word much in my vocabulary. If I had money and time and did not have to consider anyone else's wishes, I suppose that would be independence. But what I would like would be complete financial freedom and all the time I could use for my very own needs. If I got that, if just for once I could put myself first, then I am sure I would feel able to help other people.

Gerald, her husband: If you are independent you are never one-down. It means you are free of the rules. I am not independent at work, because I take orders, there are a lot of others ahead of me. Of course at home it's different, I'm independent there.

Sally: Real independence would be being able to make decisions that affected me without consulting anyone, and feeling able to negotiate with my partner on an equal level decisions that involved both of us.

Trevor, her partner: If I have autonomy that means in my firm I have a superior position. In my life? Well, yes I do have that. I make all my decisions, no one tells me what to do.

Joan: Autonomy? To me that means acting on my own behalf, feeling free to determine my own behaviour. As a couple William and I allow each other that kind of freedom, but I like us to make joint decisions about areas that affect both of us.

William, her boyfriend: If I'm autonomous I don't ask anyone's permission to do anything. I have complete freedom. At work, for instance, nobody would set any limits and nobody would control what I do. At home I try to establish that pattern.

Betty: Independence is doing what I want. It's for me to have complete choice. Having said that, I then have to qualify it by how it affects other people. I don't feel I have the right to act regardless of other people. Even if I get the choice, I am qualifying it to myself all the time. Only if I was on a desert island would I act completely independently.

I'll give you an example. When the children were born I could have either gone back to work or stayed at home. Now that really seemed like my choice. So I decided to stay at home to be with the kids for a bit. But then when I think about it, in fact it wasn't my choice, not really, because I was thinking all the time what would be best for the kids. I was not thinking what would be best for me. It's very hard to think what would be best for me.

Philip, her husband: Being a teacher, the first meaning I think of is that of a nation-state running its own affairs. On a personal level that's what it is, having the freedom to go anywhere, do anything that one wishes within the confines of legitimacy. Nothing against the law. That's what independence is and I'm not fully independent because I have a wife and family who are dependent upon me. I don't have real financial, job or movement independence because of them. The only real independence I have is in the sphere of leisure pursuits.

I think in a sense married men have less independence than women because in families like ours the whole family is dependent on the man for income. I think a man is conditioned to become 'career minded' because of the need to do his best economically for the family.

There is a remarkable consistency in the men's answers which interpret autonomy as freedom without restraint, self-determination without constraint. Men put a particular emphasis on not referring to others.

There is also a significant correspondence between the answers of the women who not only hanker for an independence which few have achieved, but also wish to retain a sense of connection. Several felt it was important to negotiate co-operatively those decisions they saw as joint.

Men's view of autonomy is based on their idea that life is a contest they must not fail. Women's view of autonomy is rooted in a desire for consensus. Women, too, are concerned with achieving independence, establishing status, avoiding failure, but they pursue these goals within a network of connections, offering support and requiring intimacy.

Relationships are an important part of the way women generally define themselves, which differs from the way men generally define themselves. Various theories have been posited to explain these differences. Nancy Choderow attributed them not to anatomy but rather to the fact that it is women who are largely responsible for early child care. Because this early social environment differs for female and male children, and is of course experienced differently by them, basic differences recur in personality development. One result is that the feminine personality comes to define itself in relation to other people more than does the masculine personality.[8]

In her analysis of mother-child relationships, Choderow believes that, with rare exceptions, children's gender identities which are the core of their personality formation, and will determine adult patterns of independence or dependence, are firmly established by the time the children are about three. Because the primary caretaker for both girls and boys is usually female, this means that the interpersonal dynamics of how children's gender identities are formed are different for boys and girls.

The formation of a girl's identity takes place in a context of an ongoing relationship with a mother, because mothers tend to experience their daughters as more like themselves. So girls, in identifying themselves as female, experience themselves as like their mothers. This means they fuse the experience of attachment with the process of identity formation. Boys, by contrast, in defining themselves as male, separate themselves from their mothers, curtailing their primary love and their sense of an empathic bond with the mother. This means that girls emerge with a basis for empathy with other people built into their fundamental definition of self in a way that boys do not. Having a strong basis for experiencing other people's needs as their own means that girls will view issues of independence differently from boys.[9]

The boy who sees separating himself from his mother as critical to his masculine development is likely to have his male identity threatened by intimacy. Girls on the other hand who do not depend on the achievement of separation for their female identity, tend to define themselves through attachment.

Erik Erikson (1968), who looked at adolescence as a stage in psychosocial development, suggested that adolescent boys celebrated their new-found separated autonomy by actively forging the kind of independent personality that is equipped to deal with the adult world of work. He sees adolescent girls however as holding their identity in abeyance as they prepare to attract the men whom they will probably marry and by whose occupation they will probably be defined, the men whom Erikson sees as rescuing women from emptiness and filling up their 'inner space'! According to this theory (which, I'm afraid, has its own in-built sexism), as far as men are concerned, an identity based on separation and independence precedes intimacy, whereas for women intimacy goes along with identity.[10]

Such theories, which attempt to explain why men tend to have difficulties with close relationships and why women tend to have problems with asserting their independence or individuality, have some relevance when we consider the kind of autonomy which women are seeking through celibacy.

These descriptions of men's identity forged in relation to the world and female identity being aroused by relationships with others are certainly not new, but they have a bearing on how and why celibate women's view of autonomy is strikingly different from the male view of autonomy. It is also relevant to what it is that women value within the notion of independence.

Women feel they have to live up to a male standard of autonomy, which is a separation from other people, a freedom without belonging, something that has to be gained aggressively at the expense of others. The male understanding of autonomy which is seen as taking control of one's life, or gaining control over other people, a method of achieving power or status, is seen as normative. The female interpretation of autonomy, of prioritizing oneself within a context of intimate relationships, is seen as departing from the norm. It is only a small step from men and women's understandings being seen as different, to women's interpretations being seen as deficient.

What is more irritating is that this male way of viewing autonomy is usually credited with the term 'maturity'.

In our society psychologists use these models of 'human' (i.e.

male) development that recognize that to achieve full 'maturity' what is needed is for people to move away from conformity, dependence and predetermined role expectations and move towards greater self-reliance and self-assertion. But because we live in a society where men get serviced and women provide that service, women are encouraged to think that attitudes of dependence and self-sacrifice are, in some sense, virtues. If as women we are constantly taught to be nurturing or to focus on men's needs, it becomes difficult to think of ourselves as autonomous beings. Subtly we begin to feel that interest in others will be rewarded, will bring meaning into our lives, whereas interest in ourselves will be seen as selfish.

Indeed interest in others, caring for others, relating to others, talking through problems with loved ones, these are attributes which *do* offer meaning in many women's lives. Most women do not want independence at the expense of connections. As, however, our developmental patterns are predicated on those of males, when girls develop differently, those differences are perceived as immature or defective. However, as Carol Gilligan has persuasively argued, women have a different way of seeing or speaking, in all senses of those words, and a woman's way of seeing the world is not worse, it is merely different.[11]

The nature of the autonomy that celibate women are grasping for is significantly different from the traditional male view. It is a need for intimacy and independence which I have termed *connected autonomy*.

As we saw from the responses of Betty, Lindsay, Joan, Sally, Jean and their partners, men have a hierarchical way of thinking, whereas women's thinking is connective. When men want to go out and play golf or snooker during a family weekend, when they want to take a job in another town, go to the pub, make love or refrain from sex, typically (though not in every case) they prefer to see these as decisions they can act out without any consultation.

It is of course not only or always men who act like this. Occasionally women act for their own good in an independent manner without any reference to intimate others who might suffer as a result. However when women do it, they are often seen (especially by other women) as inconsiderate or utterly self-centred.

According to a connective autonomous philosophy, when a woman chooses celibacy it is not because she does not care about other people (her sexual partner for instance) but because she is trying to take care of herself.

She desires both intimacy and independence.

These two characteristics are not seen as conflicting issues in the way they often are in men's lives, but as integral and related parts. Celibate women wish to stretch their sense of self without losing a sense of bonding. Many mentioned 'wholeness' as a goal they strived towards.

Why is a holistic intimacy and independence seen as hard to attain through sex? What is it about genital activity that precludes autonomy for women?

Whatever the nature of the problem, it is not solely an issue for heterosexual women. It affects lesbian couples too. Women, both lesbian and heterosexual, explain:

'I feel as wives or lovers we are constantly available. It makes me feel useful, but it also puts a stop to my dreams.'

'Motherhood takes time . . . I'm always there for my children but it doesn't interfere. It's packed lunches, or helping with homework, practical things. I can still be off somewhere in my head. But being a wife or before that when we were lovers, that crowds into my head space.'

'Jan and I have been passionate lovers for two years. But I don't always want to sleep in the same bed with her. I don't want people to ask us out together. I don't want to be part of her *family*. I've lost a lot of contact with my outside world. I need to be celibate for a time to feel whole again.'

'It's being the *sexual* partner of someone that makes them think you're always there. It isn't one way. I want to be there, it's the other part of making love. But it means I'm not free. I slowly realized that a cure would be to become temporarily celibate.'

'I feel secure being in a couple, knowing there's always one person to make love with, but I seem to be losing out as well. I can keep up obligations to my family, he does that too, but those deep friendships – well they're no longer possible. It would feel like cheating him. So I don't feel quite whole any more.'

'As soon as she went to bed with me, she used the word "we". It's ridiculous. We are not "we", she is her and I am me. I treasure our intimacy but to feel whole inside my head I must hang out for my independence.'

It seems that a 'good sex life' often becomes a life filled with helping out or helping along partners, often at the expense of our own time or energy. If help is not the issue, it may be constant attention to the minutiae of domestic living, or the emotional hothouse that can follow on genital sex. As one woman said: 'Sometimes it is hard to know where my lover stops and "I" begin.'

This idea of women choosing, through celibacy, to do something for themselves is what stands as the significant difference between the traditional view of male celibacy – men withdrawing from women, or men denying themselves women (for which denial they are then rewarded with the label 'holy') – and a contemporary view of female celibacy where men are simply *not* the focus of women becoming celibate.

Today celibacy is about women's needs. Once we recognize that women are motivated more by their own passions than by concerns to do with men, it becomes clear why labels affixed to modern female celibates are less positive than the traditional 'good' and 'holy' labels offered in the past to male celibates.

Women's search for passions that are non-genital, that have nothing to do with men, that defy the codes of the genital mythmakers, is the theme of the next chapter.

CHAPTER FIVE

Convent Girls and Impossible Passions

T ODAY women, who have always known about passion, are searching for new kinds. They believe they will find them in or through celibacy. Women talk about the 'freedom' to discover a passion that is not lust. How absurd that we should need such a freedom, that the current obsession with genital activity should make us feel that we have lost it. For women have always found pleasure in a multitude of magnificent passions. Women can be passionate about their homes, their children, their families, their extended families, whom they protect and defend fiercely and with great love. Some women are passionate about roses; others about art. Some feel a passion for God; others for meditation.

Women cannot afford to pigeon-hole their passions; they have to let them slide over the edges of their busy lives, fitting them in when there is time (and usually there is not). Perhaps celibacy is one way of offering women time for old passions, space to discover new ones.

I dare say my own passions will seem quirky to some, but to me they are compelling. They nourish my daily routine, whether or not it includes sex. I have noticed that when I am celibate my passions assume a greater significance. I am passionate about books: poetry, biography, philosophy, any time. Fiction for daytime train journeys. Crime for nights. I never leave the house without a book to read tucked into my bag. I am most passionate about the writings of Virginia Woolf. Her framed photo has been hung above every desk I have written at.

I have a passion for travel. It prevents brooding. It unleashes my imagination. Watching the waves break on the shore minimizes my own disorders. So does waiting for the dawn to break. Or there is the passion of walking in Cornwall, framed by the mountains, watching the bright turquoise of the sea turn to sombre navy with grey lines and swirls, wondering if the famous Sennen fog will soon surround me.

A passion for words. The rush and urgency to find just the right word. Will that word or this word light up a room, brush over a character? Will the words knit together, will they spirit me away?

A passion for silence and solitude. The relief of being with someone who understands without words, who goes away for long periods, and leaves me alone with my books and my pottering. The blissful knowledge that I have several days at a time, up in an attic, away from the racket of life, which no one is scheduled to interrupt or disturb. In solitude I can hang the walls of my mind with bright coloured canvases. I can be who I am beneath the skin.

By contrast the passion of good conversation; intimate friendship; the feeling of loving and being loved by friends, by family; motherhood. That extraordinary surge of sensation when I watched my (then) baby daughter swim her first few strokes in an adult swimming pool. Did I really have something to do with creating her? More than twenty years later, participating in her excitement when she purchased and moved into her first house. Over the years, sharing suppers on a tray in front of the television, with Vic, the youngest of the girls I helped bring up, both of us snuggled in on the sofa beside Fruitcake and Bod, the two black cats.

A passion for politics. The warm feeling of being with those who share the values I hold precious. Marching with other women for peace, or against male violence, or for abortion rights or to honour gay pride. In later years, working and walking in the rain at Greenham, feeling part of something that absolutely has to change the world or we are doomed. Lighting candles, braving the storms, clutching the railings, glaring at the men on the other side. Passion and politics, strength and support, everywhere one looked.

A passion for dancing. I remember as a child in the forties, my mother and my Aunt Het teaching me to do the Charleston by holding onto the back of a chair. Then the three of us dancing it together at big Jewish weddings and barmitzvahs. Today, taking a sudden decision to join a jazz dance class. Wondering if I am too old, wondering if I should have bought a leotard. Then the fever of dancing takes over, and the music that pumps out the world's energy restores mine.

Colours. I have a passion for certain colours. The flare of brown and orange Autumn leaves crackling beneath my feet, crisp in white lace-up shoes. Brown and orange taking me back in time to the flaming brown and orange sitting room in which I spent my most intense years. Memory ensures I shall always have a passion for brown and orange.

An old passion for food and a new passion for gardening. Planting sweet smelling night stock near the back kitchen, and a mass of lavender bushes by the front door. If I leave the doors open on a summer's day, there are amazing smells everywhere as I wander through the house. The excitement of picking new potatoes I had actually grown, matching them to garden radishes, leeks, and spring onions, adding Indian spices, creating another meal without going to the local shops. How proud I felt.

A passion for certain pieces of music. Verdi's *Rigoletto*, my father's favourite opera. 'Sharm El Sheikh', a piece for mouth organ and orchestra, composed for the Israeli troops fighting in the place of that name during the Six Day War. In the sixties, the memorable experience of holding my small daughter's hand, as I watched her musician father play that music for those troops.

Pop music of 1978, the year I fell in love. Joan Armatrading. The LP bought the same year. That first weekend. We were so wrapped up in conversation – what was it we were talking about? – we let candle grease drip onto the record.

The passion invoked by a sensual celibate relationship, conducted for geographical reasons, largely by post and telephone. Rushing to the door as the post arrives. Ripping open the envelopes that never have postcodes. Don't you know that without postcodes, heady tales of adventure take three times as long to reach the recipient? Waiting in, high with excitement, on the nights scheduled for phone calls. The joy of lending each other books by post, trying to read each other's minds. Spending a fortune on postage stamps.

We have no adequate framework for the feelings engendered by these sensual celibate relationships explored by women in the late twentieth century – perhaps in some ways they mirror romantic friendships of the nineteenth century – but what is not in doubt is the passion that is attached to them.

Finally, beyond or beneath these passions lurks another, new and growing. Possibly it is emerging snail-like through years of slow change and consistent challenge. Possibly it has been urged on through the writing of this book. Like many of the women I talked to, I feel that I have started on a path towards something beyond my imaginings. It is something that is not quite there, that requires constant attention, demands increasing awareness, may well be enhanced by celibacy and solitude.

Passions are as personal as fingerprints. These are some of mine. Your list will be different. Women are exploring them through celibacy throughout the pages of this book. Many of the women are quite simply passionate about celibacy itself.

Is a passion for celibacy an impossible possibility? The genital myth would contend that it is.

I raise the question because, in our sexually saturated society, the juxtaposition of those two nouns, passion and celibacy, has an incompatible sound. For in our culture the term 'passion' has largely been reserved for sexual activity, or as one woman put it, for 'great sexual love', a good example of the romantic ideology at work.

Although Polly Blue was one woman who, through living a new life infused with positive celibate energy, had arrived at a radically different and wider understanding of the meaning of passion – for her, celibacy had opened up possibilities that were a mixture of personal, political, spiritual and sexual passions – for many women, not being 'allowed' to view passion as appropriate in a celibate situation is the first obstacle they have to confront when deciding to become celibate.

I myself have had a certain struggle with the notion, which is due in part to my legacy as a Jewish girl who was educated for a brief period at a Catholic convent. This seemed to be an educational rather than a religious habit in my family, for two of my girl cousins were also sent to convent schools for substantial periods of their childhood.

As convent girls we were taught early the challenge and fascination of the convergence of impossible possibilities. The Catholic faith taught us that bodies were irrelevant, that it was the life of the spirit which counted, yet the nuns talked incessantly about bodies, about mortification of the flesh, about temptations that could only be fleshy, material, and all too human. To attain the higher potential of the spiritual self one learnt to subdue what one cheeky convent girl in an older class called 'impossible longings'. Being a girl who let her longings get the better of her, she did something in those days classed as unspeakable. In a free period when she should have been writing up her lessons, or reflecting on the proofs of the existence of Our Lord, or praying for a schoolfriend who was going through a crisis of faith, she wrote a letter to a boy, telling him in lurid detail exactly what she wanted. Inevitably she was found out, every rude word of the letter was perused by the shocked sisters, and we saw her no more. I say we 'saw her no more' because I have no idea if she was expelled, exchanged with a student from another school who did not have 'longings', or whisked away to another place on a flapping black habit. At the time, her vanishment (or banishment) seemed entirely mysterious, but I was left with the firm impression that there went a girl who would never attain the State of Grace, a girl who had failed to achieve the highest possibility. Being a young girl who had 'longings' of a certain kind myself, I became worried, but I knew without any doubt that temporarily I should have to subdue them, for I did not want to end up like her.

Another impossible possibility that faced us in those convent years, was the one about heaven. We learnt at a very young age that the possibility of going to heaven was on offer for all 'good' (i.e. chaste and compliant) convent girls, even Jewish ones, but we also learnt that there was no easy access. Struggle, a key word in our Jewish home, was also a key word in the Catholic faith. The way upward to heaven was fraught with obstacles, and riddled with restrictive rules which even the best of us, which I was not, invariably broke.

Irish writer Clare Boylan, who thought of her convent school background as a symbol of 'aspiration to the unattainable' recalls the difficulties of achieving entrance to heaven which is nevertheless regarded as a genuine possibility. She describes it as 'a universal symbol for expectation and ambition, that I think anybody with a Jewish background would probably understand.'[1]

She is of course absolutely right. Being Jewish informs a woman's consciousness for all time. However, so does being a convent girl, no matter how transiently. A literary penchant for confession was one inheritance I received from the Catholic faith, as transmitted by the nuns. An early association of intense sex with intense sin was another. I suspect my interest in goals and rewards developed from the fact that the convent would offer us encouragement and awards of blue ribbons and shiny medals for special spiritual achievement. Excessive modesty of both body and spirit was something I recall being demanded of me, but to my mortification I did not win any blue ribbons on either count.

I did however learn to slap down in myself any lurking suspicions of superiority. As humility and obedience (as well as chastity of course) were the three big moral qualities, 'acting superior' invited strict penances. Being a child who feared and eluded confrontation and punishment, I did not easily court penance, and would attempt instead to charm or bluff, with a new batch of manipulatively good behaviour, one of the less severe (and less clear-sighted) sisters. It was only later that I realized the irony of a situation where these strong, independent, tough women, who led autonomous and seemingly fulfilled lives, endlessly taught us the passive and stereotypically feminine qualities of humility and obedience. The nuns were hardly conforming housewives and mothers; they had broken the mould, why did they not expect us to?

During my time as a pupil in this North London convent, this relevant and pertinent question simply never occurred to me. Instead I would puzzle over spiritual matters I did not fully understand, as I watched the nuns marching in a long procession through the assembly hall. There was the smell of incense as they walked, and a clickety noise of the rosary beads slightly swaying. The nuns talked constantly of the virtue and suffering of the virgin saints, who became heroines to most of us. We knew that to emulate our idols we too must subdue something the sisters called 'fleshy appetites'. I remember picturing sex as a huge, squashy, red tomato!

Oh yes, we all got a clear vision very early on, about what celibacy was *not*. But what was it? Was it the same as chastity? We heard a great deal about chastity. We all knew the stories of our heroines, the amazing Teresa of Avila, and the bitterly sad Bernadette of Lourdes, both of whom had undeniably been chaste, and had undeniably suffered. Saint Teresa had been paralysed, and Saint Bernadette had died of tuberculosis and, according to the nuns, they never complained. Could we feel the same passion for the chaste state as the nuns and the saints felt? Should we have to suffer for it first? Suffering was very high up on my convent agenda, just as it was integral to the Jewish way of life. You do not emerge from the Diaspora without heavy suffering, as my Uncles and Grandparents bore witness. It was hardly surprising that inhabiting as I did these two redolently ritualistic worlds (one smelling of garlic and chopped liver, the other of fresh flowers and incense, both focused on pain and patience, agony and ecstasy), I soon began to believe that suffering was significant in itself. I think this view had something to do with my positive adoption, as a teenager, of existential philosophy with its necessary component of angst.

I remember once wondering whether it was celibacy the nuns

had tacked on with severe stitches to their austere black habits. There was certainly some indefinable aura that attached to their skirts and their presence, a dignity, a centred control, a movement of love and spiritual strength, both outwards towards us and inwards towards themselves and Our Lady, that was entirely different from the atmosphere engendered by my talkative, worldly, affectionate, bickering, Jewish family, who spoke Yiddish when they wanted to discuss matters 'unsuitable for the children's ears', which gave me a similar feeling of displacement and alienation to the one I felt when I heard Mass spoken in Latin.

At home, my father and uncles were interested in me and in my progress, but they were more interested in their business schemes, their law briefs, their tailoring schedules, and in the strange, secretive and enclosed world of the Freemasons, whose masculine materialistic rituals clashed even more strongly with the feminine and spiritual rituals of the convent, than did even my Jewish heritage. My mother and my aunties, whose own interests generally revolved around the men, food for the men, food for the rest of the family, and stories of the most successful offspring, wanted me to succeed and of course to keep all the rules. They hardly noticed that during my time at the convent (an episode which centred on educational success and geographical moves) I was faced with two entirely different and often competing sets of rules.

The nuns on the other hand noticed everything. Because they did not have men and meals to cater for, their devotion to duty, and to us, the young charges who formed a large part of their duty, was tireless and total. I felt they were interested in everything I did, and far too interested in the things I did wrong, which is how I learnt so much, so swiftly, about confession.

Today, having talked to a great many nuns, I understand that one of the greatest gifts the nuns gave to us, their girls, the gift of passionate attention, came from their celibate philosophy that 'loves all' and 'loves all well'. Their belief that not focusing on one special person made better sense of their celibate lives, allowed them to regard each of us with what seemed to a child's eyes like a very special concentration. Many years later as an adult, researching this book, I had a similar feeling when I was discussing celibacy with nuns in a Canadian theological college. In theory, I was there to interview them; in practice it was I who was put gracefully and attentively under the white light.

Novelist Jean Rhys, who at the age of fourteen went happily

as a boarder to a convent, at a later age than I did, remembers the nuns teaching order and chastity, that 'most precious possession', that 'flawless crystal that once broken can never be mended'.[2] The celibate state to young girls in convents was the state of preciousness and safety in stern contrast to sexual activity which in those days represented danger or the devil's work. I clearly recall sex as peril but I do not remember it standing for passion, because all of us knew that what the nuns were passionate about was Jesus Christ. All of us knew that he was to be the receptacle of our love also. His arms, spread over the cross, invited us to offer up our fervent, youthful, girlish passions. As Germaine Greer wrote in an essay about her Catholic childhood, Christ 'really is the archetypal lover', and convent educated girls (of whatever religion), prostrate and pining on church floors, have little trouble believing it.[3]

You do not have to be a Catholic to bear the imprint of convent life. I still think visions and voices should be taken seriously; I still believe that organization and structure is the way to contain a wanton wildness, I still find compelling in women the combination of fierce strength and unremitting modesty, which the sisters so ardently illustrated. I still find scruples endlessly absorbing. It is no coincidence that having been reared as a child on scruples and moral problems I should have elected ethics as the major paper of my philosophy degree. A favourite scruple, which I spent a long time pondering during my childhood, was what could a girl do or not do in the way of French kissing or masturbation if she wanted to avoid committing a mortal sin? Chastity, as I recall, was always part of my bargaining power with either Jesus or Our Lady. I would suggest something along the lines that if I was allowed just a trifling amount of French kissing, hardly putting my tongue inside the boy's mouth, then in return I would offer five more years' chastity. Generally Jesus and Our Lady did not deign to reply.

I grew up with a staunch and tiresome devotion to duty, instilled as much by the nuns who taught me briefly as by my Jewish family, whose teaching still lurks (sometimes uncomfortably) inside my head.

Novelist Jean Rhys recalled from her convent days the nuns' advice that to go and work very hard at something was the best way to drive out the devil.[4] My own convent inheritance in the matter of the struggle against the devil's machinations (a struggle I have frequently lost) has been this belief in hard work and duty, and a knowledge that part of my duty was to pay passionate attention to those I cared for, in the way that the nuns paid passionate attention to us, the girls they loved.

At some level I understood very early that a non-sexually active love can be just as passionate and just as absorbing as a genitally rooted one; and that such a love has at its centre the idea of being fully focused or intentional. But when I was an adolescent, many years after leaving the convent, enthralled in the first flush of unconsummated lust for the marvellous and miraculous Michael Flower (a boy much older than myself who paid me almost no attention and broke my fragile sixth former's heart), I had no way of differentiating or weighing up these two kinds of passion. As young heady girls out in the world are wont to do, I simply threw away the non-genital passion, and for several years, co-opted by the prevailing culture of my time, concentrated on the genital excitement of sex with lamentable indiscrimination, and a feverish enthusiasm that might have been better applied to my studies.

In the sixth form I developed a desire to be a saint which hotly conflicted with the guilty knowledge that for a girl like me, sin was always just around the corner. Even after a considerable period at an ordinary state school, I still believed that spotty boys would go berserk with passion if they could see the shape of my bum through my navy gym knickers on the hockey field.

I was, as you see, a child in a muddle over passion and celibacy. In the early years passion represented on the one hand spiritual devotion to Christ, a deep and caring love for those who were important to us on earth, and, most significantly in terms of the subject of this study, the independence of the strong female spirit; yet on the other hand, there was the matter of lust which lurked outside the convent doors. The outside world called *that* 'passion', while the nuns, who never made that mistake, and sharply differentiated true passion from what they saw as either temptation or sinful behaviour, were nevertheless passionate about putting it down.

A convent, as all ex-convent girls know, is the Home of Rules, chief amongst which is 'No Looseness', a rule which led me early to suspect that once you were let loose into the world, sin would await you at every corner. As writer Maeve Binchy, another ex-convent girl, said: 'I thought the world was going to be full of lust, and it was just waiting. The main thing I would have to do was beat it off because that was what the Church was all about, beating it off until the time was right.'[5] For Maeve Binchy, the time would be right within Christian marriage but certainly not before that. For a young Jewish ex-convent girl the timing was equally important, and somewhat more complex.

A Jewish background intensified the problems of passion and celibacy, the confusions that arose from sifting sex from sin from sacred states. Passion, if it existed at all for young Jewish girls, and it patently was *not* a necessary condition for a good Jewish life, was inextricably linked to sexual obedience and the marital bond to a Jewish man. In my family, as in most Jewish households, as soon as a young woman mentioned a young man's name, the first question would be 'Is he Jewish?' This was not a light matter. Gehinnom, the Hebrew name for hell, is reserved for Gentiles, and for Jewish women who have sex with non-Jewish men. Marriage to a non-Jew would be so out of the question that Gehinnom itself could not hold such a fallen Jewish woman.

If the young woman's answer to the key question was 'Yes he is Jewish', she would be told: 'So you'll make a good marriage – then, maybe, will come the passion . . .' At this point there would be a knowing sigh from a mother or an aunty. Jewish mothers and Jewish aunties know that Jewish men are encouraged to woo a woman sexually to a passionate state, so long as she is a legitimate Jewish wife. 'Win her over with words of graciousness and seductiveness. Hurry not to arouse her passion until her mood is ready, begin in love; let her 'semination' (orgasm) take place first.'[6]

If the mother or the aunty did not have great hopes of the sexual skills of the young woman's betrothed she would wink and say pragmatically: 'So if there is no passion so then instead soon will be the babies.'

End of passion. End of discussion.

As for celibacy, my Jewish upbringing utterly contradicted my Catholic school, for unlike the latter where the self-chosen celibacy of the nuns was held in high esteem, where chastity and modesty were venerated above all else, in my Jewish home celibacy was seen as a substantially more impoverished condition than marriage. Of greater significance is the fact that celibacy only applied to men. Jewish women were not regarded as celibate; they were always seen as virginal, as waiting to get married, or to be married off. This idea that virginity is merely a physiological condition, a waiting state, that is different in essence from positive celibacy is one to which I shall return.

Thomas Szasz reminds us: 'The Christian teaching against marriage and for chastity (that is for marriage to Jesus) could be regarded as an act of liberation from compulsory Jewish matrimony . . . [so] the faithful Jew finds pleasure in marital coitus and procreation; the faithful Christian in celibate chastity.'[7]

In both my childhood religions it was men (either literally or in the shape of Christ in the early years, the Rabbis in the later years) who were prioritized and served with a passionate obedience. In the secular ideologies that stand as a context to marriage and family life it is still men who are prioritized. The idea that self-chosen celibacy might be a state of independence in which the female self is prioritized, that moreover celibacy might be part of a woman's sexuality, rather than opposed to it, and that women might attach to it with a passion, as much earthly as spiritual, comes as a revolutionary idea to many non-religious women. But to the practising nuns in Great Britain and North America to whom I talked about the relationship of celibacy to sexuality, and the nature of the 'passion' attached to it, it appeared to be quite an ordinary idea.

Like the 'joyful, sexual, wise, funny and loving nuns' whom Polly Blue had known and admired, and who had been eager to tell her that 'they have bodies and are sexual', many nuns I talked to made similar statements.[8]

Two of the nuns I met were working as nurses out in communities in Canada. Sister Anne who was forty-one told me:

> My male patients know I am a nun and have taken a vow of celibacy, but it doesn't stop them from asking me out. They obviously see me as sexual. I see myself as sexual too, but in a different way. Celibacy for me is a way of life whereby I am able to express my sexuality not in a non-sexual way but in a way that calls me to love well. Sometimes it seems hard to give up the idea of being loved by one person but I am immersed in the struggle to try and love all.
>
> I see celibacy as a sexual state because I am a sexual being expressing my love, sometimes a caregiver's love, sometimes a love for a friend or relative, in a celibate way. Touch and intimacy are part of my sexuality, which the Church used to think of as negative but does not any more.

Sister Mary, a few years younger than Sister Anne, doing a similar nursing job, confirmed the importance of touch:

> As a nun out in the community, I do hands on healing in my work as a nurse. The way I heal, the way I touch people physically is a part of my sexual being. Sometimes people, well, men, expect a response from me, that I might feel but I cannot give. Centring myself on God and touching others in relationships along the way

are both parts of my celibate sexual self in service.

I asked Sister Charles, a nun who taught in another theological college, whether she saw herself as sexual.

> Oh yes, I have no doubts that I am sexual. I do not engage in sexual intercourse, but the sexuality that I live is like a pulse that goes right through me. There is an erotic part of whom I am that is lived out in deep relationships of love. It is lived out also in prayer. I think there is a strong connection between eroticism and prayer. It is a connection that scares us, that we desire, that we do not quite know what to do with. Sexuality and spirituality are both the core of what it means to be a human, and to be a woman. There was a time when I would have denied my sexuality, denied the connection between the erotic and the religious, but not now. I think many of us have denied it in the past and it has caused sterility in religious experience. We are nuns vowed to celibacy but we are also women whose sexuality is focused on our call and on the work we do.

Some nuns to whom I talked have had a more overt struggle with the problem of the blurred lines between what it means to be sexual and what it means to be celibate. Sister Angela, who at fifty-three still lives in the community where she took her first vows, explained the contradictions and conflicts of being a 'sexually celibate' nun.

> When I first entered the community, we were not encouraged to give voice to any sexual feelings we experienced. Particular friendships with other nuns were discouraged, and any closeness you might have felt towards other sisters was limited by what we all believed was appropriate behaviour for vowed nuns. I did not doubt that I was a sexual woman or that I had strong physical and emotional feelings for one or two others, but for many years there were no possibilities for anything like what you would call 'a relationship'. There were merely sexual undertones.
>
> Ten years ago the times had changed sufficiently for issues of sexuality to be raised and discussed within the community. I had become very attached to another nun. I shall call her 'Marie'. We were reaching towards each other, she perhaps because she was many years younger than me, in a more explicit sexual way. I had to face what was happening and I had to think about my celibate vocation, my vow of chastity, in the light of my feelings for my particular friend, and of hers for me.

She had been brave enough to voice them. I had finally found the courage to respond. We had begun to spend more time than was appropriate together. We touched each other, we began to focus on each other. That was the worst (although at the time it seemed the best); that focus on each other. She wanted to express her love for me in a genitally intimate way but, like me, she also wanted to stay inside the community. It was a time of agony and indecision. She began to talk about wanting to spend years alone with me. She used new words like 'home' and 'together' that did not fit our circumstances as vowed nuns. Suddenly everything I had given my life for all these years seemed in jeopardy.

Sister Angela told me that she had loved Sister Marie and had been prepared to acknowledge that love, but her profound dilemma was that she was vowed to God.

I was vowed to love all. I knew that what she and I could have if we left the community might be intense or joyous, but I felt it would be too narrow, in some way more restricted than the love and bonding of a shared celibacy that remains pure. We talked and we talked. We finally decided that we had no choice, or that I had no choice.

We stayed in the community together for three years, experiencing the bonds of love but limiting their expression to only those ways which were compatible with our vocation. We talked about it to our superior who was gentle and understanding. From her I felt given the strength I needed to continue in this way. Unfortunately Marie my friend grew restless, and more depressed. Our love, which she felt had been contained, no longer uplifted her. Eventually in deep misery she left the community. I needed all the strength our love and bonding had given me to continue to ask for grace and to commit myself to God and my sisters.

Sister Angela told me that she still loved Sister Marie, that she still thinks about her, but that she is still committed to the life of the community.

It would be facile to say that I feel better for having undergone that suffering. I don't feel better, I don't. How many times have I wished it had not brought such suffering? But my vow of celibacy means more to me now than before it had been tested. During the anxious sexually intimate times with her I felt possessed, I did not feel free to do my work for God. Sometimes now I am sad, but I am not focused on a single person. I feel I can act out my ministry in a more creative manner. My celibacy is pulsing with human emotion and spirit. I suppose that what Marie helped me to do was to integrate my sexuality into my chosen life as a nun.

It is clear from the accounts of all the nuns with whom I spoke that being celibate is a part of religious women's sexuality, and that sexual feeling is entwined into their celibate practice.

It is clear from Sister Angela's account that the difference between sexual intimacy and sexual celibacy is less a matter of genital contact than that matter of *focus*. Sister Hana Zarinah, whose controversial definition I quoted earlier ('Celibacy begins in the mind . . . I neither possess nor feel possessed'), pointed to freedom and autonomy as the basis of celibacy. Emotional or emotional and physical involvement can lead to possession, thence to lack of freedom. One woman clarified this further by suggesting that to be celibate you needed to be 'psychically free'.

Sister Angela bore this out when she said that she and the younger nun Marie 'began to focus on each other. That was the worst (although at the time it seemed the best); that focus on each other.' Later in her story, Sister Angela said that during the sexually intimate times with Marie she felt 'possessed'. Sexual possession it seems cannot be a part of the life of a celibate (religious) woman.

It is passion without possession which is sought through celibacy.

It is no longer only nuns who are struggling with this complex concept. A search for passion without possession, once associated with cloistered communities and the contemplative life of a comparatively small number of women, has become the routine 'sexual practice' of a growing number of ordinary women. Many have chosen to be single as they felt that helped them to redefine the nature and place of passion in their lives.

Listen to Joelle, a professional violinist:

I do not feel anti-sex. Making love is something I have always enjoyed and possibly shall again in the future. But for this intense period of my life, when I am with my first major orchestra, always practising, always on tour, when I need above all to dedicate myself to my music, celibacy is my best choice.

> I start to play and it is like a secret crying inside me. My head
> splits inside the sounds. I hear something else rising with the music.
> I feel . . . what shall I say . . . exalted? Nothing else matters. There
> is this purity of sound, and for that I need undivided thinking time.
> I can't get that except by living alone, and not having a lover. At
> this stage in my career I need to achieve, so my concentration has
> to be total. I am utterly wrapped up in my music; that is where
> my passion is.

For Joelle it was not the activity of sex itself which was a constraint,
but the demands made by a lover-relationship.

'I can't be focused on the sexual needs of a partner. When I
make love I get high on sex but I also become possessive, and
that sweeps other things out of my head. Now I need to be finely
tuned.'

Did she miss the excitement of making love?

> It is strange but I was surprised to find I don't miss making
> love when I am involved in my music. That gripping nerve-
> wracking feeling of possessing someone I love or, worse still,
> being possessed by them, is no longer there. Occasionally I long
> for it but I know that is being masochistic. There are big com-
> pensations. I can love outwardly when I am inside my playing, I
> can love more people in a deep way, yet still stay involved in my
> music.

In Joelle's statements there are echoes of Sister Angela and Sister
Charles who are vowed 'to love all'. Their shared philosophy starts
with an unpossessed mind.

For Joelle's sister, Peggy, who is married, the idea of celibacy is
harder. Peggy, like Joelle, started out as a musician, a cellist, but
gave it up on her marriage. She felt there was not sufficient space
in their domestic life for two passions.

> Peggy is different from me. She was never crazy about sex, but
> it was important to her to devote all her time to making a good
> marriage and family life. Today she and Gaby still love each other
> a lot, but Peggy isn't interested in the physical side. Recently she
> confessed she would love to become celibate but did not feel she
> could talk to Gaby about it in case she hurt him. So I guess she'll
> go on putting up with sex.

Though many married women (or women in long term partnerships) felt restricted in the way Peggy did, several had successfully broken down the communication barriers. First they talked to their partner about their need for celibate periods then they began a new celibate life, substituting a range of passions for genital sex.

Margaret, a senior nurse tutor in a hospital, married to Geoffrey, a surgeon ten years older than herself, was what she called 'a recently converted married celibate'. She had given up all genital activity but felt she was 'highly sensual'.

> Three years ago I took the plunge. I talked to Geoff about the fact that sex had faded out of our life. Then we both admitted to each other, and later to a few good friends, that we were bored and felt cheated by sex nowadays. What we cared about was our good companionship. There was none of the old passion left but we felt we could find it in other ways.
>
> Now we have taken on not only a physical celibacy but something I would call a 'celibacy of non-involvement'. We don't give any part of ourselves up. Although we have a passionate attachment to each other, it is a passion that spreads easily through our lives; it is not set on the act of making love; it allows the passion we feel to move us into other areas, outward as well as inward. Sexual passion in the old days, before it faded, used to be fixated on each other. We excluded everyone else. Now we are both extending ourselves outwards and having more things to bring back into what feels almost like a new relationship.

Both Margaret and her husband have joined the hospital choir. Geoffrey has taken up the piano. Margaret attends spiritual meetings.

> It is as if we are coming alive through the music and in new ways. We have so much to talk about. New things are delighting us. We aren't bored any more. I go on spiritual retreats to the country with women friends while Geoffrey is involved in his piano practice and gardening. I feel I have started to follow another path. There is passion in all parts of my life and they are welded together. I am no longer lonely. I should never have had the time or energy to find any of this out if we had continued in our old way.

Some celibate 'wives', like Margaret, are focusing themselves on their psychic needs as well as on a companionship with their partners. Some professional single women are focusing themselves on their inner lives and their work.

Significantly the passion they bring to their celibacy does not leave others out in the cold. Like Sister Mary, the young nursing nun who described herself as centred on God 'but touching others in relationships along the way', this new unpossessive emotion appears to be neither asexual nor exclusive.

Some women are now articulating their changed perceptions of what is and is not sexual and wish to reinterpret the place of passion in their lives.

Janet, a 42-year-old British lawyer, said:

> The few minutes 'ecstasy' that comes from a successful merging of emotional closeness and genital contact is no longer enough to sustain the way I live my life. It does not feel whole enough for me to trust it as a way of being. I want the kind of passion that unites my sexual self with my spiritual self. Does that sound odd? I want a genuine ecstasy that comes from an integration of friendships, love, work and personal fulfilment. My commitment to celibacy allows me this. It gives me sufficient time alone, for myself, to feel sane. I used to pour so much emotional energy into my relationship with Jenny, my live-in lover, that my other friendships started to fall apart. I often felt fractured. I was on overload at work where I felt constantly drained. I can't afford to be like that, I run a very demanding practice in family law. Three years ago I took the decision to become celibate. Jenny tried very hard to be understanding and we hoped we might be able to carry on living together. We both tried hard but it didn't work out.
>
> Strangely as I lost all my feelings of possessiveness and intensity, Jenny began to hang on to me, quite suddenly, as if she was afraid of what we might be losing. I did not feel we had to lose anything, just change things. I felt whole and strong and I wanted her to be a part of what was going on for me, but not close me in.
>
> Hanging on to something that isn't there is hopeless. What I discovered in the end was that it became too difficult to act as what people call 'a couple' and be celibate. So we separated. I hope after a long break we can get back together in some form, and be close again. She wants that too, so maybe it will work out. Meanwhile I have renewed energy for my work. I feel free to love my friends more openly, to make more space and time for them. They are very nurturing.
>
> You asked if I felt the same kind of ecstasy, that kind of lustful passion, that I used to feel when Jenny and I made love. Well, it isn't like that. It is not as private or as exclusive. It doesn't make for jealousy.

I *am* elated with my new found sense of self. It is an outward
looking passion. That lustful passion tied me up or do I mean tied
me down? Now I am celibate I feel independent. At this point in
my life, and it may not be for more than a few years, celibacy is
my own sexual choice.

Janet the lawyer has pinpointed some useful differences between
what she calls 'lustful passion' and what many women are describing
as sexual-spiritual passion, which for me, and I suspect for other
ex-convent girls, has echoes of the celibate passionate attention the
nuns wrapped around us.

The patriarchal Catholic Church has long viewed the notion of
lust or lustful passion as a dominant element in female sexuality.
The high status accorded to male celibacy has been a consequence
of the way the Church set up a celibate ideal (largely for men) to
stand for reason and moderation, which was juxtaposed with this
female sexuality seen as lustful. According to this reading, 'passion'
is labelled as out of control, immoderate and sinful.

As Marina Warner has pointed out, according to the Catholic celibatarian Fathers, Augustine, Ambrose and Jerome, chastity
became a male priestly ideal, sexual activity was sinful, and women
were marked out as sinners. Augustine suggested that because a
child cannot be conceived outside the sexual embrace which in his
view necessarily involved the sin of passion, the child was stained
from that moment. Warner tells us that the premise for this literal
connection between intercourse and original sin was the Virgin Birth
of Christ. He chose to be born from a Virgin Mother because that
was the only way a child could enter the world without sin.

'Let us love chastity above all things,' Augustine wrote. 'For it
was to show that this was pleasing to Him that Christ chose the
modesty of a virgin womb.'[9]

Augustine thus bound up three ideas in a causal chain: the
sinfulness of sex (and so the labelling of passion as lustful), the Virgin
Birth, and the supremacy of virginity. After Augustine, Jerome also
saw the Virgin Birth as the ultimate seal of approval on the celibate
life.

'Now that a virgin has conceived in the womb and borne to us a
child . . . now the chain of the curse is broken. Death came through
Eve, but life has come through Mary. And thus the gift of virginity
has been bestowed most richly upon women, seeing that it has had
its beginning from a woman.'[10]

Thus sexual abstinence on the part of men becomes holy. Paul advocates celibacy as 'good for the present distress', and he goes on to assure the Corinthians that 'it is good for a man not to touch a woman'.[11]

When Augustine, Ambrose, Jerome and the other celibatarians endorsed virginity for its special holiness, they represented much of the thought current in the Roman Empire of their day. As Marina Warner emphasizes, in this battle between the flesh and the spirit, the female sex was placed firmly and disastrously on the side of the flesh. For as childbirth was woman's special function, and its pangs the special penalty decreed by God after the Fall, and 'as the child she bore in her womb was stained by sin from the moment of its conception', the evils of sex, or what they saw as lustful passion, were particularly identified with the female. 'Woman was womb and womb was evil.'[12]

This cluster of ideas endemic to Christianity, which were an extension of Augustine's argument about original sin, meant that after Augustine, for the celibate Fathers of the Church, woman (regarded as 'the sexual') became the cause of the Fall, the accomplice of the devil or Satan, the wicked temptress, the destroyer of men. The fury unleashed against Eve and all the women who came after her gives us a highly exaggerated picture of women's sexually fatal charms and men's incapacity to resist. So Eve who is seen as cursed rather than blessed for being able to bear children, was identified with nature, a form of low base matter, that drags the souls of 'good' men down the spiritual ladder.

We can see from this that when female 'passion' is seen as low or lustful, or as liable to corrupt men, then it is condemned. When female 'chastity' is seen as inconvenient withdrawal from male lust (which, please note, is suddenly elevated to the status of 'passion') then it is condemned. If women choose to be sexually active, they are called whores; if they choose to be celibate when men wish them to be lustful or 'whore like') then they are called prudish or frigid.

Women are damned if they do and damned if they don't. Passion like chastity becomes a matter of male interpretation.

We see the genital myth at work when we look at the words 'passion' and 'ecstasy' whose strong religious and spiritual associations of the past have been transformed into their present secular and often genital associations.

In *The Gospel According to Woman*, Karen Armstrong points to the irony of the situation today where the major form of 'ecstasy' or 'passion' sought by most women is sexual.[13] As Germaine Greer emphasized, since the ubiquitous cult of the orgasm, sex has become for women 'a mystical experience which is a grace from men as Teresa of Avila was granted ecstasy by God'.[14]

We have transferred words like rapture and passion from the world of mysticism to the world of sex. Since the sixties and the cult of sexual frenzy we have invested orgasm rather than spirituality with the ultimate 'transfiguring significance'.[15]

But is orgasm the true seat of passion? I asked women what they felt at the moment of orgasm. Was that when partners felt closest? Did women who had male lovers feel close or distanced? Did they wish at that very instant to be forever bonded, or to beat a hasty retreat? What feelings do two women who are lovers have at what is held up as the closest moment of sexual passion? Is orgasm the deep connection it is so often cracked up to be?

Many heterosexual women who have now become celibate said that for them it had often been a time of loneliness rather than intimacy:

'I was always left wanting something or looking for something.'

'In the middle of sex or just at the moment of orgasm I would suddenly feel separate from him, there would be a gulf between us, just as I wanted to be close.'

'Maybe I'm romantic but I would get emotional and want to be bound up with him. What happened was this awful nothingness. Was this how it was meant to be?'

According to the genital myth it is certainly not how it is meant to be.

Some women said if they lived with partners with whom they could not communicate, then loneliness and alienation was intensified during lovemaking. It reached its highest point at orgasm.

Lesbian women appeared to have a greater variety of experiences. Many said that understanding how another woman's body feels was a critical part of a close orgasmic experience.

'It is as if I can feel what I do to her in my own cunt. I'm taken somewhere out of my mind at the point of orgasm. I have never felt that close to anyone before.'

Other women found that precise sensation too deep, too intense. It had to be held off.

'I cannot bear that feeling of being engulfed by another person, even by another woman, though I know that at some level I am longing for it. I have to retreat, I am afraid of losing my sense of self.'

Some women who live together as lovers, but who differ in the way they identify themselves, had specific problems.

Listen to Jan. She is a self-identified lesbian who lived with Anne, a bisexual woman who refused to limit herself by using a label, found men attractive, and occasionally slept with them.

> Although it is four years since Anne slept with a man, and he certainly wasn't important either in her life or in ours, nevertheless the idea of him, the idea of just 'a man' seems to enter my head at the moment when we are making love most passionately. I feel this awful jealousy. I am afraid that our relationship won't be able to withstand threats from outside. These kind of irrational feelings make a gulf between us always at the moment of orgasm.

Sometimes it is a woman's colour, and our internalized racism which produces orgasmic separateness. Sophie spoke:

> I have recently become involved with Meriel who is white. It is my first relationship with a white woman, and I think there are racial stereotypes inside both our heads. Meriel is fairly passive and I keep thinking she expects me as a brown woman to be aggressive and go ahead and actually I am a very shy person myself. When we get to bringing each other to orgasm it is as if we are both drawing back. I have to try to talk to her about it.

There were particular problems for women who were survivors of incest or rape. Both heterosexual and lesbian women said that at the point of orgasm, or just before, they would have a series of frightening flashbacks. This meant they could no longer concentrate on their current sexual experience. Many, who were in therapy, or were having incest or rape counselling, had decided to become celibate during that healing and recovery process.

As we see, despite the myth of intense closeness at the moment of orgasm, there is often a separation between partners of either sex.

So strong, however, is the genital mythology on this point that, despite their awareness of the gulf, many women still hang on to the idea that sexual passion is the way to attach themselves to their loved one. A woman may go on believing, in the face of her own experience to the contrary, that it is the most effective way. For a woman who believes this, failure will be a very deep disappointment.

Audrey was unusual in neither believing in the myth nor worrying when she did not discover emotional satisfaction at orgasm.

I do not mind that separation. I hate romantic sex. I think it's a myth. I like lustful sex. I've slept with both men and women, and you get more lustful sex with men. They don't try and eat you up. They are too concerned with what a good time they are having. Sex with men always made me feel high even though there was no connection at the big moment. I don't want my sex mixed up with affection. Sex with men was like the best kind of run, hot sweaty and relaxing. After it I'd be ready for anything. Sex with women had too much built into it. The other woman knew too much about my body. There was too big an investment. I couldn't handle that at all. As for this thing called passion, as I never found it in sex, nowadays I look for it elsewhere.

It was her need for a new type of passion which led her towards celibacy. She had been a highly materialistic person but after her fortieth birthday she began to change.

There were things going on underneath I wanted to explore. I left advertising and retrained as a counsellor. I got work counselling refugees. I began to see and hear about so much pain that it became unbearable. Sex was still fun but it had no meaning. I needed to find meaning and passion in my life. There was a Mission attached to the hostel where I worked so I began to work there too. Finally I drew a different kind of strength.

Sex began to slide away. It had no real place in the new world I was creating. In the end I became what's called celibate, though it took me months before I would use the word. What was interesting was that I went at this spirituality stuff with the Mission with all the full-bloodedness with which I used to go at sex. Being celibate gave me the space to merge what I was doing at work with what I was achieving at the Mission. It rounded my life out.

Like the women mentioned earlier for whom a spiritual search was the basis of their celibate life, Audrey too was trying to reclaim a spiritual link to ecstasy.

Women who attempt this task, however, must do so in a context where rapture and passion are no longer words that are used to celebrate women's autonomous spirit but rather words tied into women's sexual dependency.

During the period from the sixties to the nineties, when women have successfully sought new social and political rights, many have simultaneously been sexually dependent, aspiring to such goals as 'sexual fulfilment' through 'passion' with a partner of either sex.

It is a profound irony that spiritual passion which once offered women a singularly independent experience, in its twentieth century form of sexual ecstasy is a definitively, often disastrously, dependent experience. We have wonderful orgasms with someone, then we feel vulnerable, and clutch fiercely at lovers. Such behaviour, which when we look closely at it seems immature, is nevertheless seen as more reasonable than choosing independence and celibacy.

It is from dependence on sexual frenzy and this trivialized form of passion which self-chosen Ascetic and Sensual Celibates are trying to escape. By renewing themselves through their passion for celibacy, they are finding an independent experience that makes them freer from male needs, less vulnerable to male demands.

They are not denying the passions aroused by love and intimacy but they are showing a new kind of excitement for an independent existence.

Sister Anne reported how hard it was for her, even as a nun, to give up the idea of being loved by one person, to immerse herself in the struggle to love all. How much harder is it for the many celibate women today who are not nuns, who are attempting to do just that? That they are becoming absorbed by these new sensations which fuel their celibacy is a tribute to their persistence in openly engaging in behaviour still stigmatized as unnatural.

My own feeling as a child in a convent school that the nuns' passion for their celibate state was reflected both in a movement outward towards us, their girls, and inwards towards themselves and Our Lady, is not dissimilar from some of the accounts of what this new passion means to modern celibate women. 'A free-flowing outward love that is not exclusive' is how many women described it. The OED definition of passion is 'any kind of feeling by which the mind is powerfully affected or moved . . . an eager outreaching of the mind toward something'.[16] This rendering moves away from the dualism between a sexuality that is out of control (passionate), and celibacy that is controlled (and passionless).

The growth of celibate passion is a powerful outward movement towards a female-defined sexuality. A relationship between two people that is intimate and deep and may accurately be called 'passionate' may actually be fuelled by celibate energy (rather than by sexual energy). However because we have no adequate conceptual framework for female celibacy in this society, we more usually assume that if there exists 'passion' in an intimate relationship, the two people are repressing conventional sexual desire or sublimating their sexually active feelings; or we assume that the relationship 'ought to be sexual' or that it 'must be sexual' and that the two participants are wilfully refusing to recognize it.

The importance of this behaviour which men define as non-sexual and women are now defining as 'passionate' has so far received very little critical attention. If however the *practice* of celibacy is now acknowledged to be a routine part of women's sexual experience and social behaviour; and if the *desire* for celibacy, whether for long or short periods, is discovered to be as common amongst women as the need for sexual activity is generally considered to be, then we shall have to reappraise our limited definitions of femininity.

In view of the scope and potential of this issue, and its usefulness to the liberation of women, it is surprising how little serious sociological, literary or critical attention has been given to the topic, outside the popular magazine world. Recently, some glossy women's magazines have shown a series of glamorous unattached women lounging on beds in silk pyjamas, cuddling teddies, holding a glass of chilled white wine, and reading erotica. These are the New Media Celibates, elegant and desirable, on their nights in alone. Often these articles on female celibacy are positioned next to articles instructing women how to live up to male sexual fantasies, or how to get off on their own. Vibrators are a consistently recommended tool for the single woman's success in bed.

This ensures that the context in which celibacy is seen both diminishes its positive aspects and maintains firstly the notion that it is sexual activity and sexual fantasy which are primary in women's lives, and secondly the idea that the supreme (or sole) passion is sexual.

The lust that the nuns at my convent used to hint might be around the next corner, is the same lust waiting to catch the New Media Celibate unawares. For she, like the Jewish unmarried woman in my childhood family, is less celibate than virginal, although she might in fact not be a virgin. She is a transitional virgin, not one of the 'perpetual virgins' who are the subject of a later chapter.

New Media Celibates are merely women in waiting. Contemporary passionate celibates are not in waiting, any more than the nuns, who paid us passionate attention, were women in waiting. They are not waiting for men and are not waiting for sex. Absorbed and involved they get on with their lives.

Both Sensual Celibates and Ascetic Celibates see themselves as sexual beings who do not need sexual activity with men or other women to feel fulfilled. They have come a long way from the male view of celibacy as frigidity. Celibate women, who challenge society's view of what is natural and necessary, are not merely tackling an impossible possibility, they are showing other women that celibacy, far from being unattainable, can be routine, eminently desirable, a way of freeing the soul as well as the body. Celibacy can be a matter of passion.

Women have begun to integrate their sexual feelings with their need for independence and spirituality: celibacy for women is no longer locked inside convent walls while 'real' passion is played out on the fields outside.

CHAPTER SIX

···(▶━━━━➤›⦂❖⦂‹◄━━━━◄)···

Celibacy is More Than Chastity

S AINT Augustine (AD 354–430) is reputed to have said: 'Give me chastity and self-restraint but do not give it yet.' Obviously the eminent Christian leader found chastity more morally compelling than physically appealing – an idea that has found echoes down the ages largely because of the bad press given to chastity by the genital mythmakers.

What then is chastity and in what ways does it differ from celibacy?

As a thirteenth century noun, it derived from the Old French 'chastete' and the Latin 'castitas' meaning purity. With purity at its root, from the thirteenth century until today, according to the dictionary, the word 'chaste' has always denoted someone who was pure from sexual intercourse (i.e. someone virginal) or someone continent and virtuous who abstains from unlawful or immoral sexual intercourse.[1]

As I am concerned with all forms of sexual activity and not just sexual intercourse, I am taking chastity to mean the total absence of genital sexual activity between one person and another. Chastity, then, is a physical state of complete genital abstention but not necessarily a purposeful one. Only if it becomes purposeful can it be incorporated into a celibate philosophy.

Celibacy, as we are beginning to discover, is a great deal more complex. More profound. A significant factor in contemporary women's understanding of their own sexual needs, which in turn is extending and changing the way all of us will view female sexuality.

Chastity (at its simplest, when it is not purposeful) starts in the genitals. Celibacy starts in the mind. However, despite the fact that celibacy is as much a mental process as a physical state, the genital mythmakers either view it as synonymous with chastity, or they see physical chastity as the deciding factor in female celibacy.

The genital myth which coerces women through its constant stress on sex states that if women do not 'do it', if in fact they do not do 'anything' genitally, if in other words they are chaste, then they must be celibate. And, oh dear, what poor things (poor *unfeminine* things) those women must be. One mythmaster told me he saw genital abstention in women as 'useless chastity' and as an indication that a woman was not feminine.

In an era that worships sexually active performances, and demands women's constant sexual availability to men, chastity will be held in low regard (i.e. it will appear to men to be 'useless'). Chaste women will be labelled not merely non sexually active but also anti-sex and anti-men. To be anti-men in our society is to risk being labelled as ugly, ill, or, as the mythmaster pointed out to me, unfeminine.

How do celibate women view chastity? Do they see it as the bottom line in their celibate scheme? Do they agree with the genital mythmasters that chastity is the pivotal factor in their conscious decision to lead a celibate life?

Celibates can be both sensual and ascetic. Chaste women on the other hand are always ascetic. Obviously for Sensual Celibates, who may include genital intimacy, or the occasional sexually active adventure within their celibate lifestyle, total physical chastity is *not* the determining feature.

What about Ascetic Celibates? Their asceticism is partly based on a genital purity, but is that asceticism, is that stringent chastity, the predominant and causal characteristic which defines their celibacy?

Is celibacy more than mere chastity?

Investigating how chastity in women has been viewed by the mythmakers is a good place to start. Over the years several entrenched attitudes and prejudices associated with chastity have been built up and maintained. The mythmakers, always alert, have invented at least four myths around chastity.

The myth is: Chastity is a word that applies equally well to both sexes.

The fact is: Chastity has always been seen as a female virtue or a female problem (depending on which rendering is in vogue at the time).

The myth is: Chastity is a woman's free choice.

The fact is: Female chastity is always under male control. In the past this was achieved by chastity belts. Today it is achieved by the sexual double standard.

The myth is: Chastity and masturbation are mutually exclusive. If you are chaste it is hands off. Chaste women do not masturbate.

The fact is: Some chaste women masturbate, some do not.

The myth is: Female chastity is inseparable from sexual rejection by men.

The fact is: Chastity may have more to do with a woman's own needs.

These four myths link to each other and stand as a context to the fifth and most significant myth that non-masturbatory chastity is the determining factor in female celibacy.

It is time to debunk the myths. Let us look briefly at each.

To which sex is chastity affixed?

According to the dictionaries, apart from during a brief period in the sixteenth century when 'chaste' had a male-specific sense of gelded, 'chastity' has always been applied equally to both sexes.

That is all very well, but neutral dictionary definitions ignore the word's overwhelmingly feminine associations. Try saying the word 'chaste' to someone, ask them for an instant association, and you will find that the most common spontaneous answer is 'virgin'. Female. No doubt about it. The word 'chaste' rarely conjures up a virtuous male 'virgin' abstaining from sex.

As Simone de Beauvoir said, patriarchal civilization dedicated woman to chastity, and while it recognized more or less openly the right of the male to sexual freedom, woman was restricted to marriage.[2]

The perception of chastity as a vital *female* virtue, is related to the history of Christianity, but it is also related, and more significantly, to the development of women's economic position. In times when that has been insecure, in a patrilineal propertied society, chastity has become women's most highly valued possession. In 1884 Friedrich Engels in *The Origin of the Family, Private Property and the State* identified the rights of the father and the end of the matrilineal clan with the beginnings of private ownership and slavery. This change from matrilineal to patrilineal succession, contributed quite as much as did the spread of Christianity to the popular view of chastity as a womanly characteristic. Men needed to be sure of the legitimacy of their heirs to their titles and property. Women's chastity became crucial for this purpose and had to be kept under strict surveillance.

Chastity: a form of freedom or under male control?

Sexual innocence is demanded of young women but not of young men. Society's widely different expectations for men and women in the matter of chastity leads to women being controlled and manipulated. Shirley Ardener points to the fact that men are expected to chase women, and if they can to seduce them, the women being classed as 'fair game'.[3] The sexual double standard has become the modern invisible chastity belt for women. It is commonplace to find in many partnerships a situation where men are 'allowed' by both partners to stray sexually whereas women are expected to stay faithful. Partnerships between women which use this style of relationship as a model encounter similar problems.

Contemporary women's need for a new kind of connected autonomy, for being seen and accepted as equal human beings rather than as servers, does not seem to be adequately catered for in the sexual framework of most twentieth century partnerships. In many cases these relationships have not adapted to the changing and changed social roles of women and men. This could be the gap which passionate celibacy is filling.

The hidden danger of a 'good' marriage or a 'good' partnership, (i.e. one that works) is the extent to which the *woman* is expected to adapt and fit in, particularly in the matter of sex. When her husband or partner has an affair, she is either an unwilling accomplice, a powerless survivor or, too often, someone who blames herself. Her own sexual activity meanwhile is contained and belted to the marital bed.

Historically of course, in order to ensure that the actual business of chastity, just as much as the word itself, was never free from male control, men provided the women they 'owned' with chastity girdles.

Originally a medieval device, the chastity belt was imported from the East by thirteenth century crusaders at a time when protracted male absences were very common. The girdles fastened around the waist and between the legs in such a way as to preclude all possibility of infidelity during the husbands' tours in war, on pilgrimages, or on crusades. In theory this malevolent metal tool of torture was constructed with small spike holes in its pelvic fetter through which urine, faeces, and menstrual blood were supposed to pass. In practice it would have been impossible to have kept such a device clean. Skin eruptions, vaginal infections, sores, and ulcers would have been inevitable after wearing such a 'girdle' for only a short time. Imagine the effects on the bodies of women, many of whom were forced to wear them for months or even years. This blatant control of women's chastity is simply an early example (paralleled today by control measures such as sexual abuse, incest, and rape) of the ways in which male violence systematically contains and crushes women's sexuality for the purposes of male power and pleasure.

The sadistic use of the chastity belt continued as late as the nineteenth century. In 1880 a French merchandising company advertised the *camisole de force* with this slogan:

> The advantages are manifold. Not only will the purity of the virgin be maintained, but the fidelity of the wife exacted. The husband will leave the wife without fear that his honour will be outraged and his affections estranged. Fathers will be sure of their parenthood and will not harbour the terrible thought that their children may be the offspring of another, and it will be possible for them to keep under lock and key things more precious than gold.[4]

That chastity belts are still viewed as 'erotica' rather than as instruments of torture was illustrated recently when the British Museum unveiled one of its best kept secrets: a 'museum secretum' in which locked away for more than a century were remnants of what they described as one of the world's greatest collections of erotic antiques. There was a phallus-shaped Japanese glass drinking vessel for warmed sake, a Roman terracotta figure of a satyr making love to a goat, a membership certificate for an English drinking club where risqué stories were recounted, an eighteenth century condom, and several boxes of wax penises which were hung in Italian churches by men praying for a strengthening of their reproductive powers. Amongst these 'erotic' objects, centre stage, was the iron chastity belt, once thought to be medieval, now assumed to be an eighteenth century fake. Fake or antique, the purpose of this terrifying tool of torture was still the same across the centuries. Chastity, seen from within the confines of chastity belts, is about men keeping hold of women's right to sexual access. It is a direct example of male control of women's sexuality through punitive measures. It is a world away from the self-chosen chastity embodied by a modern ideal of passionate celibacy, which is about women's control of themselves and their sexual choices.

Do chaste women masturbate?

One of my ex-husbands tells a true story which illustrates the third myth (chaste women do not masturbate) and shows how some men regard masturbation by women they believe to be chaste.

It was very early in the sixties, before large scale permissiveness was the norm, when certain sexual actions were seen as taboo for 'proper women'. He had an appointment to call upon a lady friend. She was, in his eyes, and in the eyes of the world, definitively a lady, and definitively chaste. He had been calling on her assiduously, regularly, with a view to . . . well, let us just say he had been calling on her with a certain (I can only assume) agreeable persistence. He felt sufficiently knowledgeable, however, to vouch both for her chastity and for her femininity. On this particular morning, it was a Wednesday (a fact that is crucial to the tale), he called on her with hope in his heart, for this time *she* had invited him over. He rang the door bell. There was no reply but her apartment door was temptingly ajar. He walked in to hear her shout from upstairs:

'Busy. Down soon. Make yourself at home.'

He wandered into the kitchen. Suddenly he noticed for the first time a large day-by-day wall calendar. On it was written in her exquisite ladylike copperplate hand:

Monday 3pm Dentist.

Tuesday 4pm Hairdresser.

Wednesday 11am Masturbate.

(His name or the nature of his visit was not inscribed on the calendar.)

He could hardly believe the public information which greeted his gaze. In shock and horror he glanced at his wristwatch. It registered Wednesday 11.15am.

Busy, down soon, she had said. 11am masturbate, she had written. He fled.

I told the story to a sensitive male friend. His somewhat rueful comment was: 'If a man thinks a woman is chaste, he wants to keep her that way, until he is ready to take her over. The idea of a chaste woman masturbating, specially making *time* to do it, might seem competitive. After all, if you are going to put masturbation into your routine, it sounds as if you do it *well*, I mean really bring yourself off! Maybe better than a man could!'

Even though the times have moved on, taboos and secrecy still surround masturbation. There are still anxieties about appearing too assertive or too independent of men's sexual performances.

The idea that chaste women do not masturbate is, of course, nonsense. Some chaste women masturbate and some do not. Just as some sexually active women masturbate and some do not. This myth however is still one of the biggest fictions men weave about women, which subsequently women internalize then weave about themselves. Women are still loath to admit they masturbate (despite research figures, including Shere Hite's, that show only 15 per cent of women do not masturbate at all). Chaste women's reluctance to 'confess' may be because they have internalized the idea that masturbating is unfeminine. Sexually active women's reluctance may be because they have internalized the idea that masturbating is a poor substitute for penetration. Occasionally mythmakers suggest that masturbation (better if mutual) can be useful as foreplay (a giveaway word) to 'real' sex as long as it ends in orgasm for the man.

How this fiction can still enjoy such a stranglehold on women's sexuality is a mystery, set as it is against facts derived from women's own experience which tell us clearly that penetrative sex, goal-oriented to (usually male) orgasm, is not something upon which many women set a primary value or from which many derive ecstatic enjoyment.

Recent research shows that women need affection, desire intimacy, but have little regard for genital penetration. Often they buy it as part of a media maintained 'package' which they must accept wholesale in order to achieve other goals such as love or companionship. A recent *Spare Rib* questionnaire showed most of the two hundred women readers did not enjoy penetration but could not see how to avoid it. A *True Romance* magazine survey in 1986 discovered a wish for a *sensual chastity* was the secret fantasy of many women. Making love was only third on women's preferred activities, a long way after kissing and cuddling, which came first, and talking, which came second. Many women professed a decided lack of interest in penetrative sex. 75 per cent of women wanted friendship, close companionship and care far more than they wanted sexual activity. Many women who did not want sex admitted to making themselves sexually available in order to achieve those goals.

The relationship between masturbation and orgasms is another problem area for the mythmakers. Hite's 1976 study showed that only 30 per cent of women have orgasms regularly from intercourse without clitoral stimulation by hand (a further 19 per cent do manage it with clitoral stimulation), that 29 per cent never have orgasms during or from intercourse. Research by Helen Kaplan in 1974 showed that while nearly 10 per cent of women never have orgasms, of those that do, up to 45 per cent can only have them during intercourse with additional clitoral stimulation by themselves or their partner. A study in 1973 by Seymour Fischer showed 70 per cent of women were unable to have orgasms during intercourse. Recent figures from the late eighties are similarly revealing. A 1989 study in the United Kingdom of ten thousand women found that 36 per cent rarely or never experienced orgasm during intercourse, and 'most admitted faking it to please their husbands'. In a 1987 study carried out by Dale Spender and myself, we discovered orgasms were seen as obligatory, and were a form of manipulated emotional labour which women worked at in order to reflect men and to maintain male values. Though they could be achieved through masturbation, they were rarely a regular part of the genital penetrative process.[5]

Chastity, it seems, might well be covertly envied if masturbation was openly recognized as, if not integral to the chaste state, at least legitimate. For many chaste women masturbation is crucial. Sue was one. She is an Ascetic Celibate who saw her self-defined chastity as an important part of her celibacy (though she did not see it as the determining factor) and used her chaste time to explore her sexual being as well as her spiritual being. She isolated the taboo on women masturbating as one reason why women and men, or even women and women, find it hard to masturbate together.

'I was never able to reach that level of trust with a lover before I became celibate. It seemed like something you had to do in secret. I would like to think if I returned to sexual activity I would be able to let go like that with someone else there. Just go off on my own. But men, and some women, find that shocking.'

Sue believes that there is a different kind of masturbation, one that does not release sexual energy, which is enjoyed by women who see themselves as chaste, and who see their genital chastity as one part, but not the most significant part, of their celibacy.

The way I masturbate is connected to my celibacy. I have a special method which does not release sexual energy. Just before you
reach the point of orgasm, you take away whatever your stimulus
is – your hand, your finger, or your vibrator – take it away just
before you reach the peak. Instead of having the orgasm ripple
through your body, the energy goes inside and can be directed
outwards. You have control over the energy. You can direct it
to various parts of your body, or direct it to your thinking. It
is a form of tantra yoga. Some people think if you are chaste as
part of your celibacy you can't masturbate. I can and do because
it helps achieve my goal of a circled space.

Sue, who is a self-defence tutor, teaches this goal during her lessons.

We have the concept of a circle round us. Then the members of
the group decide how close they want somebody to be to them.
So with total strangers you have a much bigger circle than with
intimates. My physical chastity draws this circle round me. It
gives me emotional and sexual breathing space. My masturbation
gives me energy within it to explore. I live alone, which draws
another circle around me. Abstaining from genital sex is important, but my celibacy though it uses chastity is much wider than
that.

Celibacy for me is a time and a place. A time to explore and a
place to be safe. Also a place to be in control. Men find chastity
upsetting because they like to be in control of what a woman does
sexually.

Sue's story of a chastity which incorporates masturbation, and
which is taken on as part of her self-defined celibacy shows us
that there are *two* kinds of chastity.

One is the kind that is merely physical, is under male control,
is therefore 'useful' to men, but is not a part of a woman's celibate
philosophy.

The second is the kind that men call 'useless'. It is a purposeful,
self-chosen chastity, and may include masturbation. When this is
combined with an independent, autonomous outlook it may result
in a celibate lifestyle.

Is female chastity merely a result of sexual rejection by men?
I contend that it is not. Certainly the kind of chastity that is purposeful, which may become part of a celibate philosophy, has more

to do with women's discovery of what is important to them than it has to do with being rejected by men. Even a simple non-purposeful chastity is less about withdrawal from men than about keeping oneself pure. But the male ego cannot stand such explanations. Through the centuries the mythmakers have scorned chaste women, suggesting that they were simply women no man would find interesting.

Ovid, the Roman poet, for instance, who lived from 43 BC to 17 AD wrote: 'Chaste is she whom no one has asked'.[6] Hundreds of years later, in the eighteenth century, in another society, English dramatist William Congreve (1670–1729) reiterates the same notion: 'She is chaste who was never asked the question'.[7] It is but a short step from Congreve's 'was never asked' to Corrine Beaver's schoolboys' 'can't get any'. By this rendering, women sit 'chastely' and *wait* for men to dominate, for men to seduce, for men to fuck, for men to overpower them in scenes of possession termed 'sexual'. When the German philosopher Nietzsche (1844–1900) informs us that 'chastity is a virtue in some but in many almost a vice',[8] I recognize immediately in which sex it will be held as a vice. Not merely as a vice, but as an act of heresy in a society where sex is holy because of its role as a sacred ritual in the dominant-submissive relationship set out for men and women.[9]

I found plenty of examples in talking to modern celibate women of the ways in which men ridiculed chastity, refused to see it as a woman's decision but treated it as if the woman had either been sexually rejected or was awaiting courtship, seduction, 'a good fuck' or forcible rape.

Where 'chastity' in a woman is seen as part of her submissive waiting game, rather than as integral to her independent selfhood it is clear that language is not neutral; but in as much as it organizes the limits of our world, it is a powerful determinant of reality.[10] Language is not merely the vehicle which carries our ideas, it shapes our ideas.[11] In our monodimensional reality, into which the principle of sexism has been encoded, the assumption that the 'man's world' is the 'real world', and the way certain words are then defined, radically affects the kind of sense women are able to make of the world. The words do not ask what is this or that like for women? They state what the word means from the viewpoint of men, so where female chastity is named by genital mythmasters as sexual rejection, or as withdrawal from male interests, or as part of the waiting game for male attention, it is difficult for women not to assimilate some of these ideas.

That many women are now in fact reclaiming the word chastity and seeing it as empowering and purposeful is an indication that key areas of female sexuality are being redefined by women.

As we saw earlier in the book, the word 'celibate' in its original derivation from 'caelibatus' simply means 'unmarried'. Women today who adhere to that idea of singleness of spirit are utilizing the root meaning of celibacy as *self-determined* to challenge the genital myth of celibacy as merely and only chastity.

That chastity is not synonymous with celibacy, that it is merely a component, is confirmed by Michael Adams writing about what he calls aspects of chastity. He says 'celibacy involves chastity' which is not just a matter of bodily integrity; 'it is a matter of great refinement of mind and action; it is a matter of prayer; it is a matter not of sinning but of loving God and yourself and other people. It is active.'[12]

He suggests that chastity is not a matter of having one's sexuality neatly corralled, nor of having arrived at a tolerable plateau. Seeing chastity as active, he emphasizes that a person is chaste who is actively trying to be more chaste; whereas a person is unchaste if they are not particularly trying to be chaste.

This has echoes of the idea that celibacy begins in the mind. Adams suggests that when chastity is purposeful and is an active part of celibacy, it too is part of a mental process. In his view one significant difference between chastity and celibacy is that chastity for men can imply that they are still looking for a wife. I would suggest that 'mere' physical chastity (i.e. chastity that is not part of a wider celibate philosophy) in women, could similarly imply that they might still be looking for a husband or male partner. Celibacy, according to Adams, 'does not mean repression of sexuality . . . it is a positive joyful affirmation by which a man or woman commits himself or herself to the chastity of the single life forever.'[13] The search for a sexual partner is over. In this sense chastity becomes an integral part of celibacy which is seen as a 'gift, a spiritual gift'.[14] In his view the gift frees people to devote themselves to God.

In secular terms, celibacy that incorporates chastity can be a gift that frees some women to devote themselves to God in the traditional manner (the nuns I talked to bore witness to that), but it may also free other women to devote themselves to their careers, interests, politics, and friendships. These are the areas of genitally active women's lives which often get little attention, because women find they focus on men's emotional and practical needs, on men's hobbies, or the domestic and social consequences of men's jobs. Sexual activity brings with it a great deal of extra hard work that has nothing to do with bed.

Part of the 'hard work' of being in a sexually active relationship is to do with retaining a sense of self. It is particularly difficult if you live as part of a self-identified 'couple'. Some women attempted to solve the problem of loss of identity by deciding on total genital abstention whilst still seeing themselves within a partnership. Though all the women used the term 'chaste' to describe their behaviour, the purposefulness of the chastity of some women, and its proposed function in determining their individual identities, makes their chastity part of an overall celibate scheme.

Women such as Helen, whose story I shall tell, did not think of themselves as long-term celibates, merely as women who were utilizing chastity as a way of improving their relationships. They gave as much consideration to themselves as part of a couple as they did to their own autonomous needs.

Other 'chaste' women such as Casey, who had previously been celibate, did see their chastity as part of a celibate stance. Let us see how this works in the cases of Helen and Anthony and Casey and June. Helen decided to become purposefully chaste whilst living with Anthony. Casey's need for complete genital abstention led her to move out of the house she shared with June. Here are their differing versions. In both pairs the women's purposeful chastity was seen as positive by the woman instigating the move, but it was largely viewed and received as negative by the partner. Interestingly, Casey and June, who were beginning to define themselves as celibate, were less negative than Helen and Anthony who did not define themselves in that way.

Helen's version:

> Anthony is a financier in a big corporate practice. He was eight years older than me. The sex was always great. It wasn't sex that shackled me, I liked it. It was that through having good sex I depended upon him emotionally. I'd been like that with other men I'd been to bed with. I wanted Anthony a lot physically, but that meant I wanted to be all linked up with him. I thought about his interests, his life, definitely his work more than my own. I worried about how he could improve his practice, should we entertain his clients more, was I a good enough

hostess, did he sleep with other women on his tax trips abroad? If he did, did I want him to tell me? How much would I mind? I thought about him or about us as a couple all the time; I was never alone in my head; I began to forget who I was.

In previous relationships, being a 'woman' had meant being my boyfriend's accessory. It wasn't like that with Anthony. He said he understood my need to be myself, to have my own friends. But there was still something about the way he talked about 'us'. Something about how his friends treated us. It made me feel I was just part of a team and he was team leader. So finally I said I didn't want sex at all. Not for several months. I wanted to have a physical space around me, so that he couldn't get at my head through my body. I wanted to be free of all sexual action. I wanted to be able to have a bath and lock the door and not feel he had the right to come in and fondle me. I do a lot of thinking in the bath. I loved him and wanted to live with him, and I felt part of a couple, but I needed to reassert who I was. He has taken it very badly and doesn't seem to understand quite why I want it. But I hope things will improve.

Anthony's version:

I love Helen, but I think she's gone crazy. What does she think I am, some bloody stone? She never lets me touch her any more. I've done everything for her. I half kill myself in that practice to make sure we have a comfortable place and a good life, to show how much I care. For normal people that means you make love *properly*! Sometimes she hugs me and that's what I'm expected to be satisfied with. She wants me to *understand*! I feel like she's laughing at me secretly. She's behaving like a fucking nun yet she's smiling all the time!

Making love 'properly', to Anthony and other men, means, of course, intercourse. If women behave like nuns they are not expected to smile. Smiles are as obligatory as orgasms. Smiles are part of the way women reflect men, not the way women pleasure themselves.

How about Casey and June? Casey, a lawyer, had spent six years being celibate, had subsequently become sexually involved with June. They lived together in June's house until Casey felt their 'coupledom' was infringing her sense of self.

Casey's version:

The passion June and I had was tremendous. Heartbreaking sometimes. But there were days when I felt engulfed, as if I was in her power, as if she could treat me any old how. I would forget that I needed to be treated as someone different. Somewhere I had lost myself in the sex, and in being a sexual couple. That was how people began to think of us. I began to think of myself as 'June-and-Casey'. It was frightening. I wanted there to be a huge bold black row of dots between our names, so that people would say 'June dot dot dot dot dot dot and Casey'.

At work, in court, I was most assuredly myself. Casey Carlyle, a good lawyer, battling away, winning people's fights, getting a lot of respect for myself. At home I was constantly fighting this idea of The-June-and-Casey-Couple. The trouble was that at one level it was relaxing. It gave us both security, a sense of coming home, of being a unit that could stand up to the pressures which as a lesbian couple we had to face from outside. But ultimately it would not do for me. I had to exist for myself the whole time, not intermittently. I needed to learn things about myself and to feel a freedom that was not possible at that point within a couple situation. It may be possible later.

I wanted to stay close to June, but I wanted no more sex, an absolutely chaste spell. I didn't want to be touched in that way any more. I don't even masturbate. I am utterly off all physical expression. I am clearing the air. I moved out of the house, but we are still very close. In the future things may change but I am living firmly in the present. As a celibate I am learning to prioritize my own needs. If anyone tries to tell me what to do I get a steely glint in my eye. Nobody tells me what to do, not even June. Now that I've gone back to being celibate (remember I had six years of it before June), I know it's about what goes on in your mind not under the duvet. I think a disciplined ascetic celibacy can prepare you for a long-term solitary life. Or it can fit you better for returning to a sexual relationship. I don't know which this will be. June and I are both trying to see it as a change rather than as breaking up. I feel positive about it. It *is* a change, and I feel good things can come out of it for both of us. What's wonderful is that June understands.

How well did June understand?
June's version:

I know what she means about the problems of being a couple, I feel I get lost in it too sometimes, but I *never* want to stop making love. We used to make love all the time. Hours of it. Sucking each other, stroking each other, oh everything. Now suddenly *nothing*. She won't let me touch her, not in that way. Even when I go to kiss her properly, she moves her lips very slightly away, and her body shifts back.

How does she expect me to feel? She says she needs to be chaste for a long time to get her head together. But her damn celibacy is doing my head in! I know she doesn't want me to feel rejected. I know it's about what is going on in her mind, but she doesn't have to lie there night after night wanting her. Sure I feel rejected, even though I know in my head she is not rejecting me, she is doing something for herself. It has made me feel ugly, being unwanted like that. When she's not there I've cried my eyes out. Yes I'm trying to understand. I hope that the longer we go on like this the more understanding I may become. I don't want to give up on our relationship, I love her too much, but the house feels big and empty, and I'm not sure how I'll cope if I keep feeling like this. What the hell does she think I feel like?

For June as for Anthony, despite her greater struggle to understand, some similar emotions predominate: rejection, anger, frustration, resentment. What is positive for one partner may be negative for the other. It may, certainly at the start, be highly destructive. Messages and manipulations centred on the genital myth work to ensure this is so. It is hard not to feel that someone else's decision to be chaste does *not* imply a rejection of you. It is hard to value each other in non-genital ways when the culture puts such a high value on genital expression. As June says: 'Sure I feel rejected, even though I know in my head she is not rejecting me, she is doing something for herself.' Women like Helen and Casey are being courageous in attempting to retain passionate 'chaste' relationships within a genital society; but it is Anthony and June who need even greater strength to help make these non-conformist relationships work.

Casey's view that her purposeful chastity was 'clearing the air' had something in common with Helen's need for 'a physical space around me', her feeling that she was 'free of all sexual action'.

Celibacy becomes a freedom, a clearing house, when it involves ascetic chastity but is instigated by and bound up with an intellectual and emotional freedom. This version of an autonomous reality was mentioned by women I spoke to more frequently than any other concept. But as we have seen, women's interpretation of the word autonomy differs from the interpretation commonly used (particularly by psychologists) in delineating human (i.e. male) mature development.

Autonomy in male terms generally means a differentiated and separated independence, freedom without connection. It is a means of taking control of one's life in a decisive manner without reference to others.

Ascetic women who are reaching autonomy through celibacy, who may have lacked such independence in a previously sexually active existence, see it differently. They are designing a new autonomy which brings with it a sense of belonging. Differentiation does not necessitate exclusion. Women who have been socialized to put relationships (particularly with men and children) before their own needs, believe that bonding and intimate affiliation are worthwhile, therefore they do not contemplate a celibate philosophy which denies these characteristics. Celibate women who express a need for solitude, and find this is made easier with a chaste lifestyle, nevertheless see it in harness with certain close friendships. Similarly, an active search for independence based on a physical chastity runs parallel to a desire for intimate association.

How do contemporary nuns fit together the chastity/autonomy jigsaw in *their* picture of celibacy?

This was the view of Sister Ellen, the administrator at a theological college:

> It is a single-heartedness which is the goal we seek but do not always manage to live out. You can abstain from genital sex, and maybe that is not so hard, but you can always put other gods in the place of sex, or find other objects of gratification besides sex.
>
> In a convent or in a religious community, we equate celibacy with sexual abstinence, particularly genital abstinence, *far too much*, so that we actually miss the core of what celibacy is about: single-heartedness. This is an autonomy that is both independently determined but is also rooted in a community spirit, a place for connections.

Many ascetic women had stressed that a single selfhood, akin to Sister Ellen's single-heartedness, was hard to find in a sexually active life where energies are concentrated on relationships and responsibilities. Professor Elaine Pagels points to this problem in an intriguing study of original sin called *Adam, Eve and the Serpent*:

> Even today, an adolescent who takes time to think before plunging into ordinary adult society . . . into marriage, and the double

obligations of family and career . . . may hesitate, for such obligations usually cost nothing less than one's life, the expense of virtually all one's energy attempting to fulfil obligations to family and society, especially if one also wants to be recognized and celebrated within one's community. It is in this sense that Christian renunciation, of which celibacy is the paradigm, offered freedom.[15]

Although Elaine Pagels is writing specifically about Christians in the first four centuries, she points out that the idea of freedom which is associated with celibacy is as applicable today as it was in the past.

For many Christians of the first four centuries and ever since, the greatest freedom demanded the greatest renunciation – above all, celibacy. This identification of freedom with celibacy involved a paradox, then as now, for celibacy . . . is an extreme form of self restraint. Yet as Christians saw it, celibacy involved rejection of 'the world' of ordinary society and its multitudinous entanglements and was thereby a way to gain control over one's own life.[16]

Certainly many nuns and lay women alike today use sexual self-restraint in order to free themselves from 'multitudinous entanglement', to reject the world of ordinary matters in order to find a freer world within. Sister Claudia was another nun who saw freedom rather than chastity as the pivot for a religious celibate philosophy.

We are taught to be chaste but we must be careful not to put undue emphasis on mere genital chastity. That is not the core. A freedom for the soul to take wing, so we may be led to new paths, and a freedom of the mind so that we may take control of our inner life: that is the core. We have to cease heeding our false self; so often our false self is still imprisoned in worldly things. Through celibacy we can try and raise ourselves above what is false and worldly, and what simply gets in our way.

Sister Claudia's view is reminiscent of how the young Augustine regarded celibacy when he first made a decision to give up the world and its false selves and take on a celibate life.

The Christian convert Augustine, then a brilliantly successful young orator, was walking through the streets of Milan one night, dreading the speech he had to give the following day in

praise of the emperor. In the midst of these anxieties he noticed
a drunken beggar. Why, Augustine asked himself, did this beggar
seem so happy, when he himself was so miserable? Augustine later
described his overwhelming relief when at last he gave up his career,
his ambition, the woman who had lived with him and borne him a
son, as well as his impending marriage to a wealthy heiress, for the
freedom of celibacy and renunciation. His pagan contemporaries
regarded such renunciation not only as social suicide but as the
worst impiety and dishonour. But Augustine came to believe that
it meant no more than 'dying to the world', destroying the false self,
constructed according to worldly custom and tradition, in order to
'raise his own life above the world'.[17]

Genital worldliness can often blind us to truths. Both Sister Ellen
and Sister Claudia emphasized that women in religious communities
are apt to place too much significance on chastity, on abstaining from
lustful or 'sinful' genital sex, rather than on the search for inner truth.
This is true outside religious communities too. In a society that sancti-
fies sexual activity as a sacred ritual, that condemns celibacy as 'social
suicide', just as Augustine's pagan contemporaries did, the focus on
genital abstinence is so extreme that an automatic equation is made
between female celibacy and rigorous chastity. In non-religious life,
women have first to struggle against this insistent idea that celibacy
is anti-sex, before they can feel free to reinterpret the root of celibacy
as single-heartedness or self-determination.

It is women who see celibacy as a wider concept than Corrine
Beaver's schoolboys' 'can't get any', who are at last voicing an
interpretation that is more in line with the changes feminism has
made to women's lives.

Women who are still battling for the right to equal pay, equal
status, and non-discrimination at work; women who are striving
for equal participation within heterosexual relationships; women
who are struggling for the freedom to maintain lesbian relationships
as partners and mothers; women who are fighting male violence at
every level of their professional and personal lives, will obviously put
a high priority on their rights to independence and sexual freedom.

Seeing celibacy as primarily *a right to freedom* rather than as
a genital chastity may give women the confidence they need to
withdraw from sex if it feels abusive, or if it is inadequate and
does not fulfil their emotional as well as physical needs.

Women who believe celibacy means more than just genital withdrawal feel strong enough to get out of sexual relationships if they

feel trapped. To be celibate is to swim against the current whilst trusting in yourself to find a safe haven.

For women sexual feeling is not restricted to genitals, so celibacy is not something defined by genital behaviour. What women simply call 'sex' incorporates a multi-faceted range of experiences, which change with the biological-social factors of menstruation, menopause, pregnancy, disease, disability and ageing as well as with the socio-emotional experiences of love, desire, desperation, resentment, envy, powerlessness and hate.

Celibacy is no less culturally complex. As a form of sexuality it is linked to a woman's self-worth, associated with her intrinsic identity. Just as a woman uses lovemaking as much for reasons of hostility or aggression as for reasons of romance or tenderness, so a woman may use celibacy as much from motives of revenge as from motives of creativity. Women who feel put down, who have low self-esteem, may well use celibacy for spite. Women with high self-esteem who feel emotionally secure, are more likely to use celibacy to enhance their spiritual growth.

But whereas, no matter how low the reason, making love is not in itself shocking, being celibate, no matter how high-minded the reason, invariably is.

So telling other people we are celibate can open the door to vulnerability. No wonder one woman said: 'I am frightened to tell people I've stopped sexual relations because I'm working on who I am, because they'll laugh, or think I'm crazy.' Chastity has always been a little crazy in the eyes of the world. A celibacy viewed as predominantly based on chastity will get stuck with that label too.

To see celibacy largely in terms of non-genital behaviour, to see it, the way my male acquaintance did, as 'useless chastity' is not only to devalue other experiences which are a part of it, but also to put upon celibacy a reading which modern celibate women are *not* substantiating.

In the chapter on women's reasons for becoming celibate we heard women's voices telling us what celibacy is about. It is about simplicity. It is about dissatisfaction with sex. It is about freedom to work or study. It is about freedom from sexual anxiety and beauty problems. Remember the Fat Thigh syndrome? It is about freedom from the consequences of violence. Remember the incest survivors, the battered woman whose ear had been sliced to slivers, remember the women whose childhood sexual abuse prevented them from using tampons or even from masturbating. And countless others.

It is about regaining or taking control of one's life. It is about anti-consumerism. It is about non-genital passion. It is about spiritual growth. Remember the women for whom spirituality through celibacy was a way of bringing magic into a creatively impoverished life.

All these women became chaste as part of their celibate lifestyle. But because their celibacy included spiritual freedom, intellectual freedom, or political freedom, it became substantially broader than mere genital abstention.

Even in the past when women's celibate behaviour was more clearly separated from forms of genital activity than it is today, celibacy still embodied ideas of freedom for women. It stood for self-sufficiency, spiritual and social power.

Professor Jo Ann McNamara points out that the chaste widows and virgins who feature in her study about celibate women in the early Christian centuries chose to live independently from men.[18] Self-assertively they did so in an era when women's role was viewed primarily as procreative and when the state itself reinforced the family functions and women's domestic situation. Celibate women saw in Christianity the opportunity to make a new place for themselves in the public sphere, one which would validate their celibate condition, even, eventually, bring them praise for their way of life.

In the ancient world, before the first three Christian centuries, women's gender had severely restricted them to home and hearth. Religion and the law rigorously reinforced a rigid role structure. So for women to attempt to set up a celibate community was revolutionary indeed. For these women it was less the idea of giving up genital activity that was enticing than the radical part of Jesus' message that condemned all social barriers, including those of gender, and suggested that the ideal of a society where women were not given over like chattels in marriage could become a reality. It was not therefore surprising that by the second century many women associated celibacy with ascetic forms of Christianity and converted to both at the same time.[19]

Through this new religion, some women were trying to create a positive new identity which, though it was grounded in celibacy, was used purposefully to transcend the existing gender system.

This ancient notion of self-determination as integral to the celibate ideal is crucial to the practice of contemporary celibates. It is what lies at the heart of a theory of passionate celibacy.

The genital myth ensures that female celibacy is seen instead as a state in which women have merely made themselves sexually unavailable to men.

That women have been able to achieve a celibate lifestyle which, while insisting on connections, focuses on autonomy in the face of this kind of vociferous male opposition is quite a feat. For men see the sexual availability of women as including a social and domestic availability which focuses primarily on *them*. They are extremely reluctant to give this up. Men may talk complacently of their conviction that God loves them; but in reality what they need in their daily lives is the love of a woman. This is why so many patriarchal rules for feminine behaviour try to immobilize women into servicing men, so that women are denied economic, sexual or intellectual freedom to say no.

Cicely Hamilton, in a biting and witty book about marriage written in 1909, held the view that marriage at the turn of the century for women had not only been a trade but one that had been practically compulsory.[20] Most girls were brought up to believe that a woman's role was to be dependent, even parasitic upon a husband, and while they had no economic independence, they had no bargaining power. In other words no power of refusal. Cicely Hamilton argued with passion and conviction that while marriage remains the main source of women's livelihood, women have to satisfy male ideals of womanhood in order to succeed in this trade. She amusingly strips away all the romance surrounding marriage as far as women are concerned, and points out that it is only men who, by having far more choices, certainly economic ones, can afford to be truly romantic about marriage.

When it came to celibacy, she showed how men at the beginning of the century interpreted women's celibacy as a refusal which affected male interests adversely:

'In sexual matters it would appear that the whole trend and tendency of man's relations to woman has been to make refusal impossible and to cut off every avenue of escape from the gratification of his desire.'[21]

Cicely Hamilton was enraged that women who were trying to live celibate independent lives were dubbed 'unsexed'. She was emphatic that it did not follow that celibate women were either unnatural or unwomanly. 'Sex is only one of the ingredients of the natural woman – an ingredient which has assumed undue and exaggerated proportions in her life owing to the fact that it has for many generations furnished her with the means of livelihood.'[22] In other words women were forced into trading their sexual services and domestic skills in marriages for the sake of survival. The trade was the exchange of their person for the means of subsistence. As Cicely Hamilton saw marriage as a job, she thought it perfectly legitimate to look at the position of the women workers in that particular job market. She found the conditions insupportable: sexual subordination, occupational hazards (such as venereal disease), long hours, and complete lack of payment. She concluded that the regulations governing exchange and barter in the marriage market, therefore, were necessarily framed in the interests of the employer – the male.

Her solution, at the time, was that more women should remain unmarried, should take up celibacy. Predictably, men's response was to adopt what she described as 'uncompromising and brutal attitudes' towards spinsters, lashing out at them viciously in the hope of driving women back into marriage.[23] Men's contempt for celibate spinsters was summed up in their description of them as creatures who were 'chaste and therefore inhuman'.[24]

Hamilton describes this contempt as arising from fear of economic competition, for if a woman was economically independent such a situation might bring with it the 'power of [sexual] refusal'.[25] Cicely Hamilton suggested that men's relentless 'savage dislike' of celibates 'must have had its origin in the consciousness that the *perpetual virgin* was a witness, however reluctantly, to the unpalatable fact that sexual intercourse was not for every woman an absolute necessity.'[26] (My italics.)

For some women, in fact, it is genital abstention that is the absolute necessity. But whereas the genital myth sees abstention, or chastity, as the linchpin of celibacy, it is not necessarily the deciding factor in a woman's view of herself as celibate.

CHAPTER SEVEN

Perpetual Virgins

HAVE you ever asked your teenage son what he thinks about virgins? Or even *if* he thinks about them. Maybe you asked your nephew? Perhaps you discussed it with your neighbour's kid? Or your sixteen-year-old daughter's boyfriend?

Maybe you think in the nineties, since the second wave of feminism, boys neither care about being virgins themselves nor talk about girls' virginity – well, not unpleasantly, at any rate. These sixteen-year-olds are the glorious Sons of the Women's Movement. These sixteen-year-olds, true heroes of the liberal feminist age, surely have learnt better. Not for them paying lip service to the genital myth which divides women into virgins and whores, the sweet girls and the sluts; which constructs virginity as a battleground for a male takeover. Thank goodness those punishing days are over.

Or are they?

Writer Cynthia Heimel, mother of sixteen-year-old Mark, certainly thought so. She had great hopes for this generation. For years she had carefully cultivated Alan and Evan, her son's friends, feeding them chocolate milk, letting them watch TV until dawn, so that the day would finally come when she could persuade them to tell her about their sex lives. As the author of *Sex Tips for Girls*, a street-smart bestseller, she had a professional interest in the subject. She had known Alan and Evan since they were grimy-handed, milky-faced seven-year-olds. Now they were cleaned up sixteen and could not talk to their own Moms about sex, so they opened up to Mark's mother.

'I don't think I have any friends who aren't virgins,' said Alan.

'Most, well, a lot of my friends aren't virgins,' said Evan.

'At this age of sexual inexperience, the most attractive aspect
of a girl is willingness,' continued Alan . . .
. . . 'Girls are people, *maybe*,' said Evan, a baby-faced hulk
with bleached hair. 'Most boys my age don't think about the true
value of a woman. They just think about sex.'
'There was this girl,' said Alan . . . 'We thought we could
pull it off.'
'She was very sexual,' said Evan. 'She offered me, Alan and
this other kid . . .'
'Let's just say a motel, tequila, and fun and pleasure entered
into it,' said Alan . . . 'Anyway she was just leading us on.'
'She was aggressive,' said Evan . . .[1]

According to sixteen-year-old boys, aggressive girls are those who
are not pushovers. Aggressive girls are those who won't let boys
'pull it off'. Have I not heard this somewhere before?
   " 'There's one kind of girl you have sex with,' said Alan,
'another kind of girl you have a crush on.' "
   Oh no! As optimists and mothers we thought the times had
changed. Cynthia Heimel looks in horror at those she has nurtured
on chocolate milk, and whispers to herself: 'Oh guys, please don't
tell me this.' Relentlessly however the boys continue.
   " 'The girls I have liked I have only liked from a distance,' said
Alan. 'None of them have been aggressive. Sweet girls. But the girls
I go out with are pretty aggressive . . . If a girl sits on my lap and
wiggles her – ah – well, it's easier to ask her out.'
   'That's why sluts are easier', said Evan."
   Sluts? Cynthia Heimel, raunchy pro-woman writer that she is,
mild mother of Mark that she has trained herself to be, is deeply
shocked.
   'Sluts? Oh my God . . . I had hopes for this generation . . .
sons of single mothers, sons of women with demanding careers.
Sluts? Has anything changed? What about feminism?' she asks the
boys.
   " 'Throw it out the window,' says Alan.' "[2]
   It is clear that in young men's eyes the genital myth still divides
women into sweet girls and sluts, virgins and whores. Does it also
still construct virginity as an arena for attack?
   First let us look at the meaning of virginity. According to the
dictionary the primary meaning of 'virgin' is 'a person, especially
a woman, who has never had sexual intercourse'. Secondary meanings include the notion of an unmarried woman who has taken

a religious vow of chastity in order to dedicate herself totally to God. Then, interestingly, something (someone) 'not yet cultivated, explored or exploited by man'.[3] So the commonsense version of virginity is simply the state of being an untouched, unsullied maiden. As a physiological condition therefore it is distinguishable from celibacy because being a virgin does not necessarily imply making a positive decision. Where girls and women see their virginity as a possession to be mislaid, or a commodity to be sold, their virginity is *transitional* and does not begin in the mind. Only when virginity is *purposeful* could it become connected with a celibate lifestyle.

If there are two distinct but linked types of virginity, there are also two possible methods of. attack:

Transitional Virginity, the playground of the sixteen-year-old Alans and Evans, historically has long been open to sorties and siege, assaults and encroachment. Transitional Virgins are women in waiting. Women, waiting, willingly or unwillingly to lose their virginity.

Perpetual or Purposeful Virginity is open to a more subtle form of attack, that of vilification, calumny, castigation and contempt. These punitive measures are taken because the heroines of perpetual virginity are purposeful virgins who make a 'profession' of their virginity, who see it as a positive part of their sexuality, and in so doing fail to comply with the coercive messages of the genital myth. Compulsory congress and constant availability to men are communiqués which need a transitional rather than perpetual virginity for effective functioning.

One school of thought on virginity sees it as a spiritual blessing, another school sees it as a psychological hang-up. Many are content to view it merely as a neutral physiological state. My interest has been not only in the question of whether today's genital myth still constructs virginity as a battleground for male control, but in two related questions: firstly, in what ways does virginity as a category significantly differ from chastity or celibacy, and secondly, can we view some virgins as chaste and others as celibate?

I perceive perpetual virgins as having a significant connection to Passionate Celibates, while in the main transitional virgins do not.

Remember Cicely Hamilton on the subject of men's attitude to perpetual virgins:

'That active and somewhat savage dislike must have had its origin in the consciousness that the perpetual virgin was a witness, however reluctantly, to the unpalatable fact that sexual intercourse was not for every woman an absolute necessity.'[4]

That was written in 1909. My interest lies in whether perpetual virgins today reap similarly brutal responses from those whom their purposeful virgin state is not designed to please.

Here by contrast is journalist Audrey Slaughter (who in the sixties edited the first two teenage magazines, *Petticoat* and *Honey*) recalling a transitional virgin story which other journalists still wickedly recount about her. During her editorship of *Petticoat*, Audrey Slaughter gave her journalistic fashion team careful instructions on how to choose the young teenagers who were to be used on the magazine covers. According to members of the team not only were the teenagers to be highly photogenic but they had also to be virgins!

Significantly one of the cover illustrations for a *Honey* magazine (January 1965), which Slaughter edited during that period, subtitled 'Young, Gay and Going Far' (a title whose unambiguous words show how long ago and far away the sixties are) offers two bright young virginal things in pink cover-up undies, all frills and invitation, with the caption: 'How Far Will You Go? It's a Year for the Daring.'[5]

Whether these young models, too, were virgins by editorial request is less significant than the fact that they were dressed and photographed to appear as transitional rather than perpetual, decked out in pink, smiling and seductive, ready to be captured. How-far-will-you-go slogans were part of the frenetic, frivolous, pretty and playful image of the sixties. Flower Power was in the air and on the ground; by 1961, the pill was marketed and approved for prescription first in the United States, then in Great Britain; virginity was a testing ground as never before. Virgins and non-virgins alike wondered just how far they *could* go with the new apparent 'permissiveness'.

What the Genital Appropriation Era actually permitted was more access to women's bodies by more men; what it actually achieved was not a great deal of liberation for women but a great deal of legitimacy for male promiscuity; what it actually passed on to women was the male fragmentation of emotion from body, and the easily internalized schism between genital sex and responsible loving. The how-far-can-we-go virginity programme was often how-far-can-we-go-to-please-men?

Today, thirty years further on, we may ask how the politics and progress of the last three decades have affected attitudes towards virginity. Already we have heard the voices of boys in the nineties, the young and caustic male tones of the violent backlash against feminist thinking. What about feminism? Throw it out the window. What about virgins? Sluts are easier. What about sluts? There's one kind of girl you have sex with.

Now let us listen to the voices of the young women who are their peers. How does virginity appear to them?

'Being a virgin at school was really bad news!'

The speaker was Joey, twenty-two years. She described the pressures encountered by the girls:

> It was really heavy. Some of us didn't care about losing it, but some of us didn't want to. Obviously we all wanted to be thought cool. But you couldn't be a virgin and be cool – the boys saw to that. They made up to us, made us feel we'd be quite something if we did it with them for the first time. So a lot of us did it. I suppose it was to please them, but you didn't exactly think like that. You thought you'd get some status. But it was just a trap. As soon as you'd done it with a boy, he'd tell the others. Then they'd kind of despise you or call you names. Slag you off. Thinking about it now, you wonder why you didn't warn your mates but you didn't. Some of us thought it was our fault. Like you hadn't been sexy enough or you'd come on too strong the first time. So maybe you deserved it. You thought mainly about yourself. You didn't sit and think oh yeah it's happening to all of us.

Joey is British, her school a mixed country boarding school. Girls and boys roamed the adjoining woods and fields after school.

> In our crowd, fourteen-year-old girls went around with older boys of sixteen. Everyone would go and get drunk down the fields. We all had bottles stashed away in the dorms. It was one of those 'free' schools so they didn't check up on you much. At first some of us lot would try and clan up – we'd go around in a gang. We actually weren't that interested in the boys – they weren't that good to talk to – but they wouldn't have that. They soon sorted us out.
>
> Their idea of a good time was to get the most clannish girl really drunk, do a load of sweet talk on her, so she thought the boy felt something special about her. Mind you, to be fair, some

of them did. But I bet they didn't tell that to the other boys. Then they'd go in the woods and he'd lay her. Maybe in a one-to-one (they always *told* you it was going to be one-to-one, but you just knew sometimes they were lying!). Some of the time another boy, or maybe two or three would be right behind the trees watching. Two of the boys were the worst, they said they watched a lot, I don't know if they really did, but they'd boast about how much blood they'd seen and how many screams they'd heard.

But you didn't really know all that was going on. You were like in the middle of this experience. I don't think anyone minded much about the pain, not everyone felt much pain, you were like glad to be getting on with it. I didn't feel it much, I'd done it in my head so many times that when it happened well it was kind of a let-down. One of my mates said it was really painful but she didn't care because it was a big relief to have it over. I remember thinking I was being smart! SMART?

Joey struck an attitude of incredulity. She sat thinking, in silence for a while, then she said:

Being a virgin definitely wasn't smart but, honestly, not being one wasn't smart either. The boy's attitudes to the girls who did get laid were gross. To their faces they'd be nice as pie but behind their backs they'd call them cunts and tarts. Afterwards the older boys, the ones that ran the show, said the girls that had got drunk in the woods and done it were just rubbish. They said they might just as well be passed around. So the boys would look out for an ex-virgin and say to one of their lot: 'Oh look here comes Marg, it's your turn now, she's quite a cunt.' The girl who thought she'd done it with this boy because he'd said he was crazy about her, would find she was being treated as a cheap lay.

The girls who stayed clannish got it worst. They were told they were prick teasers or piss-offs, or the boys called them abnormal, or prudes, or said they'd turn into lezzies. You couldn't win.

Joey's experience of school attitudes to virginity, and what it means to be a young virgin, is not pleasant. Nor, it seems, is it untypical.

Sandy is Canadian, nineteen years old, her school a state high in a large North American city.

In our class, around thirteen or fourteen, there was terrible pressure on us to lose our virginity. Some of us didn't want to. We were kinda young I guess, there wasn't a real special reason, other than some of the guys being pushy. But we didn't stand much of a chance. I went around in a gang. We were close buddies, but the guys hated us ganging up and not caring what they thought. So they just made it impossible for us to stick together.

They wanted us to lose it, it was push, push all the time. It was kind of heavy. Your virginity got to be a goddamn handicap so you had to give in and lose it. Sometimes they were clumsy so it didn't happen the first time, it was just more like fooling around. You'd be told it was your fault. You'd be done over again. After the first time I guess I was still a virgin but it was okay. I was hanging around with a guy I liked so we fooled around again a lot more, and he was kinda nice to me that time, so it was more or less okay. I liked him a lot so it made it feel better.

The experiences of some of Sandy's friends were not quite as straightforward as her own.

A couple of the other girls tensed up the first time and couldn't relax at all. They just couldn't let it happen. So one guy came in his pants. Another guy came all over her thighs, it was gross. Then they got mad, and wanted to do it again. The girls really tensed up and didn't want that. Then a few days later one of these guys, well, he got an older guy who was really experienced, and he just sorted them out good and proper so that then the first guy he went in and had a ball.

After that it was hard to be the same gang any more. In fact we didn't want to then. Everything changes once you go with a guy, you sort of belong to him. It's kind of a good feeling, but it's also bad for you. You've stopped being free. It's like they've got this power over you. You want to be around them.

So what happened was, after we'd all done it, we couldn't talk about losing it any more, or what it might be like, or even about fun stuff, going down cycle trails, going to the movies, cross country ski-ing, hanging out on the beach, all that good stuff. It was just all heavy dating talk. That's all we did, talked to each other about the guys. We even discussed their dicks. We stopped talking about us. At the time it seemed the regular thing to do, looking back you realize it was quite smart of them.

If we look closely at the two accounts by Joey and Sandy we can see the way male control of transitional virginity operates at many levels including control of the women's conversations. We can also see where it coincides with male control of chastity which I looked at in the previous chapter.

The two young women live in different countries thousands of miles apart. They have been educated at very different kinds of schools. Yet there are significant similarities in their stories.

For both girls the state of virginity is not seen as a precious possession but rather as an undesirable burden. Joey describes being a virgin as 'bad news'. Sandy confirms that 'your virginity got to be a goddamn handicap'. It was mainly a handicap because in both accounts many of the girls would rather not have lost it. Sandy says 'Some of us didn't want to', while Joey tells us 'Some of us didn't want to but obviously we all wanted to be thought cool.' In both cases the boys put pressure on them. The guys in Sandy's high school put 'terrible pressure on us to lose our virginity . . . it was push, push, all the time', while the boys at Joey's boarding school put pressure that was 'really heavy'.

In both schools the girls lost their virginity because it was seen as cool or smart 'to please the boys'. Each time it was 'just a trap'. This is the genital trap set for unwary women trying to avoid the messages of the genital myth. Each time the girls are trapped into believing they are at fault. Sandy said if a guy was clumsy and a girl didn't lose her virginity the first time, she was told 'it was your fault'. When the sexual episodes went wrong in Joey's school, the boys led them to think it was 'our fault. Like you hadn't been sexy enough or you'd come on too strong the first time. So maybe you deserved it.' As in other situations, the girls are damned if they do, and damned if they don't.

It is significant that in each school the girls are part of a closely knit group which the boys see as territory, like the girls' bodies, which they have the right to invade. The genital myth works on the assumption that a woman's control of her body and her sexuality does not lie with herself. Joey tells us the girls 'would try and clan up', they would 'go around in a gang', but the boys 'wouldn't have that'. What did the boys do? 'They soon sorted us out,' says Joey, recognizing when she is recalling the events, though not having realized at the time, that it was because 'we actually weren't that interested in the boys'.

This is paralleled in Sandy's story. In her school, the girls 'went around in a gang'. They were 'close buddies', but the boys in her school were not having that either. 'The guys hated us ganging up and not caring what they thought. So they just made it impossible for us to stick together.' All the boys wanted was the girls 'to lose it', and all the boys did was to 'push, push'. The boys, of course, did not only want the girls to lose their virginity, to be taken over by one of them, they also wanted the girls to lose interest in each other and to start paying attention to the menfolk.

In both accounts the girls are treated not only as the property of the boy to whom they 'lost it', who can if he now wishes treat them as 'rubbish' (Joey's story), or as second hand goods to be 'sorted out good and proper' (Sandy's story), but also as the property of other boys who are invited to watch or to participate in the young virgin's first sexual experiences.

The participation of the other males, although instigated and encouraged by the boys, nevertheless takes place with the acquiescence of the girls, is another illustration of the workings of the genital myth, which suggests that losing one's virginity is deemed, by men, to be as much a public act as a private sexual experience.

On a broader level, the watching of women by men, socially and sexually, has been recorded throughout the history of Western culture. Writer John Berger's well-known statement that 'Men look at women. Women watch themselves being looked at. This determines not only the relations of men to women, but the relations of women to themselves,' has never been more accurate.[6] When men watch women with sexual fascination or sexual intent, or when men, having gazed their fill, make social judgements, those verdicts are internalized by the seen sex.

In a short story by Margaret Atwood, called 'True Trash', set in a boys' holiday camp, fourteen-year-old Donny and his voyeuristic schoolboy friends take turns watching the camp waitresses bask in the sun 'like a herd of skinned seals, their pinky-brown bodies shining with oil. They have their bathing suits on because it's the afternoon. In the early dawn and the dusk they sometimes go skinny-dipping, which makes this itchy crouching in the mosquito-infested bushes across from their small private dock a great deal more worthwhile.'[7]

The waitresses know they are being looked at. They can see the bushes jiggling.

'The boys are only twelve, or thirteen, fourteen at most, small fry. If it was counsellors, the waitresses would giggle more, preen more, arch their backs.'

Even so, even with only an audience of small fry, they rub

oil on one another's backs, toast themselves evenly, turn lazily this way and that, causing the small fry to groan and drool.[8]

The waitresses are not professionally trained for their job, but are high school students, employed for the summer. As they lie around, sensual objects of the small boys' scrutiny, they read a diet of *True Romance* magazines, the true trash of the title.

The trash mag heroines are sleazy rather than glossy. According to the workings of the genital myth as accepted by the great gods at *True Romance*, these paper goddesses are virginal, weak, fall helplessly in love with the Wrong Men, eventually Give In, become Fallen Women, are inevitably jilted, and end in tears.

They wear dresses that are a 'dream of pink', somewhat reminiscent of the sixties' *Honey* magazine dresses that were how-far-will-you-go? virginal pink. The trashy heroes' eyes are 'burning and determined'. In general, the burning determination of all trashy heroes is to get the girls out of their dream of pink dresses, just as the burning (but less likely to be fulfilled) determination of the small fry watchers would be to get the waitresses out of their sun-oiled swimsuits.[9]

The girl, whom young drooling Donny slobbers over the most, as he squints through the binoculars, is 'Ronette the tartiest, Ronette the most forbidden'. Back at the camp, when Ronette is on waitress duty, leaning over to clear the plates, Donny, like the other boys, tries to look down the front of her sedate but V-necked uniform. She smells of hair spray, nail polish, something artificial and too sweet. 'Cheap, Donny's mother would say. It's an enticing word. Most of the things in his life are expensive, and not very interesting.'[10]

Donny feels he doesn't stand much of a chance with Ronette, not like Darce, an older boy, a counsellor, a young man with fraudulent charm, and 'a reputation as a make-out artist'.[11] All fourteen-year-old Donny can do is gaze, salivate, and wait for the waitresses to strip off and skinny-dip.

The summer progresses. The waitresses and counsellors double date in canoes. Joanne, the retiring, the resolute, the perpetual virgin who won't make out, is paired with Perry, the fervent, the frustrated, who will probably tell. Ronette, whose every sensual sway is watched by grubby boys infantile with lust, is paired with Darce, whose every pushy thrust is watched by salivating small fry eager to emulate. Soon Darce and Ronette are a couple. Everyone watches, everyone knows.

One night, Donny and Monty, another fourteen-year-old spy, owner of the infamous binoculars, sneak out of their sleeping bags to see what is worth watching. This time it is the counsellors who are their prey. They hear the older boys talking. Loudly. Lewdly.

'It's about Ronette. Darce is talking about her as if she's a piece of meat. From what he's implying, she lets him do anything he wants. "Summer sausage" is what he calls her.'[12]

Monty sniggers and Donny knows he will tell the other boys that Darce has been porking Ronette. Though yesterday Donny himself giggled insanely over the expression 'porking' suddenly he does not want it to be used about Ronette. Suddenly he loves Ronette. Love: the ultimate grade six insult, to be accused of loving someone. What can a fourteen-year-old turncoat spy do under the circumstances? If he charged out of the bushes and punched Darce he would both look ridiculous and get flattened. Instead he decides to punish Monty by pinching his binoculars and sinking them in the lake. He gets found out and is sentenced to expulsion.

Before he leaves he drifts disconsolately down to the beach. Ronette is there. She tells him she is sorry for him. " 'It was because of you,' he says. 'What they were saying about you. Darce was.' " Is Ronette moved by the young boy's championship and its consequences? Maybe. Anyway she begins to untie her apron. Then she takes Donny by the hand, leads him around the hill of rock, out of sight, lies down and arranges his hands. Her blue uniform unbuttons down the front. Donny cannot believe this is happening to him, in broad daylight. 'It's like sleepwalking, it's like running too fast, it's like nothing else.'[13]

It is a secret seduction. They are not a couple. Nobody knows. Donny leaves the camp in disgrace over the binoculars episode. Ronette tells Joanne she is 'in trouble'. Joanne assumes 'it' is Darce's. Ronette is scathing. " 'Mr Chickenshit. It's not *his*.' " But protectively, she will not say whose it is. She plans only to leave school, to keep the baby.

Three years pass. Joanne is less retiring. She has become a writer. Unexpectedly Darce phones her, recalls her as the waitress who wouldn't make out, asks her to a party, because his girlfriend has dumped him, and Joanne was 'the kind of girl you could talk to'.

'Do you ever hear from Ronette?' she asked him.

'Who?' he said . . . he really didn't remember. Joanne found this blank in his memory offensive. She herself might forget a name, a face even. But a body? A body that had been so close to your own, that had generated those murmurings, those rustlings in the darkness, that aching pain . . . it was an affront to bodies, her own included.[14]

Darce continues the affront. He throws up on her borrowed dress. Perpetual virgins who don't make out, who are only there to listen to the men, seem to get that treatment. Joanne stuck him with the cleaning bill, 'but even so there was a faint residual stain.'[15] She has been stained by his careless grotesque behaviour, just as Ronette was stained by his callous aggressive labelling. Girls who 'do' are summer sausages. Girls who 'don't' can be vomited over. They can all be watched. They can all be labelled. They all have something in common with Joey's 'rubbish' and Sandy's 'second hand goods'.

Margaret Atwood continues the story. Eleven years after Donny and his grubby pals had first watched the waitresses, he accidentally bumps into Joanne. She is now a successful freelance copywriter, he a respectable lawyer. They go for coffee. Remember Joanne, the perpetual virgin, was in Darce's view 'the kind of girl you could talk to'. Now it is Donny who begins talking.

" 'We used to spy on you,' he says. 'We used to watch you skinny-dipping' . . .

. . . 'Did you?' says Joanne absently. Then, 'I know. We could see the bushes waving around.' "[16]

" 'What about Ronette?' he says, which is the only thing he really wants to ask."

He tells Joanne that Ronette had once been 'really nice' to him, when he had been turfed out of camp. For Joanne it is a major piece of information, the missing piece in the story. For Donny it is only a minor irritation.

'He's feeling guilty, because he never wrote her. He didn't know where she lived, but he didn't take any steps to find out. Also he couldn't keep himself from thinking: **They're right. She's a slut.**'[17]

Like sixteen-year-old Evan said to Cynthia Heimel: sluts are easier.

Joanne, the perpetual virgin, the clever and creative girl who wouldn't make out, has been slotted into one type of category, overlooked, treated disgustingly, designated as useful for only minimal male needs. Ronette, the transitional virgin, who showed her appreciation of a fourteen-year-old's protectiveness in the way she knows he wants, is vilified by both Darce the aggressor (at the time) and Donny the protector (all those years later). Darce could not even recall the name that went with the body of the girl he slept with, the girl he porked. Donny, unknown to himself but in all probability the father of her ten-year-old child, recalls her name very well, but decides in retrospect she had after all been one of the summer sluts.

Thus do the men and boys who gaze at the girls with the golden tans, deliver their verdicts.

In the 1990s, Donny and Darce, like Alan and Evan, divide the world into sluts and sweets and penalize both. The tale of waitresses Joanne and Ronette has much in common with the accounts of the schoolgirls Joey and Sandy. Both accounts show us that girls who lose their virginity easily, for love or 'status', get no better deal than those who less easily or less willingly lose it.

The most significant feature which follows the loss of virginity was summed up by Sandy. Girls, she says, couldn't be 'the same gang any more'. Indeed the girls no longer wanted to be part of that gang. 'Everything changes once you go with a guy, you sort of belong to him.'

For girls this is seen as both positive and negative. At one level it offers them positive feelings of security, of belonging: 'It's kind of a good feeling,' Sandy says. She has bought into the genital myth which decrees that women should necessarily associate emotional closeness with sexual activity. This ensures they will find it hard to contemplate periods of celibacy. On the negative side however, Sandy realistically sums up: 'But it's also bad for you. You've stopped being free. It's like they've got this power over you.' There is a level, always, at which women do know just what is going on, just how they are being conned, but it is seldom represented as in women's interests to make such knowledge visible. This makes it hard for women to acknowledge it to themselves.

Fortunately not all schoolgirls' experiences matched those of Joey and Sandy, or reflected those of the fictional waitresses Joanne or Ronette. Several contented young women reported that their first sexual encounter had been with a boy they were fond of or to whom they were mutually attracted. In their cases, the experience of losing their virginity had been pleasurable.

'I knew it was time to lose it and I was wild about my boyfriend. He was very careful with me. It didn't hurt at all. I didn't get much out of the actual experience but I felt we got closer.' (Fifteen-year-old.)

Several young women saw losing their virginity as a matter of indifference.

'You knew you'd got to do it, like homework, so you just went through with it. The boys got off on it so that was okay.' (Fourteen-year-old.)

Some saw this hurdle to be overcome less as a matter of romance than of farce.

'We had a terrible time trying to get rid of my virginity. We had to have several goes. It just would not work. My boyfriend and I were awfully inexperienced, and I'd never been one for tampons, so we just fell about laughing. When it did happen he got a lot of pleasure so I felt it had been worth it.' (Fifteen-year-old.)

What is significant about these more heartening experiences is that they echoed the negative ones in the way that all girls saw virginity as a handicap, or as an obstacle, something to be rid of. For them virginity is transitional. Several used phrases like: 'You knew you had to get rid of it so you chose the sexiest boy to do it with.'

In order to explore the differences between the transitional virginity of these young women's accounts, and perpetual virginity which may be a part of a purposeful celibate philosophy, I listened to dozens of accounts of what it meant to young women to be a virgin.

Of the girls who saw the experience as positive, most of those did not view their first sexual experience as an event in which they were equal participants. Rather, they perceived it as either something boys did to them (one girl said losing one's virginity was promoted as 'for your own good'; several girls said it was 'to give the boys pleasure'), or as a means for boys to control, not only the girl whose virginity was being taken, but the whole group of girls to whom she belonged. In this respect the more favourable accounts mirrored the more overtly negative.

Many accounts showed that from an early age, boys promote the cardinal message of the genital myth – that girls' virginity is under male control. Some girls have internalized this idea and therefore appear to lack a sense of self. They do not act as autonomous young women. Those girls who did perceive their virginity as more 'purposeful', who decided to stay 'clannish' or self-protective, who refused to give in to the boys' sexual demands, were labelled bad or deviant. Such stories mirrored Joey's, where at her school the 'girls who stayed clannish', were abused as 'abnormal prudes' or were told they 'might turn into lezzies'. It is these clannish 'perpetual virgins' who have a connection to female celibates. Though transitional virginity shares with celibacy the idea of genital abstention, because it is not autonomous it cannot be equated with passionate celibacy.

Like certain kinds of chastity, transitional virginity is either willingly or unwillingly under male control. Traditionally, it has (like chastity) been open to male testing procedures. 'Virginity tests', for instance, which are gynaecological examinations performed by a physician or some other 'expert', supposedly to determine whether or not a woman is a virgin, have functioned, like chastity belts, as a violent method of social control. In practice they have been used to police women's behaviour in many cultures and historical periods. They have been used to determine whether a young woman is 'acceptable' for marriage, her acceptability/virginity being part of a body-examination system over which she has no rights.[18]

During the seventies, the UK immigration service routinely performed these tests on Indian women, and other women of colour, who were trying to immigrate to Great Britain. Tests which distressed and humiliated women were used to restrict immigration.

It is probable that this territorial behaviour associated with virginity is more often found in men than in women, but women are not exempt. The genital myth works not only through males, but also through females whose mindset is manipulated by male attitudes and values.

Women who have power within a sexual relationship with another woman can also feel and may express some of these territorial attitudes, although in these relationships the power is not institutionalized.

Take the case of Franca and Ginnie. Franca was a university professor, head of department, member of several key committees, a very powerful woman. For ten years she had lived discreetly and affectionately with a painter called Alice. Unfortunately for the household finances Alice's abstract paintings were highly praised but infrequently sold. Franca shouldered their financial burdens and felt this gave her the right to run their partnership much as she ran her department. With authority. Towards the end of the decade, rows over control were gradually replacing the early rapture. Alice retreated into her art. Franca spent more time at work.

Enter Ginnie. A mature student of thirty-four at the university, who fixed upon Franca an eager gaze and total admiration. There were two curious features about newcomer Ginnie. One was that in the decade before her return to study she had headed a highly prestigious firm of accountants and statisticians, and being of a solitary disposition with few friends, she seldom went out or spent money, so had amassed a considerable private income. (After life with talented impoverished Alice, this had a certain appeal to Franca.) The second curious feature was that throughout her adult life Ginnie had never taken either a male or a female lover. At thirty-four she was a virgin. Having never dated anyone, she seemed unaware of the ethics involved in social relationships. That Franca was, in old-fashioned parlance, an 'attached' woman did not count at all with Ginnie. Having fallen in love with Franca, the virginal statistician set about informing her of the fact.

Knowing that Alice was painting at a farm in the country, that Franca was about to join her for the vacation, Ginnie suggested to Franca that she accompanied Franca and spent her holiday with the two women.

> She'd made her feelings obvious [Franca said]. I knew this was a dangerous situation but I felt excited by that amount of admiration. So I said yes. We travelled together. It was a long journey. On the train Ginnie talked incessantly, telling me she had never experienced these emotions for anyone. She made extraordinarily passionate statements out loud on the train. I wondered who else she had slept with. Suddenly she said 'I'm a virgin. I have never known what to do about it.'
>
> I tried to think of Alice, my partner. About our life, our ideal of monogamy. But all I could think of was conquest, the vision of power, of taking this girl over. It is strange, she was over thirty but she seemed like a very young girl, almost a child in some ways. In the end that's what happened. We waited till we got to the farm. I talked to Alice about it before Ginnie and I made love. I had hoped everything would stay the same, that my relationship with Alice would carry on. We tried, but everything changed. There were terrible consequences for all three of us. Alice and I finally broke up. I never had much of a relationship with Ginnie. It was one of those awful mistakes. But that actual moment of taking her to bed. Honestly I have never had such fierce feelings before. It was like owning someone's body, possessing every inch of them.

As we see from Franca's admissions, the feelings of power and control that can be engendered by a woman's virginity do not lie entirely with men. In this case, a woman obsessed with the small power she is allowed, has internalized the message that a woman's virginity can be 'taken over' if it is part of a sexuality that is not under her own control.

Initially most of us are likely to associate virginity with chastity, because as we saw in the previous chapter, the root of the word chaste is 'pure' and there is an integral association between 'purity' and the Virgin Mary. As Marina Warner comments, 'the price the Virgin demanded was purity, and the way the educators of Catholic children have interpreted this for nearly two thousand years is sexual chastity.'[19]

Unlike my own convent school, where we only received blue ribbons for special spiritual achievement or excessive bodily modesty (and gallingly some of us did not), in Marina Warner's convent school she and all the other little girls wore blue ribbons round their necks with medals of the Sodality of Our Lady, presumably whether they were excessively modest or not, because blue was the colour of the Virgin. At their convent the ribbons merely signified that the wearer was a child of Mary, had dedicated herself to the Virgin, 'and promised to emulate her in thought, word and deed: her chastity, her humility, her gentleness.' The Virgin was of course 'the culmination of womanhood'.[20]

Given these somewhat passive and feminine attributes for the blue ribboned group to imitate, it is hardly surprising that Marina Warner's father, said to be a witty agnostic, bitingly pointed out that Catholicism was a good religion for a girl.

It is hard to emerge from a convent and not to recall the Virgin as the culmination of true femininity. It is difficult even in later years for young women to shake off both that idea and that ideal. In a child's confused and often troubled world a convent upbringing, if it does nothing else, offers a few basic certainties of which the Virgin, her chastity, her beauty, are paramount. Perhaps it is a convent education which makes both virginity and celibacy seem familiar and valuable as well as irritating, reactions which girls who go to schools similar to Joey's and Sandy's do not necessarily recall or share.

What I remember about the notion of virginity was that to be virginal was to be blessed. That was the sacred script running through my childhood. As a highly competitive young girl, whose aim was to win as many gold stars as possible, I did not lightly cease to be a virgin. I did not rush to be first in the queue, at what in those days was seen as the rather risqué family planning place. Let others hurtle along and give up their 'precious pearl' without the proper prize. Not me. Unlike Joey and Sandy my virginity was always more of a blessing than a burden, if only because the surrendering of the virginal state fell foul of both the Jewish and Catholic systems of punishments and rewards, on which I was centred for many years.

A religion focused on the Virgin, the sublime model of chastity, implies that virginity is as Jean Rhys puts it, women's most 'precious possession', and like many other possessions precious to women (their self-respect, their creative talents, their friendships), can, for the right price, be taken over.[21] Yet simultaneously the teaching of the Catholic Church, the example of the Virgin Mary herself, and the concrete presence of the nuns, offer us a vision of perpetual virginity devoted to a spiritual ideal.

As Professor Jo Ann McNamara observes in her study of early celibate women, virginity is usually a 'transitional phase in the life of a young girl', but when women choose to 'define virginity as a voluntary profession' then it can be identified as part of the celibate ideal.[22]

We saw earlier that certain religious or cultural mores make it difficult for celibate women to define their virginity in a purposeful way. Judaism is an excellent example. In Jewish tradition, spinsterhood, which was assumed to be virginal, was seen as a form of barrenness, as something that brought upon a Jewish woman a shocking stigma. Thus single Jewish women not in obvious sexual relationships, and not necessarily young, are more likely to be seen by others as transitionally rather than as *occupationally* virginal, as waiting for marriage rather than avowedly and happily celibate. Not only that, they are much more likely to see it that way themselves.

In the first three Christian centuries however, young Jewish women (for as Jo Ann McNamara points out, the first women to embrace Jesus' message were Jewish), did manage to choose virginity as a profession. By making it part of a celibate stand they incorporated it into their independent lives. Jesus' message held an inherent hatred of social barriers, an anarchistic impulse to turn the world upside down. The idea of a new world where marriage and being given in marriage were no longer priorities or necessary truths by which women should live their lives, a society conceived neither as male nor female, appealed to many young women.

One of the attractions of this unstructured new religion was its strong individualistic message which was used by some women to break the barriers of 'otherness' and to create a positive new identity rooted in celibacy. Men at that time tended to see women as 'the other'; in terms of archetypal temptation or extreme purity, the early Christian versions of our contemporary summer sluts and girls who won't make out.

However, a group of emancipated women decided to ignore the barriers between men and women that in the ancient world had been fortified by restrictive gender roles, legal restraints, and religious taboos. They set themselves up as celibate, a situation which transcended the existing gender system which rested firmly on the belief that the female body was inferior to the male and periodically polluted. Such a belief made it almost axiomatic that women's minds were perceived as feeble and their morals hopelessly corrupt, which in turn led to a public sphere inhabited largely by men, who sealed it off and secured it against the contaminating influence of women.

Thus when early Christian virgins and widows, outcasts and ascetics, decided to embrace the celibate life as part of their Christian belief, these women 'conceived and carried out a revolution of vast proportions. They forced the social structure of antiquity to incorporate the celibate woman in a secure and even superior stratum.'[23]

Some women consecrated to virginity began to teach, others to prophesy. Philip the evangelist, one of seven deacons, had four unmarried daughters who prophesied. What the stories stress is their virginal status. Though virginity was not a requirement for prophetic status, this emphasis strengthens the idea that virginity was already in vogue amongst early clever Christian women, who knew their condition of perpetual virginity endowed them with a charisma lacked by women subject to husbands.

Such charisma does not go down well with the genital mythmakers. Although a few men were friendly, consecrated to the new ideal themselves, most of the men who commented on the process were hostile, fearful of the new order they saw developing in their midst. Hardly surprisingly, given what we know about penalties attached to women in any period in history who try to live outside the area of male control, emancipated women of the first three Christian centuries were treated with 'savage contempt'.[24]

Most of the women had no appropriate language and no new concepts with which to respond to the attacks, or define themselves. When a virgin takes up a purposeful stance and 'converts' her acceptable transitional virginity into a purposeful celibacy, she does not have an identity because there is no space for her within the world bounded by the genital myth.

As McNamara says of these women, 'they remained simply "unmanly" possessors of all those negative personality traits unsuited to the virile identity.'[25] In a sense, a perpetual virgin of that era 'became a man' but without initially the status or power that real men had, and the more she threatened to acquire it the more open to attack she became.[26]

As this female celibate group grew in strength, and took up positions within the new church, men became more frightened and attacks, both verbal and symbolic, or actual and aggressive, on perpetual virgins and celibate widows increased. What was it that these women found in Christianity and in the celibate life which they embraced, which gave them the strength they needed to combat the scorn and contempt of their time? To take on the profession of perpetual virgin, to deny themselves the physical and emotional satisfactions offered by marriage and motherhood, could not have been an easy choice. Jo Ann McNamara suggests: 'A fear and hatred of men is the possibility most ready to hand. Gnostic literature, the apocryphal gospels, and the tracts in praise of virginity . . . all advance the humiliation of sexual intercourse and the pain of childbearing as reasons to turn away from the procreative life.'[27]

Many women may have been eager to leave the burden of housekeeping in favour of a life of spiritual devotion and active involvement in the infant church. A third suggestion is that in those days even the most congenial marriage was (as it is today) in many respects limiting, as is even the most fulfilling maternal experience. Having children may bring women joy and pain but it does not necessarily stretch the mind.

The large milieu of virgins and widows attracted to Christianity points to a widespread impulse for women to free themselves from the bonds and obligations of marriage without falling into the prostitution that was its usual complement. By the second century, young women were living in a society where they were forced into marital beds by parents or guardians whose power was reinforced by the paternalistic state. McNamara suggests that sexual activity was seen as revolting by many young virgins, and their fears would have been increased by the fact that they had no control over their procreative processes. Not all women take to maternity, but not only were these women's wishes about pregnancy discounted, but their husbands had uncontested legal power to decree whether or not the ensuing baby would live.

In the second century AD life for many women entailed enforced virtue or enforced vice. When prophets preached the flesh was evil, many women felt their own experiences or those of their sisters could testify to it. So when some saw a mystical route to escape from the flesh, they took it.

The idea of giving women the option to reject marriage in that period was almost inconceivable. But so popular did the situation of those described as 'ever-virgins' become, that Ignatius of Antioch was forced to suggest that women needed to be counselled against adopting the virgin life out of hatred of marriage rather than for the 'proper reason' of religious devotion.[28] Proper or not, the reasons mounted up.

The conditions of those women's lives which confined them to their homes severely limited the range of relationships open to them. Women who were perpetual virgins were able to break through society's limitations, sometimes to discover emotional relationships with women which they were unlikely to have known before, sometimes to achieve relationships with men that were of a completely new order. Without a genital basis, these male-female relationships were more equal, more life enhancing.

One example of a celibate partnership between a young virgin and a man vowed to chastity is the story of Thecla and Paul, the celibate pair who sometimes travelled together, sometimes lived separately, who shared a profound spiritual union which grew out of a mutual devotion to a higher purpose for which Thecla the perpetual virgin died.[29]

Paul's letters to the Corinthians indicate that perpetual virginity was being promulgated as a possibility among the believers in Corinth, apparently the first experimenters in celibate Christian lifestyles. Soon this radical innovative idea was heard in other cities.[30]

Thecla, a young virgin about to be married, heard Paul preach and was instantly converted to a life of virginity. She broke off her engagement. She defied every parental effort to force her to honour her obligation. She abandoned her home, her family and her fiancé. Finally her parents turned her over to the court to be executed for her refusal to marry. She escaped death twice, and embarked on a long career as a missionary. Finally when Paul, despite her heroineism, refused to baptize her, she baptized herself whilst awaiting martyr-dom in the arena where the savage beasts were about to be let loose on her.[31]

For Thecla and other perpetual virgins of that period, the genitally chaste life was seen as a divinely bestowed liberty, to be used in the pursuit of higher ideals. The legend of Thecla, soon to become a popular melodrama, illustrated the ideal of Christian chastity as a device to liberate women from the sexual demands of their husbands, and perpetual virginity was seen as an escape from the villainous plots of parents. Many women and men maintained that Paul through the living (and dying) example of Thecla gave women licence to teach and baptize. By the third century, widows and married women who had left their husbands were beginning to formulate a concept of virginity as a way of life. The rejection of sexual activity was but the beginning of a new adventure. They threw off certain wearisome domestic responsibilities and they lived as independent women taking on 'masculine' roles in the Christian communities in which they lived and worked, in places as far apart as Rome and Africa.

Gradually the notion of virginity came to subsume all sorts of women who lived without sexually active expression. It became a profession not a physiological accident. McNamara points out that the condition of virginity had come to transcend the flesh, to be accepted as a condition of the soul which depended on the consent of the practitioner. It was this definition of virginity which rested on *purity of intent* rather than mere physical integrity that allowed the virgin ranks to be opened to widowed and separated women.

It was this new definition of virginity which is akin to that of passionate celibacy which begins in the mind. It was this challenging definition of virginity which meant that while female virgins began to hold a special place in the community, they also became objects of fear and suspicion to men. Male clergy saw them as a challenge to their superiority and authority in the Church, lay men saw them as a challenge to their superiority and authority in the home.

Challenges by women cannot go unanswered.

Perpetual virgins who challenge the male genital myth of their time show a celibate strength. This means they see themselves as autonomous, self-willed, beyond capture. It is significant that Mary Daly renames virgins as women who are 'never captured'.[32]

It comes as no surprise that men will then attempt to capture and overpower them. Historically there have been many and bitter occasions when militant virgins have been irrevocably captured, subdued, taken over, and grievously disempowered.

Perhaps the most dramatic example is that of Joan of Arc: soldier and military thinker; illiterate and brilliant, courageous and faithful. Faithful to her God, faithful to her voices, whom she first heard aged thirteen, and to whom she promised to keep her virginity for as long as it should please God. One almost forgets, Joan was not merely a soldier and a strategist; there were other small matters. Additional facts. She was also a woman, a woman from peasant stock vowed to militant and perpetual virginity, a woman who was without a shred of doubt a passionate celibate.

One should not forget these small matters. One should not overlook these additional facts. For Joan, born 1412, who died at nineteen in 1431, was killed for these small matters, was burnt alive for these additional facts.

The young girl who had routed the English from much French territory, who had devised the stratagems for their eventual expulsion from French soil, who was responsible for getting Charles VII crowned King of France, who helped him become Head of State and establish a French nation-state, was tortured and convicted by the Inquisition, was sentenced to death by the Catholic Church, was burnt at the stake as a witch.

One of the small matters was that of her clothes. At seventeen she escaped her father's house and authority, obeying her voices that told her to go to Vaucouleurs to find Robert de Baudricourt who would take her to Charles. She arrived in Vaucouleurs wearing a red peasant dress. She left the town without it, dressed in men's clothes, determined never again of her own volition to dress as a woman. She had a man's job to do. At the trial her captors asked her over and over why she refused to wear women's garb. She replied that it was 'but a small matter, and that she had not taken it by the advice of any living man; and that she did not take this dress nor do anything at all save by the command of Our Lord and the angels.'[33]

She never did take the advice of a living man. She never did behave like most living women are compelled to behave. So she was killed. Killed for her politics, killed for her faith, but most of all killed for being a woman dressed in men's clothes, a woman who refused to wear women's clothes, a woman who refused to make babies and made wars instead, a woman who refused to get fucked on the battlefield, or off it, a woman whose perpetual virginity was as much a rejection of the social subordination of women of her time, as it was a rejection of the sexual activity on which it was based.

Her perpetual virginity was that of a rebel in a society that could not and would not countenance one.

She resisted at all times the male takeover of her body, the right of which is an underlying premise of male dominance, just as she resisted at all times the religious and political takeover of her mind. She resisted the trap of being merely female. 'And as for womanly duties. She said there [were] enough other women to do them.'[34]

As Andrea Dworkin says, the resistance of this virgin 'was not a puerile virginity defined by fear or effeminacy. This was a rebel virginity harmonious with the deepest values of resistance to any political despotism.'[35]

Dworkin, in an impassioned review of Joan's life, makes it clear that despite the existence of a cultish worship of virginity as a feminine ideal in that period, Joan's purposeful and sustained virginity was not an expression of some aspect of her femininity or her preciousness as a woman. It was a self-conscious and militant repudiation of the common lot of women which as Dworkin emphasizes 'then as now, appeared to have something to do with being fucked'.[36]

I see Joan's virginity as purposeful, as an essential element of her virility. It was based on and it illustrated her autonomy. It defined her as she helped to define it.

'She refused to be fucked and she refused civil insignificance: and it was one refusal; a rejection of the social meaning of being female . . . Her virginity was a radical renunciation of a civil worthlessness rooted in real sexual practice.'[37]

In other words this perpetual virgin refused to be feminine. She did not therefore stand a chance.

I wish she was not merely the most dramatic example of a perpetual virgin punished by the patriarchal process of the genital myth. I wish she was the only example. Of course she is not.

Anthropologist Fernando Henriques gives us more evidence. All of it barbaric. Evidence that sickens, that shocks, that makes one want to stop up one's ears; stories about perpetual virgins that we would rather not hear. But stories that it is imperative we know. In his work *Prostitution and Society* Henriques tells tales of the way in which sacred virgins who inhabited ancient temples were horrendously forced into becoming 'sacred prostitutes'.[38] Henriques tells tales of ancient Phoenicia where 'their virgins also were presented for prostitution to the strangers who resorted there.'[39]

He tells of the atrocities perpetrated against the sacred virgins of Heliopolis when Constantine abolished the 'custom' of giving over sacred virgins to prostitution:

> They stripped the holy virgins who had never been looked upon by the multitude, of their garments, and exposed them in a state of nudity, as public objects of insult and derision. After numerous other inflictions, they shaved them, ripped them open, and placed inside them the food usually given to pigs; and the animals thus devoured these human entrails in conjunction with their ordinary food.[40]

Henriques believed that the citizens perpetrated this barbarity against the holy virgins from motives of revenge, on account of the abolition of the ancient custom of yielding up virgins to prostitution.[41] It is a brutal physical form of the psychological revenge we have seen enacted against perpetual virgins throughout the centuries.

Many of these unattached, purposeful virgins who reaped severe attacks were of course nuns. Among the many verbal and physical attacks on convents and nuns during, for instance, the Protestant Reformation, were frequent charges of looseness. Religious women at that time were condemned for their 'unnaturalness' in living apart from men.

In one of Martin Luther's letters, he gives his explanation of why nuns were supposedly abandoning their cloisters during the Reformation.

'Women are ashamed to admit this, but Scripture and life reveal that only one woman in thousands has been endowed with the God-given aptitude to live in chastity and virginity. A woman is not fully the master of herself. God fashioned her body so that she should be with a man, to have and to rear children.'[42]

This is the view bonded to the genital myth of that period.

Luther was not the only male expert to voice this view. Male attackers who both preceded and followed him were also afraid of women becoming 'masters of themselves'. A celibate lifestyle is a threat to a masculist society's values. When virginity is seen to be purposeful or even 'professionalized', when it becomes the key to a celibate lifestyle, it too becomes a threat.

Men wish to view virginity as a state that is under their control.

When virgins do not act in this way men become disturbed or angry. We saw this clearly in the case of Joey and Sandy's 'clannish' schoolfriends. We saw this bitterly in the story of Joanne and the 'True Trash' waitresses. We heard this all too audibly in the conversations of sixteen-year-old Evan and Alan. Men rarely pay more than lip service to the idea of esteem for the blessed state of virginity. When that virginity too obviously lies outside their control all respect for it melts into anger, curls with contempt. It is an outrage based on male fear of women's clannishness, male anxiety about women's indifference to male interests. Sexologist Albert Ellis wrote in his *Journal of Sex Research* in 1969: 'I would call the preservation of virginity an overt display of arrant masochism.'[43] There you have it. According to the Ellis, Kinsey and Comfort school of Genital Appropriation 'preserved' virginity cannot possibly be in women's interests because it patently and blatantly does not serve men's.

CHAPTER EIGHT

Endangered Species

So far I have looked at celibacy as a social phenomenon affecting individuals. But what models does history provide of celibate *communities*?

The Shakers are a useful example. Yesterday and today they have been reviled and revered, persecuted and praised.

They have aroused interest and attracted notoriety, partly because Shaker women and men who live together as a community stick passionately to an ideal of celibacy, and partly because they work on the provocative premise that celibacy can raise women's status in any male-female group. They even believe that celibacy can begin to change women's position in the world outside.

Who were the Shakers, and how plausible or relevant are their ideas to us today?

The Shakers started as an eighteenth century American utopian religious community who adopted celibacy instead of intercourse as their motivating symbol. Not content with using it as a symbol, they organized everything from the design of their house to the design of their life around it. Seeing the nuclear family as a structure which helped to subordinate women, they banished it in favour of a communal system. Men and women were encouraged to treat each other as platonic brothers and sisters; they prayed together but slept apart. In the old days they even ate apart. Shakers felt such measures would privilege female spiritual status, would improve women's position, and would offer men and women more equal social relationships.[1]

In the genital climate of the late eighteenth and nineteenth centuries, such bizarre ideas meant that the celibate Shakers always attracted attention. They did so then; they do so today. For there are still a few of them left. Initially they were a large organization, with branches spreading across the United States. At their peak, in 1840, they numbered about six thousand. Today, however, in an ancient Shaker residence on Sabbathday Lake, a remote, often snow-covered, spot in north-eastern America, there are just nine Shaker women and men left, who still act out the stringently simple celibate lives of their predecessors.

The Shakers first came there in 1783, converted a group of local farmers, and with their bare hands and aching limbs built the village in which the original Shaker dwelling still stands. They hewed the trees, made the bricks, and began to chop and cut and nail and paint until on Christmas Day 1794 a small group sat down for a modest meal and prolonged worship.

'People see us as an endangered species, a bit like the whooping crane,' one of the remaining Shaker sisters said. 'They are always asking: how many of you are there left?'[2]

A Shaker brother at Sabbathday Lake confirmed that so many people in the outside world think they are extinct that when they visit the community and find the practising celibates alive and well they are deeply shocked. They think of them as creatures of a bygone age. The members at Sabbathday Lake tell the amusing story of Sister Elizabeth sitting on the back porch of the Shaker dwelling house about seven or eight years ago snapping beans. Night was falling. It was serene and peaceful. A tourist drove up. Knowing that the 'quaint' religious sect lived there, he stopped at the porch. 'Oh you're just like the Amish, you don't have any electricity,' he said.

'And what do you think this is?' she said acidly, pointing to the light pull and the telephone cord.[3]

People in the outside world however remain unconvinced, either of their existence, or by their views. Indeed, today Shakers are better known for their exquisitely proportioned and simple furniture than for their religious beliefs or celibate lifestyle. Shakers have become part of the American vernacular culture. You cannot open a magazine without seeing twentieth century goods based on ancient Shaker products, or decorative arts which draw for inspiration on Shaker designs. At auctions throughout the country their furniture which, like their life, pared things down to essentials, now sells for thousands of dollars. The nine remaining Shaker women and men who live monastic lives praying, cooking, working and providing spiritual and domestic comfort for each other, find these material excavations of their past extraordinary. As the group, who have not made furniture for more than a hundred years, lay the old Shaker table for a moderate repast, they know that the table itself could fetch more at an auction than they spend on food and living for months at a time. Today most of the Shaker antiques are more likely to be spotted in a wealthy American home than at Sabbathday Lake. As far as the last Shakers are concerned, this current craze for their furniture symbolizes an American myth that says you can buy into a special way of life without committing yourself to its goals or its hardships.

In a complex commercial and genital society, Shakerism as an ideal of simplicity and anti-genital principles has become collectable – if you can afford the price. A hundred miles from where the last Shaker community, with its religious commitment that embraces Christian poverty, still finds it difficult to make ends meet, I met a Canadian businessman who told me proudly he had just acquired an antique Shaker chair for over a thousand dollars. The irony was lost on him. 'You can get Shaker stuff really cheap, really cheap,' he said excitedly. 'Look at how perfect it is, how honest, how delicately proportioned and balanced, a delicious example of the Shaker way of life. Such honesty, such simplicity.'

He did not mention the Shakers' dedication to joyousness in all aspects of life from shovelling manure to scrubbing floors, nor their antipathy to everything costly and commercial, nor their denial of personal property, nor their disapproval of the American nuclear family. He certainly did not mention their hostility to intercourse, their stringent abstention from genital activity and from any form of sexual expression – all of which are somewhat more meaningful examples of the Shaker way of life.

Listening to this enthusiastic Canadian businessman I suddenly understood why Sister Mildred, one of the last celibate sisters, an Elderess at Sabbathday Lake community, said sadly before she died in 1990 that she did not want to be remembered as a chair.[4]

Today, as in the past, this endangered species, who work together and sleep apart, define celibacy as strict genital abstinence. Today, their furniture is seen as relevant, their values as outdated. Some of these values, however, could be relevant to those of us interested in genuine social change.

It is not insignificant that the Shakers were a group led by a woman. Strong-minded, controversial, and often in trouble, Ann Lee, the Shaker founder, was an illiterate British blacksmith's daughter who shocked first Britain, then America, with her defiant doctrine that God was bisexual, that intercourse was original sin, and that she was the female Christ spirit. Needless to say, she met aggression and uproar head-on wherever she went. She believed that the path to spiritual harmony, social peace and a genuine unity between the two sexes could only come about through celibacy in houses constructed to keep them apart sexually but together spiritually.

In the America of Ann Lee's time, heterosexual intercourse symbolically associated women with childcare, domesticity and low prestige, just as it does today. The cultural context against which the Shakers prayed and danced, was a symbolic system that opposed men and women and devalued women, just as it does today. When the Shakers looked outside their own whooping crane organization at mainstream America, they would have seen intercourse standing for the nuclear family, for private ownership of property, for capitalism, for the class system, just as we see it today. Most significantly, they would have seen the separation and hierarchy of the two sexes: men who were viewed as dominant and acted accordingly and women who were viewed as submissive and suffered because of it.

Ann Lee's view was that celibacy, by altering women's relationship to reproduction, could therefore associate women with production and leadership rather than with consumption and a degrading submission.[5]

The key problem for the Shakers was the power dimension in *all* sexual relationships, and the particular power problems that occurred in relationships that involved intercourse. Today writer Andrea Dworkin asks: can intercourse itself ever be an expression of sexual equality?[6] The Shakers felt it could not. They believed that the power dimension, present in all sexual relationships, diminishes or changes when sex is absent. Although it was their religious beliefs which led them to practise a purposeful chastity, they felt strongly that using celibacy as a unifying symbol allowed them to argue forcefully for social and political equality between the sexes, and to practise it in their domestic lives.

A purposeful chastity of course does not always or necessarily entail a fairer attitude towards women. Several mixed celibate societies have furthered the purposes of the genital mythmakers because, unlike the Shakers, they did not include women's emancipation as part of their celibate philosophy. A brief look at earlier celibate groups, from as far back as the first three Christian centuries will show us that historically there has been a frequent association between female celibacy and female freedom, but that it needs creative thinking such as that of the Shakers to ensure that celibacy is used in women's interests.

Celibate women have always had a more autonomous identity than their genitally-enslaved sisters. Those who escaped motherhood and marriage into celibacy through religion, did not merely raise their status in spiritual matters, they also gained a social power unavailable to non-celibate wives and mothers of the time. Professor Sally Kitch, who researched early connections between sexual equality and a determinedly chaste lifestyle pointed to the time of the Roman Empire when women who did not wish to become prostitutes (which was one alternative to the authority of husbands and fathers) decided instead to embrace celibacy. If they were Christians they chose it primarily for religious reasons, believing that celibacy cleansed them for an active spiritual life. More significantly their celibacy elevated them to a high status within the Church, not open to their married sisters, who were controlled by the genital myth of the day. It was a myth whose consequences were not so different from our own.[7]

Then as now, women who opted for sex with men found that it was not merely intercourse, it was also cooking, cleaning and nurturing. Then as now, women who opted for sex with men discovered that the domestic demands that accompany sexual activity have abysmally low status.

Some Church Fathers found virginal celibates particularly threatening. Clement, for instance, warned men to avoid contact with unmarried virginal women because they were likely to prove a special temptation. Tertullian, another esteemed Church Father, thought married or widowed celibates were less dangerous than virgins because they had 'travelled down the whole course of probation whereby a female can be tested'.[8]

Tertullian believed (and he was not the only man to do so), that the lifelong independence of perpetual virgins was so threatening that it weakened the case for classifying them as 'proper females'. Jo Ann McNamara points out that there was so much doubt about whether or not unmarried virginal celibates could be considered women at all, that the fear grew amongst men that such unwomanly females might actually have to be treated as men. They might, forsooth, even become equals to men in the Church hierarchy.[9]

In the Catholic Church it is a matter of debate whether celibate nuns have been looked on as the equals of celibate monks. The nuns I talked to were in no doubt as to the answer. They felt that in a society where male activities and male gender characteristics are

valued above those of females, the Church does not stand immune
from these misogynistic values.

In the Protestant Church, several communities experimented with
celibacy, but without relating it to such feminist goals as equal
opportunities or increased power for women. In America, celibate
utopian societies were set up at Ephrata, Zoar, Harmony, Amana,
and New Jerusalem. However neither in the way their religion was
organized nor in their domestic structure did they advocate leadership or decision-making for women. The Amana Inspirationists
founded at Ebenezer, New York, in 1843, then transported to Iowa
in the 1850s were contemporaries of the Shakers, but unlike them
they did not consider celibacy as a crusading symbol for improving women's position, or valuing women's activities. Far from it.
Although well known for their celibate doctrine, in practice the
Amanans watered down their celibacy by tolerating marriage for
those members who did not wish to enter the highest ranks of the
community. As for their views on women, their lukewarm celibate
philosophy did not stop them attacking their sisters. Amanan leaders
warned their male believers to 'fly from the society of women-kind
as much as possible, as a very highly dangerous magnet and magical
fire.'[10]

As the Shakers realized, merely adopting a celibate lifestyle in a
community does not always or necessarily improve women's chances
within that group. Nor does it necessarily offer a radically different
ideal to affect and influence the world outside.

The important thing is that it *can*.

When it is the basis for the way a community works, celibacy
can diminish the power dimensions between men and women.

It is significant that the communities which did not succeed in
achieving greater independence for women were those who did not
consider celibacy as crucial to *every* aspect of their group's organization in the way that the Shakers did.

Sex and celibacy, far from being simple concepts, acquire meaning and significance from the culture surrounding them. To the
eighteenth and nineteenth century Shaker women, celibacy meant
abstention from all forms of genital activity or physically demon-
strative expression. This is a very different interpretation from that
of twentieth century Sensual Celibates who endorse masturbation
and physical embraces.

In the society from which the Shakers withdrew, social forces
shaped sexual activity as they do today. Fathers were revered as

workers and heads of households while 'ordinary' and 'good' (i.e. married) women were restricted to the unprestigious home, where they were economically dependent. Single women who had to earn a living turned to the few dead-end, low-paid jobs open to them. Suffragettes, who were not considered either ordinary or good (they after all fought for women's rights), were termed unfeminine, unchristian, aggressive and emasculating. So 'ordinary, good sexuality' between women and men was constructed on the model of the loving paternalistic male ruler and his willing submissive reflective wife.

For the Shakers intercourse stood symbolically for the subordination of women in the outside world, with that subordination made sexy in bed. In the light of this, it is curious that the prevailing myth about intercourse is that it connects and fuses the two sexes in a joyous union.

This then was the system in which Ann Lee was brought up. These were the entrenched ideas she felt she must fight. It was no wonder she did not fit comfortably into such a society.

Ann Lee had been out of step with her time and her community from a very young age. She was born in 1736 in Manchester, England, which at that time was a city gripped with experimentation and religious nonconformism.

Texts and stories suggest that Ann Lee had been hostile towards sex and reproduction from early childhood. She disliked any mention of it and had a positive aversion to any practical examples.[11] According to Shaker legend, when she was still a young child she even tried to dissuade her parents from having intercourse. Predictably neither her mother nor her father welcomed her suggestions. Later her father retaliated by physically abusing her.[12] She was coerced into marriage with a man called Abraham Stanley and experienced what seems to have been great pain in four childbirths, followed by desperate grief over the deaths of all four children. Three died in infancy and one at the age of six in 1766 when Ann Lee herself was only thirty.

Scholar Edward Horgan suggests that she believed the deaths of her children to be a punishment for sexual indulgence.[13] Henri Desroche, a Shaker historian, suggests that as she joined a religious group only two years after her last child's death, she chose celibacy and the spiritual life as a palliative for her grief.[14]

This might have been the initial impulse, but her steadfast commitment to celibacy, and the celibate dedication of her followers, few of whom felt her revulsion towards sex, probably stemmed as much from intellectual and religious reasoning as from genital aversion.

Certainly, from the time she was a young woman she would preach to anyone who would listen to her that God was half male and half female, that sexual intercourse was original sin, that celibacy was the way to be saved, and that there was no reason why women should be unequal to men in the eyes of her bisexual God. She regularly disrupted church services in the Cathedral and was just as regularly thrown into prison for disturbing the peace.

In 1770, still struggling with the loss of her children, during her second stay in prison she had a vision that she was to become a spiritual leader and that her destiny and that of her followers lay in America. One account of her conversion says that Ann Lee 'fell upon her knees, her eyes blinded by the supernatural radiance. The conviction was borne in upon her then . . . that the life of the celibate . . . and the taking up of the cross against the world and the flesh was the only way of regeneration.'[15]

She was thirty-four and ready for a new life. Believing that America would be more receptive to her challenging ideas, she set about inspiring her group. By 1744, aged thirty-eight, she and eight converts set off for New York. The believers did not encounter much more tolerance in the New World than they had in the old.[16]

The group, whose official title is The United Society of Believers but who were called Shakers by observers entranced by their rocking, rolling, shaking dance movements, performed as they worshipped, settled into the New World and began shaking up the ideas of the residents. The colonists retaliated by harassing them, sometimes violently, for their strange beliefs. They were accused of treason because they would not take up arms, even in the War of Independence, and of even greater heresy for their radical social views. For a woman to set herself up as a temporal religious leader was provocative stuff. For that woman to see herself as a female Christ who believed in equality for women in the fight against male lust was really too much.

Despite the opposition to the Shakers, within two years Mother Ann (as she was then called) and her converts had raised enough money to buy a swampy plot of land in Watervliet, near Albany, New York (where today her gravestone stands). In 1776 she set up her ministry there and in nearby Mount Lebanon.

Because Ann Lee was non-literate, there are no written records by her, and most of what is known comes from fond memories on the part of her followers and critical memories on the part of her opponents, recorded as much as thirty or forty years later by believers. The image handed down however is striking. Ann Lee was a very tall, powerfully-built woman, with a substantial figure and apparently extraordinary gifts of the spirit. Her genuine charisma was greatly enhanced by her followers' (possibly mythical, but certainly compelling) claim that their female Christ spirit had the gift of tongues and spoke seventy-two different languages.

One description of her, written in 1816 from a compilation by those who knew her, says:

> Mother Ann Lee was a woman of strong constitution rather exceeding the ordinary size of women, rather thick but very straight and well proportioned in form, of light complexion and blue eyes, her hair of a light chestnut brown. In appearance she was very majestic and her countenance was such as inspired confidence and respect. By many of the world who saw her without prejudice, she was called beautiful.[17]

A very early account describes the Shakers quietly seated in the large room. Mother Ann entered, threw her head back, started singing and praying and moving her body in time to the music. Within minutes the seated men and women began to move their hands rhythmically back and forth. Then as Ann Lee's charisma started to flow through the whole community, the singing got louder, the movements stronger. Tempestuously she sang and swayed, tempestuously they rocked and rallied. Finally, with the chairs tilting off the ground, she led the brothers and sisters into an elaborate series of spontaneous routines. Nothing less than a spiritual holy rolling!

This then was the woman who forcefully set about converting the inhabitants of New England to an anti-genital pro-woman way of life.

Her critics thought she was deranged, possessed of the devil. Her followers thought she was the second coming of the Christ spirit with all the necessary apostolic authority. What everybody made no mistake about was her clear and consistent identification of celibacy with women's rights as well as with religious harmony.

From the time Ann Lee became their leader, through to her death, then throughout the years of ministry which followed, Shakers were unswervingly articulate about the connection between celibacy and ideals of sexual equality.[18]

Ann Lee began with the matter of lust. She consistently taught her converts to equate sex with sin and celibacy with salvation. Shaker legends describe Mother Ann's nine years of 'constant travail of spirit and body' over the question of sin. Only when she had a vision of 'Adam and Eve in the Garden of Eden committing the act that resulted in their expulsion from the Garden and in saddling mankind with a heritage of sin' did she see that her role lay in promoting celibacy as the way to reverse the sexual curse on mankind.[19]

Her view of the curse offered her Shaker followers an interesting departure from conformist Biblical lines, which also helped to raise women's status. Traditional Christian society viewed women as the first in sin; Shakers however viewed women both as victims of sin, and as capable of redeeming the world from sin. This gave women an enviable and powerful metaphorical position in Shaker philosophy. Shakers saw the world poisoned by lust, and by male domination which they closely associated with lust. Women escaped both these evils and thus within Shaker spiritual affairs female virtues were privileged, and a kind of female spiritual superiority was promoted.

To Shakers, sex was fleshy, sex was bad, sex put women down. Lust tainted all family relations, lust limited women to inferior roles. It was genital activity which reduced women to stereotypical passivity, housewifery, and economic dependence. Sex, in their view, equalled irrationality, it created disorder. Where you saw a woman only as a sexual creature you also saw her as less than a rational being. They believed if you had physical passions you would be excluded from higher mental and physical life and they wanted both women and men to participate in the life of the mind and spirit. Offended by the gross materialism produced by lust, what they wanted was co-operation in the sharing of worldly goods and labour. At least that way women would benefit.[20]

Today we have a Western media notion of 'romantic love' based on the ideal of intercourse. In practice this means women are emotionally and economically dependent upon 'sexual love', most acceptably from men who are or will become their husbands to whom they have to be sexually accessible at all times. If they are not, financial insecurity or violence may ensue.

The Shakers believed that total celibacy on the part of both sexes removed this pressure.

In the West today there is an assumption that women resent any sexual deprivation, that they always want sex and need to be constantly genitally available to men. Male convenience is very well served by such arrangements, whilst the fact is that many women do not actually feel deprived at all. Shaker women certainly did not. Shaker men, too, felt there were great spiritual and social compensations for sexual abstinence. In fact they probably saw them less as 'compensations' than as benefits. (It is interesting that despite my commitment to this study, the twentieth century frame of reference out of which I write encouraged me to use the term 'compensations'.)

Readings of Shaker texts show that many Shaker women had already encountered and despised obligatory genital sex within marriage. They recognized that marriage was meant to legitimize sex, but they did not see it as justifiable. Marital sex they found selfish, non-egalitarian, exploitative. Marriage itself they saw as an attempt to justify lust that in serving male interests destroyed spiritual values. If people were to be saved and women's lot improved, marriage, like capitalism, needed wiping out.

Marriage, however, was not the only sin founded on sex. The selfish gathering and keeping of personal property was a second. War was a third. These created divisions between the rich and the poor, the bond and the free, on the basis of categories called 'male' and 'female'. Shakers wanted to do away with the consequences of those categories, so they did away with sex because that is where they saw those categories rooted.

Sex to the Shakers was more than sin, it was a central evil in American culture. It divided families, it divided women from men, it established a vicious class system. Even capitalism they saw as founded in the selfishness of the nuclear family. Heterosexuality the Shakers saw as competitive, avaricious and impersonal. It separated society into two different realms: nature (home, hearth, love) where women were exploited, and culture (money and the workplace) where men were valued. Shakers thought women's exclusion from cultural prestige was the direct result of their reproductive and sexual relationships with men. To rectify this, they undertook not to reproduce. Obviously this philosophy, which meant that the Shakers had to recruit in order to maintain their numbers, rather than rely on children being born to the group, was a contributory factor to their decline.

One interesting connection between Shaker women and women in mainstream America, was that women outside Shakerdom were increasingly interpreting ideas of feminine morality in terms of chastity and modesty. Such an interpretation, although limiting in many ways, had one useful spin-off. It helped to reduce women's experience of the hazards of childbirth and limited the number of children they had to rear. Both groups of women saw voluntary control of reproduction as a means to autonomy.[21] There was, however, a problem which they had to overcome. In that era celibate women who chose not to reproduce were thought to be 'unnatural', and Shaker women who chose to be single to free themselves were unable to throw off this notion that they were unnatural.[22]

That many considered themselves unworthy as non-mothers has parallels of course today. It was and is a paradoxical situation, for mothering has low status, almost no 'practical' rewards, yet it is considered 'natural' therefore approvable. Shaker women saw that given their society's structure motherhood could be a hindrance to women's independence, yet they also saw how important many maternal characteristics were both to women themselves and to the part they intended to play in redeeming humanity.

What they did was to construct a metaphor of spiritual motherhood which was an image which connected celibate women with Ann Lee their spiritual mother, and through her to the divine 'infinite mother' or Holy Mother.[23] This allowed women to retain nurturing images of motherhood but gave them an additional prestige not usually associated with biological motherhood.

One of the lifelong champions of women's rights, Shaker writer Anna White, defined the maternal spirit as a force for unifying the universe's 'spiritual, intellectual and humanitarian' elements and for instilling sensitivity, tact, sympathy, and spirituality in the daily lives of her children.[24]

This was clever because it built on the traditional source of women's power – the ability to give birth – but it transcended it by translating biological (natural) motherhood into spiritual (cultural) terms.

Shakers were convinced that the 'cursed family' system, in which men controlled women, had its roots in the same curse as that responsible for lust and sin. According to writer Nicholas Briggs, when God told Eve that her 'desire should be to her husband' he also required that the husband 'should rule over her'. Thus God created male dominance as well as lust in the 'cursed family'.[25]

In the new Shaker 'family', sibling love was not merely less sinful, it was more open to sexual equality. Being a sister or a daughter became more important than being a wife or a mother. This meant that women often qualified for prestige on their own merits rather than through those of their men. The two sexes were good friends rather than enemies or lovers. Though the brothers and sisters slept and ate apart, their commitment to an equal mixed-sex society was the reason they shared houses, rather than living in single-sex communities.

The democratic approach they established, which still operates today at Sabbathday Lake, meant that every decision had to be taken communally, whether it was to admit new members, choose what vegetables to grow, or go out and enjoy themselves. Women's voices had an equal share in the running of the community.

Today the Sabbathday Lake Shakers, involved in local schools' programmes, explain to schoolchildren that being brothers and sisters means taking care of each other equally and for the good of all. They are still working on the precepts of the ancient Shakers who in the words of Frederick Evans of New Lebanon in 1878 said 'Those who admire husbands and wives, more than they do "brethren and sisters in Christ" should not consider becoming Shakers.'[26]

Sabbathday Shakers today report that the children's response is often intense curiosity about why the brothers and sisters do not marry as they are not actually related. Several of the Shaker sisters noticed how incredibly important sex is to thirteen-year-olds and how freakish they thought the concept of a celibate family was. 'Don't you miss having children?' the last Shaker women are often asked. One of the remaining young Shaker sisters who only recently joined Sabbathday Lake, and who loves babies, told a BBC crew that it took her a while to get over the fact that she would not have children. However, after several months in the community she has seen the benefits to women of the brother-sister philosophy. 'I guess I have kind of lost that mourning, that need to have children. We do have quite a number of children who come here in the summer to help out as volunteers. We work in schools. It is not as if we are without children altogether, they are just not our children.'[27]

Apparently it is not the concept of celibacy so much as the concept of community and social justice for women which is what outsiders who make prolonged visits to Shaker communities find most difficult today. Members of the generation of the great I-am and the great He-Man suddenly find they are expected not to do what they want but only to do what is good for everyone.

Chores are communal. Each brother and sister does his or her own washing on a special day. Meals are communal, cooked on a rota system, often for very large numbers. Part of Shaker philosophy is never to turn anyone away, in case it is the Christ. This can pay off, as a humorous Shaker story shows. Many years ago when Sister Aurelia Mace was the Trustee of the Sabbathday Lake community, a tramp appeared at the back door. He looked bedraggled, tired and hungry, so she fed him, helped him to clean up, and finally sent him on his way with a box of food. Several weeks later she received a beautiful sterling silver box from Tiffany's, New York, signed: 'From Your Tramp. Charles Tiffany.'[28]

Togetherness-without-intercourse relied on the idea of adoption rather than blood. According to Sarah Lucas, a Shaker writer, adopted love was an impartial 'expansion of love, not requiring us to love our natural relations less, but to love others more, and all on a different and higher principle.'[29]

Celibacy which was not limited by ownership or fidelity created voluntary families, formed rationally through selection and choice. What it did specifically for women's position was to infuse family life with voluntarism and reason.

The Shakers, who concentrated on an egalitarian ideal, reflected this in the organizational design of the houses. Male dormitories complimented female ones. Beautifully designed meeting houses became the architectural jewel of each community, because that was where the brothers and sisters came together most often, most purposefully. They set up a governing system which had male and female leaders. There were elders and elderesses, deacons and deaconesses whose status was identical. Elderess Antoinette Doolittle together with Elder Frederick W. Evans joined the New Lebanon community in the early 1830s and jointly edited the *Shaker and Shakeress*, the society's first periodical published between 1873 and 1875. Inside the magazine they promoted equal rights for women both in Shaker communities and in mainstream America, equal education for both sexes, as well as the abolition of capitalism, and the inalienable rights of citizens to land.[30]

When Ann Lee used the phrase taking up the cross *against the world* as well as against the flesh she was identifying the means by which celibacy could be used to promote social rights for women. She had a very clear understanding that because women were socialized to focus their desire on men, they became subjected to them, and that meant that their social and political rights were easy to infringe. But before Ann Lee had time to see her creative feminist dreams translated by the administrators amongst her followers into institutional structures, she suddenly died.

It was 8 September 1784, only ten years after her courageous and ultimately triumphant arrival in New York state. It was not a triumphant death. But it was not entirely inappropriate. Ann Lee, who as a young girl had regularly disrupted church services with her unorthodox views on sexual intercourse and roused to anger clergy and lay people alike, died from terrible injuries sustained when another angry mob attacked her after a characteristically controversial religious meeting.

She was but forty-eight years old. In her ten years of fiery ministry her converts had grown from the original eight to well over a thousand. Her death initially inspired a sudden expansion of Shakerism with its idealistic hope of fairer lives for women. Three years after her death, in 1787, Watervliet where she had started her organization, formed an official Shaker community. Nearby Mount Lebanon later became the site of the Central Ministry that governed all Shaker communities.

It is bitterly ironic that today Mount Lebanon has become the site of the annual Willis Henry Shaker auction, America's largest, most prestigious sale of Shaker antiques. There is a dreadful element of black humour about the fact that in order to persuade rich and famous buyers to snap up Shaker artefacts at up to $35,000 a piece, the organizers play tapes of early Shaker sisters singing such hymns as ' 'Tis a Gift to be Simple'.

The few remaining Shakers living today at Sabbathday Lake in Maine must be glad that at least Mother Ann is spared that particular gallows joke. She was also spared the unspiritual excitement of the television company who filmed both the Shaker antique industry and the Sabbathday Lake community. At this event someone remarked on the strange coincidence that every time there is an auction the rains pour down. The tart reply from a Shaker member that 'It's the old Shakers crying,' would have done credit to Mother Ann herself.[31]

This charismatic and quirky spiritual leader did not live to see her vision of a land rainbowed with the promise of celibate communities dedicated to revising and improving what it means to be female. But as the Shaker founder died, so Shakerism and celibacy blossomed. Between 1776 and 1826 nineteen celibate communities in half-a-dozen states were established. A further ten branches called 'out-families', and several short-lived groups rose during the same period.[32] By 1830 twenty-three celibate communities had spread across the fifteen hundred miles from Kentucky to Maine, all of them firm in the belief that through a religious commitment to celibacy, women would become men's equals, in work, home, education and religion.

Estimates for the number of Shakers converted by 1840 ranged from 3600 to over six thousand.[33]

Whole families decided to join the Shakers, largely because they were not a virginal sect. Records show that married couples, often with more than a dozen children, joined enthusiastically, but in most cases the husbands left within a few weeks. For wives this lifestyle was appealing as it meant the removal of childbearing demands and a huge improvement in their position. The American husband was perceived almost as the woman's employer. In the alternative celibate system women were not seen as employees under male supervision, but as equally paid and valued co-workers. The loss in terms of power to the husbands is obvious. We can see why a great many left. Some men found the idea of transforming 'marital love', which included power over marital rights, into brotherly-sisterly love not at all to their liking.

Given these opposing movements towards and against Shakerism it is not surprising that from 1840 onwards women converts consistently outnumbered men. If we compare Shaker demographic statistics with those in the population as a whole, we find that in 1840 Shaker women comprised almost 58 per cent of the Shaker population across America compared to the general white population of the USA where women comprised only 49 per cent. By 1900, though, while the percentage in the general white population had remained at 49, in the Shaker movement women were comprising 72 per cent; nearly three-quarters of all Shaker members.

Interestingly, their honest, self-supporting lifestyle was rooted in making and selling produce, furniture, medicine, and manufacturing tools, based on 'feminine' domestic merchandise, utilizing specifically female skills. Inevitably this helped to promote women's status in the groups whose motto was 'Hands to work and hearts to God'. In their attempts to blend home and workplace, Shakers manufactured products inspired by their own domestic needs, and marketed goods based on 'housework'. Preserved food, wool and herbs were among their early products. In the early Shaker days men raised and harvested the herbs whilst the women dried and packaged them for sale. Today at Sabbathday Lake they still continue to dry and package herbs that sell throughout America, with one of the Shaker sisters in charge of production.

To ensure that working time became shorter, so that more time could be released for worship and reflection, the Shakers invented many labour-saving devices, designed to aid what today we see as 'women's work' but which they saw as family labour. We have them to thank for the apple corer, the clothes pin, and the flat broom, as well as the circular saw. They were granted patents for three intriguing inventions: a counterbalanced window sash, a large industrial washing machine, and a singularly Shakeresque idea, a tilting mechanism for chair legs so that Shakers could tilt and rock their chairs as they sang without splitting the bottom of the chair or harming the floor.

Their unified 'social plan' insisted that equal male-female co-workers had to meet the work standards of the group, to be judged by their labour and not by their sex. 'Female' domestic work was transformed into productive paid work that was essential to the group's survival. The expansion of female domestic skills into the public paid arena provided a major portion of each 'family's' income. Because there was economic interdependence in the work of the two sexes, Shaker brothers actually valued the 'feminine' characteristics and skills of Shaker sisters which were an integral part of that work.

Belief in educational opportunity ensured that girls and boys were educated to the same standard. They were not however taught together nor even at the same time of year. Girls were educated in the summer so that they could work at preserving fruit in the winter. Boys were educated in the winter so that they could work on the land in the summer. The Shaker leaders did not offer the same work to boys and girls but they were strong in their pronouncements that the work of each sex carried equal importance. Apart from the practical reasons they gave for separating boys from girls, their underlying philosophy of celibacy was reason enough. Sex was an evil with a compelling lure. The young had to be encouraged to resist its temptations. So free mixing of the two sexes socially or at work was not allowed.

It is true that Shaker concepts of gender difference led them to prescribe separate and distinct gender roles, so that men worked outside while women performed indoor domestic chores, and women often served the men, made beds, mended clothes and prepared food. Even today, in the last remaining community, it is the sisters, Frances, Minnie and Marie who more often than not cook the lunchtime meal. But although these traditional roles resemble mainstream gender roles, unlike our society which interprets domestic roles as lower status women's work, Shakers did not see the performance

of domestic tasks as evidence of the weakness or dependency of one
sex upon another or as evidence of the greater value of non-domestic
tasks performed by men. They felt able to hold onto this radical
view because celibacy had abolished the unequal power dimension
between the sexes. The workings of their lives reflected a unity and
equality not to be found in the genital world outside.

Women's Rights advocate Anna White, one of the most influential
women writers of any period in Shaker history, wrote in 1891:

'The occupations of men and women may differ very materi-
ally; but does this go to prove that those of women are of the
least importance? Not by any means.' She suggested that men's
duties may be 'sterner' but that women's duties were 'all important
responsibilities'. According to Anna White and other Shaker writers,
'the man is as equally dependent upon the woman as is the woman
upon the man.'[34]

What Shakers did was to reframe the world in which they lived.
They reframed the meaning of gender distinction. They reframed the
meaning of sex separation. They saw hierarchy as evil. They thought
difference *could* be divine. But it could only become divine by means
of a steadfast celibacy.

To ensure that celibacy was constant and effective, strict house
rules were introduced which limited male-female interaction. In
the early days they were not allowed to spend more than fifteen
minutes in one another's company. Because spiritual unity was the
goal of their gender differentiation, Shakers insisted that men and
women lived under the same roof, so family groups occupied large
communal houses in each community. But inside the houses the
ideal of an egalitarian society dedicated to celibacy was carefully
reflected in their physical design so that men and women would not
'accidentally' bump into one another. They ate in the same common
room but at different tables. They slept apart at different ends of the
houses in order to avoid sexual temptation.

Several writers saw the Shakers' form of celibate cohabitation
as an improvement on the celibacy in Jesus' era. In 1883 writer
Giles Avery said that traditional cloisters and nunneries tended to
'abnormalize the sexes' whereas the Shakers learnt to live as men and
women together but in a spiritual rather than a sexual harmony.[35]
A progressive Shaker leader, Frederick Evans, mentioned this idea
by writing in 1866 that the useful thing about Shaker communities
was that in them, 'the males and females, instead of coming under
vows of perpetual chastity, and then being kept so separate that they

could not infringe them, are all together as are brothers and sisters in a natural family.'[36]

Today at Sabbathday Lake, their focus on genital abstinence is still reinforced by the structured layout of their house. Begun in 1883 the dwelling house was constructed so that the south end is largely inhabited by the brothers and the north end by the sisters. More rooms are shared in common today than in the early days: there is a large communal kitchen, dining room, meeting room, music room and family library. These are all in the centre of the L-shaped part of the house. There are also communal work spaces, store rooms and a print room. Like their spiritual ancestors, they are not encouraged to intermingle. Mealtimes and prayer meetings are the only occasions when the community comes together. During the rest of the day the sisters and brothers sit at separate tables, use separate doorways, go up and down separate staircases. They sleep, of course, in separate 'retiring rooms' at opposite ends of the house.

Part of the Shaker philosophy is that everything should be rectilinear, orderly, equal and balanced, so Shakers are not only expected to sleep in sex-segregated rooms, they are also expected to sleep straight in their beds.

Today some of us might find curious their segregated sleeping pattern but it has parallels and similarities in many parts of the world, past and present.

In many traditional New Guinea societies men sleep together in men's quarters, women and children sleep in a separate compound. This means that intercourse is not a matter of casual propinquity but must be deliberately sought out and only on specified occasions. It is celibacy that fills in the spaces. Among the Maring community, men and women have no contact at all at certain times and always sleep separately. In many traditional New Guinea segregated societies where genital abstinence is common, the nuptial bond is much less important than social bonds between men.

One of the most abstemious groups ever to be studied, whose rigid restrictions about marital intercourse result in lengthy celibate periods is the Dani of Irian, Jaya, Indonesia, whose males and females sleep in separate compounds. Anthropologist Karl Heider observed the Dani for thirty months and learnt that sustained periods of celibacy were the norm, that weddings took place only on the major pigfeasts which occur every four to six years, that the wedding night has no sexual significance because couples are not allowed to have intercourse until two years after the wedding. Most nights the men sleep in the loft of the men's house while the women sleep in their all-female compound. After the birth of a child there is a further celibate custom of total abstinence from intercourse for several years. Interestingly this code never appears to be infringed.

Karl Heider's conclusions about the Dani bear out the idea that where genital abstention is culturally invoked there are absolutely no problems attached to it. He reported that the Grand Valley Dani's four to six year post-partum genital abstinence is invariably observed, that such a long abstention is neither supported by powerful explanations nor is it enforced by strong sanctions, that most people have no alternative sexual outlets, and seem to need none, and that no one shows the slightest sign of unhappiness or stress during celibacy.[37]

Germaine Greer comments that there was no evidence that these people's sexual energies were being sublimated into artistic activities or warfare which she notes is the usual 'compensation'.[38] She seems to have fallen into the same genital trap I fell into earlier. The Dani, wisely, do not feel that genital abstention needs to be compensated for. They seemed to have both a low interest in sexual matters and a very low activity level. What perplexed Heider the most was that this remarkably low level of sexual activity combined with a highly controlled celibate programme was not enforced by any powerful system of either social or religious sanctions.

In our twentieth century, Western, secular society where sex replaces religion, those who believe that sex is the world's most potent or unstoppable force also believe that genital abstinence is virtually impossible and where successful is merely a matter of repression. Freud's libido theory, which has become part of the Western folk model of sexuality, holds that repression of the libido, though it may have connections with cultural creativity, on an individual level frequently leads to neurosis. Acceptance of this, in my view, damaging idea means that orgasm-oriented Westerners find it hard to believe that female and male celibates do *not* spend their waking hours struggling to mistress or master their uncontrollable genital urges.

As Germaine Greer comments:

It does not shake the faith of the orgasmist one iota to point out that total celibates are not more deranged, inefficient, unhappy or unhealthy than any other segment of the population. Many people simply believe that celibates are not celibate; that priests have liaisons with nuns ... just as the protestants of the sixteenth century believed that convent fishponds were full of the skeletons of aborted foetuses.[39]

Research on the Shakers shows evidence that their celibate philosophy brought them not only good health but also long life. In the late 1880s writer Giles Avery assessed the effect of celibacy on longevity in several Shaker communities. He found that compared with the average lifespan in mainstream America of less than sixty years, in the celibate Shaker community of New Lebanon, 'the number of deaths from 1848 to 1850 was 29 persons and their average age was 70½ years – this included both sexes.' He also found that among two hundred Shakers in Alfred, Maine, one hundred were more than seventy years old, thirty-seven were aged eighty to ninety, thirteen were aged ninety to ninety-seven. The average age of the two hundred Shakers was '62 years, 9 months, 6 days, 2 hours'. More significantly he discovered that all of these elderly Shakers had 'good use of their limbs, [were] able to go out of doors, and [were capable of] a good day's work of choice.'

Life expectancy at that time in the general population was only fifty-six years for men and a few years older for women.[40]

Both the Shakers, an absolutely celibate sect, and the Dani, a semi-celibate sect, lived long and healthy lives, were free from stress, and appeared contented. Heider's conclusion from his two-and-a-half year observation of the Dani was that Freud's assumption that there are 'normal' levels of sexual libido for all people irrespective of culture and socialization is, quite simply, wrong. He suggested that sexual activity is learnt in response to patterns of stimulus and if these are absent then the sexual learning is of a different order.[41]

Today in our society we are all constantly pressurized to see ourselves in terms of genital acts, even to regard them as the core of our inner being. But what is sexual in one context (or to one person) may not be so in another. The definition of what is 'sexual' constantly changes to serve the social order. The way we apply socially learned meanings is what makes some experiences sexual and others not. What goes on in our heads is often much more erotic than what our genitals get up to. The development of certain cultural forms stimulates sexual fantasy or desire. As these forms change so do the fantasies. In our pro-pornographic society, media presentations of women with scarves bound tightly over their eyes, covered breasts but no knickers and a male hand holding a knife somewhere in the background is typical of what is supposed to constitute a 'turn-on'. Imagery like that is meant to turn on men, but the effect of such imagery on women's attitudes towards themselves can be devastating. Our 'desire' which is usually followed today by a burst of genital activity is also constructed by society's norms and expectations. To take an obvious example, our culture's fat hatred means that the goal for desirable females is a slim body proportioned to specific measurements. So fat women are not desired in the same way as slim women are, or are not desired at all.[42]

We have seen how in the West today, heterosexual desire is predicated on the dominant/submissive expectations we are fed, and that that form of desire is not restricted to heterosexuals, but can also be expressed by gay males or lesbians.

So where there is a very different cultural pattern of chastity maintained and encouraged by sleeping arrangements that segregate women and men (as with the Dani and the Shakers) 'desire' and passion may be of a very different order. Genuine celibate desire may turn towards sleep, meditation and good sound dreaming, rather than towards stealthy contemplation of how to violate the celibate standard.

Obviously segregation by itself neither equals nor necessitates celibacy, or even chastity. After all, women and men can creep up the wrong stairs in a Shaker house, and add a cloak and dagger excitement to what is often the somewhat banal experience of intercourse. However segregation can achieve two purposes: one practical, one symbolic. In practice it allows attempts at genital forays to be overseen and monitored. For the Shakers this supervision by fellow members strengthened their own motivation towards ascetic chastity. Symbolically it reinforces by separation and ceremony the importance of celibacy to the worship, the workings, and the ideals of the community.

It is, however, not only the particular construction or style of 'desire' that changes from culture to culture but it is also the *degree* of sexual activity which is subject to cultural change. Different societies express sexual activity in different ways. Some have what is called 'low activity level' (where there is infrequent genital expression) and 'high affect level' (where people talk and think about sex compulsively). Other societies have 'high activity level' (a great deal of genital expression) and 'low affect level' (which means people are not particularly preoccupied with sex verbally, pictorially or psychologically.) Still others, like the Dani, have very low activity levels, and very low affect levels, and appear perplexing to outside observers.

Despite our acknowledgement of these differences, until the mid-seventies there was an assumption, even in some academic explorations of sexual behaviour, that across cultures we could find a uniform total of sexual energy in human beings that was ready and available to be expressed.[43]

Then in 1973 John H. Gagnon and William Simon advanced what was at that time the revolutionary theory that the *level* of sexual activity itself is determined by social and cultural circumstances. Their work suggested that sexual energy is *not* constant across all societies but develops in response to stimuli at different levels in various cultures.[44]

Shifting levels of sexual activity, and the likelihood of *no* activity being validated in a particular society may be influenced by that culture's high or low affect level. In our post-Freudian society, we are all slaves to a culture with an obsessively high affect level. Sex is our major conversational topic and our biggest consumer industry. Who is doing it with whom? Why aren't John or Joan doing it? Or are they doing it and not telling anyone? When will Jane move from being 'just' a friend to being a lover? All these pieces of chit-chat symbolize what is and what is not acceptable sexually. What is not acceptable, what does not even rate as a matter for discussion is celibacy, because in sex-as-prescription terms it cannot be acted out. It is, as it were, an act without meaning.

Both Freud's somewhat lower affect society and our high affect one were and are hostile to women's interests, sexual and social. Women, once victims of Freud's theory that the genital organization of 'normal' female adults involved a transition from the 'immature' clitoral orgasm (that pleased women) to the 'maturity' of the vaginal orgasm (that pleased men – indeed is intended to enhance men's pleasure and neutralize women's) were later thankfully saved from such pernicious propaganda by Anne Koedt's discovery that the clitoris was where it was at.[45]

Women today, however, have become victims of something worse. Post-Freudian culture treats women as pornographic objects for male sexual consumption whilst simultaneously prohibiting women from pleasuring themselves in ways that do not reflect men's egos or give life to limp penises, and, more significantly, prohibiting women from *not consuming at all*.

Low sexual activity, prescribed in the late nineteenth century for women labelled 'passionless' is now considered pitiable. The women are in need of treatment. The sexual wheel has come full circle. Sex therapists thrive at women's expense. **No sexual activity is today considered freakish except NO sexual activity.** It is hardly surprising that in such a compulsively coital society women do not find private or public acknowledgement of celibacy either easy or appropriate.

It is hardly surprising too that people today find it easier to understand the value of Shaker furniture than to understand the value of the Shakers' lifestyle. Looking at the Shakers through the genital lens of the nineteenth century, we saw how they were perceived as sexless wooden people making wooden chairs. We saw also that through their own wide angle on sexuality they viewed themselves as sexual beings in motion. Love and energy dancing together. It was a dance that affronted a genital society. The biggest affront came from the Shaker women who defiantly denounced sex instead of meekly submitting to it, who brazenly took up with pretend brothers instead of real husbands.

One of the last remaining Shaker women at Sabbathday Lake community who said they were looked on as an endangered species added: 'Our life style is considered irrelevant. People have written us off.'

I think their celibate stance makes them not so much an endangered species as a dangerous species: dangerous to those with an interest in preserving the genital myth. Many people see them as irrelevant, but a celibate philosophy used in the cause of a fairer society, an increase in female rights and status, may indeed be highly relevant. Most of all it may be crucial to the development of a new way of looking at relationships between women and men.

CHAPTER NINE

Celibate Sisters

I N their challenge to a genital society, Shaker women had one thing on their side: Shaker men.

Living with men, even as celibates, allowed the women a certain limited prestige and public acceptance, which they would not otherwise have had. This was because the nineteenth century (like our own) favoured male activities and attitudes above those of females, which ensured that male membership of a group gave that group status. So celibate Shaker women did not merely benefit from the specific support of their Shaker brothers, they also benefited from their *association* with them. Other groups of women at that time, who attempted celibacy without this male crutch, attracted substantially more hostility, and presented a far greater threat.

One such group was the stormy Sanctificationist Sisters, tough Texans, mainly ex-wives and mothers, led by the charismatic Martha McWhirter, who set up an unofficial celibate commune in 1879 which they officially incorporated in 1890. Needless to say, it was violently resisted by outsiders.

The sisters, perceiving the nuclear family and the American way of life as selfish, narrow and sinful, struck out at these two sacred cows. The townsfolk, appalled, struck back at them. They were ridiculed, vilified, and ostracized. At least at the start . . .

Their biggest failing in the eyes of the town was their attitude towards sex. For the sisters saw sex as more than sin; in their view it was the pivotal evil in American culture, a symbol of the distressing way women were treated. Celibacy they saw as sanctification, as purity, and, in practical terms, as the best way to prevent the spread of the family's poisonous influence on society. According to researchers such as Professor Kitch they understood celibacy to be much more than genital abstinence; they saw it as the cornerstone of social reform which included expanding women's rights.[1]

Martha McWhirter's vision, which the group implemented with fire and flair, was to do away with nuclear family life and adopt instead a communistic style of living that mixed domesticity and work. Living as co-workers and 'sisters', the group substituted spiritual bonds for genital bonds, and through those measures aimed to transform the sexual power politics which they felt oppressed women.

Although they were actually *less* overtly critical of mainstream culture than the Shakers, the fact that they set up a commune that was for all intents and purposes single sex, meant that in practice their radical stance against the cultural norm of their day was that much more striking.

Nineteenth century society, though it allowed for 'Boston Marriages' between unmarried women (usually of financial means and therefore independent of men), was nevertheless a society dedicated to sex and marriage.[2] It was a society which mocked female celibacy. It was a society aggressive to women who prioritized women's interests at the expense of men's. Above all it was a society hostile to and threatened by outspoken women-only groups.

The Sanctificationists had stepped outside their prescribed roles in every possible way. It was no wonder that George Pierce Garrison writing an account of the Sanctificationists in 1893, only three years after their formal inception as a community, reported:

'Among the marks of this society's growth are households divided and families broken up. It has excited the deepest of human passions to culmination in violence; and one would think it fortunate, if he considered their intensity, that they were appeased without the sacrifice of human life.'[3]

Eight years later a somewhat naive journalist wrote defensively: 'The women have no politics and do not pretend to be reformers.'[4] This was laughable in the face of the stir they had caused in several cities, and the fact that their commune had become a form of living politics based on celibate values in total conflict with and critical of every important established norm.

The group themselves, to judge from their few remaining texts,[5] saw themselves as reasonably and intelligently utilizing celibacy to fulfil their religious purpose, increase women's power, improve women's status, and as a sane and satisfying means towards sexual equality. Nothing at all to get excited about. A great deal to applaud.

Obviously we have here a perfect example of a women's group

setting themselves up against the genital myth. Let us look further at the founder of this rebellious community.

Martha McWhirter, like Ann Lee the Shaker leader, was a stimulating example of how celibacy focused the quest of strong nineteenth century women for independence. Assertive, and deeply spiritual, she stood up for a better deal for women. Believing that the way to get it was for women to become celibate, she led her crusading corps of sanctified sisters in a fierce fight against the sexual double standard of her age.

Like Mother Ann, Martha McWhirter was a highly religious woman, initially a member of the Methodist church and a believer in the Wesleyan doctrine of entire sanctification. Curiously, also like Mother Ann, whose sexless crusade was undertaken after a beatific vision following the deaths of her four children, Martha McWhirter too had a vision following the deaths of her brother and two of her children. One account, collected by Professor Kitch, describes how after these tragedies, McWhirter in terrible grief over her losses, spent the night tormenting herself about her lack of faith. The following morning when she was busy kneading biscuit dough she suddenly felt faith stream right through her, infusing her body and soul.[6] She immediately interpreted her vision and her tragedies as a sign from God that she must purge her life of sin, including the sin of sex. This, combined with her acceptance of the Wesleyan doctrine that sanctification should cast out 'carnal nature', led her to believe that because of her ongoing intention not to sin which would be evidenced every day and night by her stringent commitment to celibacy, she would be in a constant and continuing state of sanctification. As would any of her women followers who took the same celibate route.[7]

The orthodox Methodist doctrine of the time did *not* in fact prescribe celibacy. Wesley, who had discussed the importance of sanctified people turning passion into meekness, and hatred into love, and who had emphasized the throwing out of what he called 'Old Adam' and 'carnal nature', nevertheless made no explicit suggestions about believers living celibate lives. This immediately threw McWhirter into conflict with her Church and its elders.

Trouble erupted on the religious front in 1870 when the Belton Methodist Church tried to convert the Union Sunday School run by Martha McWhirter and her husband George into an exclusively Methodist institution. The McWhirters and other women supporters of what was in effect Martha's school, refused to join. Though most members of the group were Methodists, there were a few Baptists, Presbyterians and other Christian sects. The official Church's school plan disturbed Martha McWhirter because her belief in Methodism was based not merely on celibacy but also on ecumenism, an ideal to promote unity amongst all churches of the world, which she felt was threatened by this plan. The Belton Church officials argued, but McWhirter's largely female group stood firm, committed to non-denominational principles and a celibate philosophy. Finally the group broke from the Church. The Union School was abandoned by everyone except McWhirter's followers. By 1874 they were the only people who met there.

Just as her strong belief in ecumenism had alienated her from the official church, so her views on celibacy began to estrange her from her husband George. She and the other women who shared her beliefs attempted to change their physical relationships with their husbands into spiritual ones, while they demonstrated their anger at their economic dependence by asking for a fair share of the family income. Initially they were prepared to continue their domestic duties whilst refusing to have sex. Their original commitment to celibacy – based partly on the same biblical text (1 Corinthians 7 v12–15) which Mother Ann used to justify Shaker celibacy – did not require them to dissolve their marriages. The marriages, however, did not improve. The more McWhirter preached the new gospel of a share in the family business and separate sleeping arrangements, the more the men tightened the purse strings and physically abused the women.

It is not clear whether George McWhirter abused his wife or was merely hostile to her revolutionary ideas. Martha did in fact continue to maintain a relationship with George long after the sex was over. It is possible that she believed they could transform the sexual love they had had for twenty-five years into the celibate affection of sister and brother. Perhaps he hoped so too. Certainly he stayed on in their home for a few years after she had committed herself willingly and him unwillingly to celibacy. Eventually however Martha McWhirter said that 'a stone wall grew up between us, he on one side and I on the other, and both of us loving each other.'[8]

Despite her initial agreement to continue to cohabit, she was never for one moment prepared to maintain a family system at the expense of celibate freedom. Nor did she think her women friends should do so. In 1880, by which point the women's continued insistence on celibacy and women's rights as the core of their marriages had resulted in many of the husbands abandoning or divorcing them, she said stoutly: 'If a husband should go to a wife and ask her for his sake, for the sake of her children and the peace of society to surrender her belief . . . I should say for her to do no such thing.'[9] Martha also angered George by insisting on being the breadwinner for her and her children during their short life as a celibate couple.

Soon an exasperated Martha was saying that though the women were happy to perform wifely and motherly duties whilst practising celibacy: 'If the husband chooses to leave us on account of our religion, we let them go.'[10]

As the women one by one discovered just how the injustice of private ownership affected them in practical terms, when they tried and failed to gain control both over property jointly owned with their husbands, and also property they had separately owned before marriage, McWhirter stepped up the attack. All control of women by their husbands was evil, she pronounced. Such control was grounds for terminating the marriage.

'It was no longer women's duty to remain with a husband who bossed and controlled her. God made man and woman equal, and to women in these last few days he has revealed his will concerning his own elect few.'[11]

By late 1879 to early 1880 so many of the women had either been divorced or separated from their husbands because of their beliefs that for the sake of their economic survival they formed a commune.

The sisters started to earn their own bread by actually baking and selling it. They said their bread was sanctified, which earned them the derisive nickname of the Sanctificationists from the critical townsfolk who nevertheless bought the bread. Then in the face of storms of protest and often violent abuse from the town, the sisters moved on from selling goods such as eggs and butter, to making and selling rag carpets and firewood, and opening and running laundry services, dining rooms, and boarding houses. Once the ventures based on their proven domestic skills proved successful, they expanded into non-domestic areas of dentistry, millinery, shoemaking and teaching.

Knowing from hard personal experience the reality of domestic servitude, they established a routine of communal housework. Understanding all too well the evils of economic injustice they decided on co-operative business methods. They insisted on the right to property ownership (with all property and income shared equally amongst them), and set professional membership standards. Unlike men who start up businesses, the women decided to mix domestic arrangements with financial interests, both in the content of the work and in the way it was done. Their constitution required all the women to perform some manual labour for the community, and to contribute all income from their outside jobs to the group. This meant that though their domestic labour was still unpaid, it was, unlike that of married women, identified as an economic contribution. By being required to contribute money for the whole group's support the sisters were taking on the identities of male breadwinners rather than female homemakers. In their previous roles as wives they had earned their economic security through sex and reproductive duties, now they gained it through their own work. This made a significant difference to the way they viewed themselves.

Their business interests also brought about a change in their social status. As wives they had been judged as middle class, because of their husbands' middle class occupations. Initially, as independent breadwinners doing menial jobs, they became working class. Though their first jobs were dull and routine, they nevertheless offered the women the self-esteem which the genital myth suggests women only get from marriage. Eventually their business success and upward mobility returned them to middle class status, but on their own terms, which became a source of great pride.

As the sisters prospered, some enraged and incredulous husbands attempted to buy their wives back. All of them failed. Martha McWhirter's son-in-law first abandoned her daughter Ada Haymond then went to court complaining that the sisters had alienated his wife's affections. He sought divorce and custody of their children, partly on the grounds that Ada was refusing to submit to sex in marriage. In 1887 Ada, who joined the sisters after her husband left her, testified in court during her divorce proceedings that her husband's offer of money to persuade her to return to the marital bed was absolutely 'no inducement for her to live with him'.[12]

To the women who had begun to taste economic independence, such offers were hardly an attractive prospect. The men, however, found this attitude utterly incomprehensible, and they were prepared to take strong measures. When the sisters made it a rule never to seek or accept financial help from former husbands, one woman, Sister Johnson, was committed to an asylum for refusing to take her husband's insurance money.[13]

By dissolving their marriages, as Professor Kitch points out, the sisters were in the anomolous position of being not quite female and not quite male. From the Belton townsfolk's point of view they had become a socially threatening group of loose women, which meant that, at the start, they suffered extreme social ostracism. Their celibacy did however make them acceptable as business owners. Men apparently found it easier to talk money with not-quite-women.

The sisters' business acumen resulted in their extending their talents from operating small outlets like the bakery, to owning and running the major Belton Investment Company, and acquiring their first hotel. 1891 saw the incorporation of the Central Hotel Company, the culmination of several boarding houses, hotels and other businesses owned and run by the women in Belton and Waco, Texas, during the preceding decades. (In 1929, thirty-one years after the sisters had moved to Washington DC, their Central Hotel in Belton was still known as the 'earliest and most successful venture of women into business activity in the state of Texas'.)[14]

The Belton townspeople, who started by rejecting and ridiculing the women on the grounds of their sexlessness and unwomanly behaviour, were ultimately won over by their good food and professionalism. First they patronized the dining rooms, then they recommended their comfortable accommodation to visitors. Finally McWhirter earned the respect of her male business colleagues when in 1894 she was asked to serve as the first woman member of Belton Board of Trade.

By 1898 they renamed their family and business unit the Woman's Commonwealth, which by then was a highly successful corporation with a board of trustees of which McWhirter was president until just before her death in 1904. It was unusual only in that it was run entirely by women using traditional female domestic skills and professional 'feminist' methods, which were connected to their root belief in celibacy.

With the profits the group made they purchased a large home in Washington, followed by land in Maryland which they farmed and used as a retreat. Finally they built a house on the land as a retirement home for the group, and after McWhirter's death, surviving sisters continued to run their celibate community until their own deaths. The last member, Martha Scheble, was still living in the Maryland house when she died in 1983 aged 101.

Though most of the celibate sisters lived to a good age, unlike the Shakers, whose numbers spread across America, the Sanctificationists were never a large group. At their height in 1880 their numbers reached fifty; in 1890 they became an official community, but by 1891 membership averaged thirty-two and after 1898 despite their successful business enterprises, numbers slowly dropped.

Though two or three men joined (and swiftly left) the community during its one hundred year period, the Sanctificationists were for all effective purposes single sex. Their constitution theoretically accepted male members as long as they undertook to abide by the women's conditions. In 1902 McWhirter said 'They are welcome if they are willing to live the life we do.'[15]

In practice almost no men could or would qualify for such a membership. According to McWhirter the men could never fulfil the conditions because they suffered from 'bossism'.[16]

The smallness of their number in no way impeded their passionate politics. Their women-only membership meant that their fierce beliefs had an early feminist ring. Though they never envisaged God as a woman, they did believe in female spiritual power based on intuition and receptivity, which they saw as specifically female traits. As the years moved on, the sisters moved further and further away from standard Methodist beliefs and began to serve as their own authorities on religious matters. McWhirter said firmly 'I know that what we teach is right. We are perfect. There is no adding anything new to what we have.'[17]

Increasingly they used their own consciences as a source of spiritual guidance. McWhirter finally decided that sanctification required her to rebel against any church practices, including marriage, that did not respect the sanctified woman's control over her own spiritual life. By setting up spiritual autonomy based on celibacy for themselves, they achieved a female form of religion throughout the community.

Although their celibacy had its origins in religion, they believed it had ramifications far beyond religious practice. Becoming celibate, *and having feminist goals as part of that celibacy*, would start to put right the errors of a genital culture whose focus on intercourse and coupledom produced ownership instead of partnership, competition instead of co-operation and selfishness instead of privacy. (It is interesting that some celibate women today are saying something similar.)

To achieve these ends, the sisters felt that what was needed was physical separation. Unlike the Shakers, whose separation hinged on gender, the Sanctificationists being a single-sex group, had to base separation on individual autonomy. So while they insisted on a separation between the sanctified women members and unsanctified men in the world outside, they also insisted on physical separation between the women members themselves. This, they felt, would begin a path toward a spiritual unity and a social equality between the two sexes as well as equal partnership between women members. They aimed at spiritual and economic partnership not sexual relations. They believed that non-genital intimacy could be passionate and strengthening but that it allowed for no jealousy, no possessiveness, and therefore offered a possibility of greater equality.

How did they achieve this in practice?

Firstly they made a rule forbidding sisters from any intimacies with outsiders. Secondly they prescribed limits on women's expression of intimacy within the group. These rules were based on the notion of *disinterest*. Having given up marriages where 'interest' equalled sexual activity, which made women dependent on men, they saw disinterest as a way forward. Their idea was somewhat similar to the Catholic rule that nuns should not have 'particular friendships'. The sisters' behaviour was strictly regulated by the group's by-law which stated: 'Members shall not show any interest in one another, other than that of a purely friendly nature, nor shall they permit any person not a member . . . to show them . . . any special attention or interest other than that of a purely friendly nature.'[18]

Thirdly they had a rule about sleeping accommodation. Unlike the Shaker women who slept in single sex dormitories, the Sanctificationists had individual bedrooms, or occasionally a room for two women. The bedrooms opened into common workrooms or dining rooms. This gave the women a feeling of privacy which contrasted with the communal warmth of their shared work and leisure pursuits. It also segregated them at night time when more physically intimate associations might have sprung up.

The sisters modelled their lifestyle with its deliberately impersonal bonds on that of Jesus and his disciples, interpreting discipleship as a mixture of sibling love and friendship that does not need sexual activity to be spiritually successful.[19]

They tried to turn all possible relationships between the women into those of siblings. To be a 'sister' was to be a spiritual partner. To be a co-worker was to be an economic partner. Genital interaction spoke to them of dependency, and they were determined to allow no hint of dependency to creep into the group. They did however recognize their obligations to care for each other. Another rule said that all family members could expect to be provided with food, lodging and clothes and with 'care and attention in sickness and misfortune, and in infancy and old age'.[20] Even the children who belonged to several of the women were cared for communally, so that mothers had little opportunity to indulge in partisanship.

This deliberately dispassionate context was particularly curious, and I suspect not very easy, because so many of the women were blood relatives. Each year the community membership lists showed a surprising proportion of sisters, mothers and daughters, none of whom were allowed to use their kinship to express any demonstrativeness or special affection.

In 1880, out of twenty-nine members, twenty-one had a relative in the community. In that year there were seven pairs of mothers and daughters and five pairs of blood sisters. In 1896, out of twenty-five members, only four of the women had no blood relation to the community. There were eight mother-daughter groups (some mothers had three or four daughters with them), and four groups of blood sisters. This meant that when the 1902 prohibition against 'special attention or interest' was issued, women had to abide by it in the face of considerable potential for kinship intimacy. This was made more difficult for the women because Belton was a small town in which most of the women had grown up and had been close friends as well as sometimes relatives.

Though the sisters' constitution does not specifically discuss sex with other women, they were so resolute about establishing a community based on disinterest which offered no affectionate preference to any other woman, not even daughters, that it is safe to extrapolate from this principle, that all forms of physical demonstrativeness, most especially genital activity, which might well lead to preference or 'interest', would not fit their celibate philosophy.

If the women expressed themselves fulfilled by a life without sex, outsiders in Belton Texas found it hard to credit. When the sisters first set up their community, townsfolk saw them as sexual anomalies and held them up to ridicule. Because they were running businesses, which was men's work, outsiders assumed they would have male sexual values, and must be suffering from sex deprivation in a commune with no men. When Ada Pratt, one of the members, eloped from the community, it was seen as 'defection', her escape was headlined by a local reporter: SHE MARRIED THE FIRST MAN SHE MET, the implications being that Ada Pratt was a desperate and repressed nymphomaniac.[21] The facts were different. Far from rushing into bed with the first man she set eyes on, Pratt had met and known many men by the time of her elopement. She had always been a troubled member of the community, and when she finally fell in love with a particular man, after considerable reflection she gave up her celibate communal life.

What is more interesting than one woman's 'escape', but was certainly never seen as newsworthy, was how few women during the hundred year period appeared to have had any inclination to run away. There is in fact very little evidence of any sexual discontent in the group. According to the testimony of Martha Scheble, the last survivor, most of the forays which women made out of the community resulted not in sex or marriage but in the women's return to the group with renewed confidence in its celibate scheme.[22] Martha Scheble herself left the community for several years in 1901, but finally decided she did not after all like what went on in the outside world, and she returned and renewed her celibate life in the commune, outliving all the other women.

The women who appeared most contented as celibates were those who had been married prior to joining. This certainly suggests that the best training ground for celibacy in the nineteenth century may have been the sexual and economic hardship women found in their marriages.

Something else may have made it easy for the sisters to feel fulfilled through sexual abstinence and that was the nineteenth century ethos of female sexual purity which was popular with feminist and non-feminist women alike, and which could be seen as linked to the sisters' own goals. Equally, in the nineteenth century abstinence was the only truly effective form of birth control.

Today in a society that permits birth control while it over-values sex for individual pleasure, celibacy may seem locked into some nineteenth century moral framework. But seeing feminist goals as an intrinsic part of female celibacy can still raise some provocative issues.

Our genital framework makes viewing the sisters difficult. The modern heterosexual perspective would label them anti-sex and therefore deficient, whereas a twentieth century radical lesbian perspective might ask why were not all or at least some of the women actively lesbian as part of their politics? Both of these attitudes are ill-founded because they are enmeshed in today's genital myth. The views are simply not appropriate for the nineteenth century sisters who though they patently shared some of the ideals held by contemporary feminist groups, were critically different in that their resistance to the genital myth of their day was based on a total opposition to all forms of sexual activity, with celibacy as their key symbol. It is hard for us with our genitally fixated vision to imagine a purposeful feminist group that does not involve sex with either men or other women. But the sisters' goal was something quite different: they wanted to transform all sexual desire into economic, religious and personal power and status for women.

Because as yet we have no celibate framework from which to approach such a group, even if imaginatively we can understand them, we have no context by which to value them. In our society women do not count, all-women groups do not count, and groups of people who are not genitally active do not count.

In a technological age, where we no longer *need* intercourse for reproductive purposes, and where, despite massive changes for the better in women's position, women still suffer from participation in reproduction and intercourse, we can perhaps take from the example of the Sanctificationists several key ideas:

> The refusal to accept as primary or necessary the heterosexual couple.
> Celibacy as a symbol of spiritual union between the sexes.
> Celibacy as a way to reduce jealousy and possessiveness.
> Celibacy as a means to improve women's cultural status.
> The use of female characteristics in work and economics to increase their value in other spheres.
> That passion may be found as much in shared celibate enterprises as in a shared bed.
> That celibacy offers women greater social gains than it would offer men, because male reproductive and sexual behaviour does not limit men's social choices or status to the same extent.
> That social roles embedded in intercourse remain harmful to women's interests.
> That culture and all forms of sex are interlinked.

Celibacy alone does not necessarily increase women's prestige, but the successful practice of celibacy linked to the goal of improving women's position, as demonstrated by the Sanctificationists, may well do so. What is indisputably relevant to those of us struggling in the twentieth century with many of the same problems is this vision of celibacy as a new symbol on which to base social change.

CHAPTER TEN

Creative Solitude

SOLITUDE, like celibacy, does not serve the genital myth.
Solitude is the seat of quiet conversations with an inner world; solitude is the rocky retreat where if one digs deep enough one may find an unimagined self (one may not like it, but at least it is something new to work on); solitude is a sanctuary from the lives and needs of others; solitude, even when it is impossible in its silence, galling in its forty-eight hour day, offers women a space outside the coupling yoke.

Coupledom, however, is the fantasy palace of our sacred sexual congress. A pairing palace, or a pairing semi, or a pairing mid-terrace, whose occupants, whether they actually genitally pair and repair or not, nevertheless subscribe to the genital myth homemaking insurance policies.

The capacity for solitude, the capability of celibacy, each ensure a growth in independence. Each competency strengthens and empowers the other. Each threatens the social order which would have women in sexually dependent situations sublimating any jaunty, captivating or creative ideas to male needs. One begins to see why women who live alone, staunchly, sometimes without mirrors or irons, sometimes admitting to intellectual thought, or a fascination with the self, tend to be looked on with a certain suspicion.

To be alone and yet be content, to be celibate and yet rejoice – how these attitudes strike at the sexual and social norms that the mythmasters would have us kneel to.

How the mythmasters ignore the facts that what goes on in bed may bore, that what goes on in company may fatigue, how they would have us bend to the notion that what goes on between two people genitally and emotionally is not merely of paramount importance in gossip's daily round, but that it is what provides life with meaning, with significance, and keeps us in unique psychological health!

I believe that what goes on in a woman's mind when she is entirely on her own is of comparable value. Our current stress on intense relationships means we disregard the processes which take place in solitude. Those solitary shifts of thought may invest a woman's life with an entirely new meaning.

This is, of course, true for men too, but in our society men are given more leeway in how they choose to live and how they apportion their time. If they want long stretches of solitude they can probably take it. Fishing, which has very little to do with pike, trout, or salmon, and a great deal to do with men's desire to sit unharassed for hours at a time, is a fine example. If men want to live alone, they do so, and are rewarded with the flattering label of a 'bachelor existence'.

Many celibate women, attempting to return to an interpretation of celibacy as independent singleness, seem prepared to put up with less flattering labels in order to test out solitude. Some are creative women who need many hours of dedicated work alone, who have found the demands of conventional partnered sex intrusive on their imaginative growth. These are women who *choose* a life alone and are therefore more likely to become enriched (as well as occasionally frustrated), by the experience.

There are, however, women who live as celibates in solitude but who have chosen neither situation. They may be widows, divorcees, single mothers, women who have been deserted, or those who are suffering loss, bereavement, or a radical and often punishing change of circumstance. All of them will discover they too are up against the forces of the genital myth which interprets celibacy as misfortune and solitude as loneliness.

The myth works efficiently because we are still focused (some would say stuck!) on Freud's view that the capacity for orgasm leads to sexual fulfilment, which in turn brings other forms of fulfilment. Inability to attain the genital stage is regarded in women as neurotic. Absurd though it may be, in the nineties this view is still in vogue. Psychoanalysis along these lines has become so widely influential that even those who do not agree with its theories nevertheless use its idiom in discussing the merits of people's personalities. This roots the discussion rather in terms of sexual relationships than in terms of ideas.

How often, for instance, might you hear a friend saying something like: 'Martha thinks Joe's got an Oedipus complex. No wonder their marriage is on the rocks'?

Now compare that with the likelihood of your hearing a friend saying:

'Martha has just read Hélène Cixous, and I honestly think she's a better person for it'?

Since Freud advanced the idea that heterosexual fulfilment is the highest standard of mental health, and since the genital mythmakers have established the notion that genitally intimate *attachments* (i.e. sexual couples) are the acme of normality, someone who rates their hobbies higher than their sex life, who values impersonal ideas above personal relationships, who actually prefers their own celibate company to that of a lover, is regarded as unbalanced.

Yet historically humans have always been as much directed to the impersonal and non-sexually active as to the personal and genitally fixated. This is why so many of us gain immense satisfaction and self-esteem from playing chess, doing the pools, train spotting, badminton, bingo, pottery, writing books, playing the viola, gardening, sculpture, studying for a diploma, sailing, taking photographs, wood carving, upholstering chairs, yoga, Egyptian dancing, designing computer programmes, or looking at old churches.

I would further warrant that many of us find our impersonal passion quite as absorbing as, though possibly less tempestuous than, a sexual relationship. But it does not do to say so. Many of our interests may be learnt in company but they are indulged in solitude. As we get older, they may fascinate us more, as human relationships become less important, perhaps as a prelude to the necessity of having to deal with loss and death.

There is nothing wrong with the fact that in our society we set a value on the capacity to form attachments on equal terms, on the ability to have successful intimate relationships. What is highly dubious is that these are seen not only as the sole source of human happiness but as evidence of emotional maturity. As Anthony Storr points out, it is the absence of this capacity which is seen as pathological, and the capacity to be alone is seldom taken into account when judging criteria for emotional maturity.[1]

The aim of this book has been to show that the assumption that a woman's happiness and health depends on a satisfying genital sexual life is absolutely wrong. Genital sex and coupledom can no longer be the touchstones by which we evaluate women's maturity or their emotional wellbeing. The capacity to be celibate, and the capacity to live in solitude must also be acknowledged.

What then is solitude?

Solitude is the state of being alone, and is not to be confused with loneliness. Yet many people do confuse the two. Loneliness *can* result from solitude, but it does not have to. There are times I have never felt more lonely than when at a large noisy party. At other times I have felt a deep joy at being on my own. For me, solitude is a place of recovery from what is going on in the rest of my world. Too much time spent with other people ensures my desperate need of a retreat. I suddenly, and substantially sooner than even my good friends recognize, *have* to be by myself. It is as if with the coin of fun and companionship I let other people buy small pieces of my soul and I can only retrieve them by spending time alone.

On these occasions I have a *need* to be on my own, which is different from the *capacity* to be alone. I have always had that need, which I used to fulfil by removing myself from a busy family household and going to Cornwall for weeks at a time to live alone and write. It is only in the last few years that I have developed the capacity to be alone. Anthony Storr points out that many extroverts, those characterized by an open, confident relationship with others, contrary to people's popular conceptions, have this need of solitude because they may lose contact with their own subjective needs by becoming over involved with or losing themselves in their objects.[2]

This situation attacks women more often than men because convention demands that a woman should constantly be empathically alert to the needs of others without regard to her own needs. As feminist writer Gloria Steinem, former editor of *MS Magazine*, said in an interview:

'Women's problem is empathy sickness. We put ourselves into someone else's position all the time. Men's problem is empathy deficiency. They can't easily feel what other people are feeling.'

Steinem's solution is that women and men 'each need to move in the direction the other has been'. This is exactly what celibate women, many of whom live autonomously in solitude, are trying to do.[3]

Many people however are aghast when a woman wishes to give up on empathy, and live alone. Living alone is seen not merely as missing out, but in a deeper sense as deserting what is still viewed as a woman's duty – servicing men.

Even women who practise celibacy in a house with a relative, an aunt, a sister, or a mother, no matter how talented or strong, are still seen as strange, their life designated not as valuable but as lonely.

The poet Stevie Smith, whose zany humour pointed up the pain of life, resided from the age of three until her death at sixty-eight, in 1971, in the same house in unfashionable Palmers Green, with her Lion Aunt as her constant companion. In the first of her three novels: *Novel on Yellow Paper* (1936) she commemorates her aunt with the words: 'Darling Auntie Lion, I do so hope you will forgive what is written here. You are yourself like shining gold.'[4]

Stevie and her golden aunt were always looked upon as somewhat comical, Stevie for having missed the marital boat, the aunt perhaps for staunchly protecting her. The facts however were different. For Stevie, living a life without a husband, without the duties of a wife for which she frequently reported, with immense satisfaction, that she was not suited, was a decisive choice, the act of a solitary writer who knows under what amiable conditions her rare sensibility best flourishes. She was a woman who insisted that her own best element was friendship not love.

> My spirit in confusion,
> Long years I strove,
> But now I know that never
> Nearer shall I move,
> Than a friend's friend to friendship,
> To love than a friend's love.[5]

The year before her death she told a friend that he must correct people's misconception of her, that 'because I never married I know nothing about the emotions. When I am dead you must put them right. I loved my aunt.'[6]

Stevie Smith was not comical. She was nervy, bold and grim. It took nerves to practise in celibacy and solitude her unusual love. It took a certain grimness to continue with her wry dry writing throughout her fatal brain tumour, through the loss of her powers of speech, through the last weeks when, with death approaching, she wrote boldly her last poem: 'Come, Death. Do not be slow.' As, unable to speak, she handed over the typescript of the poem, she encircled the word 'death' to indicate that she did not wish her own life to be further drawn out.[7]

In the unforgiving times of the genital myth, the courageous boldness of Stevie Smith and other women, like Emily Brontë, who established the rare love of relatives alongside the unflinching life of the mind, have been misrepresented.

Emily Brontë was often called the sphinx of English Literature, hardly flattering in feminine terms, as a sphinx is a monster with a woman's head and a lion's body, but a real giveaway as to how people see women whose fierce and unfettered routines illustrate their utter disinterest in womanly behaviour. What critic Katherine Frank calls the 'purple heather school of Brontë biography', sentimentalizes Emily as a rhapsodic storm-tossed poet and dismisses her as the passive victim of nineteenth century patriarchy, a forbidding mystical woman who was essentially *lonely*.[8]

In fact Emily Brontë was anything but passive, anything but lonely. She had a 'world within', a fantasy world of the kingdom of Gondal, home of the imagination and secret writing. It was a safe interior realm that protected her from all the lures, disappointments and broken dreams of the 'world outside'.[9]

In the early years Emily had her pet birds Rainbow, Diamond, Snowflake and Jasper, two pet geese Victoria and Adelaide, and Hero, her tame merlin hawk, whom she had found on the moors, wounded, unable to fly, then nursed back to health. She had her lifelong scribbling on the Haworth kitchen table, littered with nutshells, turnip ends and peel from apples prepared for the perfect apple pudding. She had sisters and a father who loved her. She needed no man, no company outside. She was a determined headstrong woman who deliberately chose seclusion and celibacy as a way of life.

By 1842, after an unhappy spell abroad as a teacher, during which time she discovered that everything she needed to learn could be self-taught at home, she recognized finally that she simply did not require outside stimulation, nor the approval and praise that others need in order to learn or feel good. Katherine Frank suggests that Emily suffered when exposed to any such outside influences or to the company of strangers, that she felt threatened, even violated by their demands. It was this fierce independence which led her to see herself as a solitary 'ocean rover' who would 'sail a desert sea'. Only at home, alone by preference, or with her sisters, was she at ease and contented.[10]

By that winter of 1842 she had written fifty of her best poems, secure in the knowledge that she had not only a room of her own, but the whole house to manage, and in which to eat, cook, sleep and write, a total control over her life and environment. In one of her most famous and self-revealing poems, she tells us she is a 'chainless soul'. The poem is a proud explanation of the solitary life she had chosen and would be faithful to until death.

> Riches I hold in light esteem
> And Love I laugh to scorn
> And lust of Fame was but a dream
> That vanished with the morn –
>
> And if I pray, the only prayer
> That moves my lips for me
> Is – 'Leave the heart that now I bear
> And give me liberty.'
>
> Yes, as my swift days near their goal
> 'Tis all that I implore –
> Through life and death, a chainless soul
> With courage to endure![11]

Her courage indeed was immense. Her will inflexible. She made her own trenchant choices, unusual in her day, unusual in ours, and stuck to them, caring absolutely nothing for the opinion of others. When she died aged thirty, with her one great novel *Wuthering Heights* misunderstood and condemned, she died in silence and, despite the presence of her sisters, essentially alone. Katherine Frank uses the term 'unassailable integrity', which suggests that the triumph of Emily Brontë's life was not that of the mystical spirit but that of a woman who was never yoked to the fates of others. I see her as a woman who led an existence of unique and awesome autonomy, who compromised neither her celibacy nor her solitude.[12]

It is of course this autonomy, this celibate chainlessness which, when it occurs in a woman, will provoke anger or disbelief in men. Strength will be looked upon as eccentricity, a life alone distorted to one of loneliness. Josephine Tey in her remarkable crime novel *The Franchise Affair* deliciously illustrates how this works.

The Franchise is the gaunt and isolated country house in which live two singular and single women: the elderly acerbic Mrs Sharpe, she of the malicious tongue, cold, blue, seagull's eye, and billowing white hair; and her forty-year-old unmarried daughter Marion. Wild like a gypsy, with an 'odd air of being self-sufficient', Marion, much given to vivid silk kerchiefs that flaunt her swarthiness, disconcerts the locals by driving a golf ball like a man, using her thin brown wrists like a professional, and mocking any potential suitor with a fine line in sarcasm.

These two women, who appear perfectly content living a solitary life with only each other for occasional company, are suddenly thrust into the community's headlights when a fifteen-year-old schoolgirl accuses them of abducting her, keeping her locked up for a month in their attic, beating her viciously with a dog whip and starving her to a state of sickness. The locals, already wary of eccentric solitary women, one of whom looks like a sibyl, the other like a witch, are more than ready to believe the girl's story.

Enter respectable Robert Blair, the unmarried local solicitor whose every whim for more than twenty years has been catered for by his devoted and doting Aunt Lin. Robert the rescuer pledges himself to their defence, and whilst solving the case falls in love, or fancies he does, with the indomitable Marion. Throughout the book Robert and Marion keep a physical distance bridged by humorous banter. Despite this, it never crosses Robert's conventional mind that Marion might refuse to wed him. She is, after all, unmarried and living the life of a recluse with an ageing mother. She ought, runs the sub-text, to be grateful for the opportunity.

He decides to ask her three pages from the book's finale, at the ninth green on the golf course. She decides to refuse. She points out with pertinent accuracy that he is used to being spoiled by Aunt Lin 'and would miss far more than you know all the creature comforts and cossetting that I wouldn't know how to give you – and wouldn't give you if I knew how.'

Placatingly, Robert assures her that it is because she does not cosset him, because she has 'an adult mind' that he wishes to marry her.

" 'An adult mind is very nice to go to dinner with once a week, but after a lifetime with Aunt Lin you would find it very poor exchange for good pastry in an uncritical atmosphere.' "

Don't you care for me, Robert persists, unable to credit her apparent refusal.

" 'Yes; I care for you a great deal . . . That is, partly, why I won't marry you. The other reason is to do with myself.' "

Robert is taken aback. He is unused to single women who have 'selves'.

" 'With you?' " he says.

You see, I am *not* a marrying woman. I don't want to put up with someone else's crotchets, someone else's demands, someone else's colds in the head. Mother and I suit each other perfectly because we make no demands on each other. If one of us has a cold in the head she retires to her room without fuss and doses her disgusting self until she is fit for human society again. But no husband would do that. He would expect sympathy . . . sympathy and attention and feeding. No, Robert . . . what I say is good sound sense.

Robert will have none of it. His predictable retort illustrates exactly how men view women who live alone or with relatives:
" 'But, Marion, it is a lonely life . . .' "
Her answer is the answer many celibate women who live alone today are giving:
" 'A "full" life in my experience is usually full only of other people's demands.' "
Robert grinds his teeth, and consoles himself with the thought:
" 'She was right: perhaps her mocking habit of mind would not be a comfort to live with.' "
Then he returns to chew on one of Aunt Lin's delectable pastries and on this devastating new idea that a single woman should be quite in possession of her faculties and not apparently in want of a husband.[13]
Robert's reluctance to accept that Marion's situation suits her admirably is based on his philosophy that a woman should live with a man to bring him comfort. He is at some subterranean level unable to take in Marion's view that a woman's life without a partner may have its own considerable comforts.
What then are these comforts? Celibate women scattered through the pages of this book have repeatedly talked of space, of peace, of setting their own routines, adhering to their own rituals. Author Jean Rhys, in a short essay called 'My Day' points to the *unimpeded* choice of food as one of the comforts of those who live on their own:
'When the post comes, the day starts . . . Later on I can plan a long elaborate meal, my first if I'm hungry. Settle for bread, cheese, and a glass of wine, if I'm not.'
If a woman has emerged from an overtaxing couple or family situation, where her responsibility for catering and cooking meant she had to meet the requirements of others, being free to choose the time she eats, and what she eats, may be for her, as it was for Jean Rhys, a small but consistent delight.

In the later period of her life Jean Rhys lived alone for many years in a remote part of Devon, sometimes at ease, sometimes with tragic difficulty. When she first moved to the country there were times when the rest of the house was intolerable, the kitchen becoming 'the one place where I could stop feeling anxious and depressed, where the silence was bearable'.[14]

She fought off loneliness by having a huge assortment of literature (including thrillers, books of marvels, wonders, mysterious apparitions and plagues of grasshoppers) at the foot of the bed. Sometimes she would read long into the night, often she would be awake before dawn reading.

After the success of her first batch of novels in the twenties and thirties, including the subtle and haunting *Good Morning Midnight*, she virtually stopped writing until after the Second World War. Then, late in the fifties, she fitfully began again, until inside the silence of her patches of solitude, after a gap of twenty-seven years she once more found a magnificent voice in the award-winning *Wide Sargasso Sea* in 1966. By 1975, in a short book of essays on old age, solitude and memories, now thinking of herself as an old woman, she describes her feeling of triumph that she has survived another night, which is followed as the sun rises by a new feeling of pleasure in a solitary existence.

> It is then that time stretches, time you're free to spend exactly as you wish. You can eat what you like when you like, drink what you like when you like or not at all, for no reproving warning glance forces you to drink out of defiance. You can spend a couple of hours dressing, or slop around, not bothering to dress at all, reading passages from 'King Solomon's Mines' or 'Lady Audley's Secret'. Or wander about in what passes for a garden. The intoxicating feeling of freedom repays you a thousand times for any loneliness you may have endured.[15]

Though she remained until her death in 1979 haunted by chronic obsessive despairs, she was not, as her friend and literary executor Francis Wyndham confirms, 'the hunted *lonely* woman who figures in her novels . . .' but a 'slant-eyed siren with whom one could enjoy the full intensity of a treat as with no one else'.[16]

I have always seen her as a woman who did not choose solitude, but struggled with it, often despairingly. Who wrote, almost against her will, within it, about it, finally wrenching from the solitary process the knowledge that it can be a powerful weapon for survival. Four years before her death, she was able to say: 'Isn't the sadness of being alone much stressed and the compensations left out?'[17]

I would call the fruits of solitude rewards rather than compensations, and it is on these finally I wish to focus. Writers like Charlotte Mew, Beatrix Potter, Rosemary Manning, Alice James, Marianne Moore, Harriet Monroe, Harriet Shaw Weaver, Emily Brontë and Stevie Smith are some of the women who for long stretches of time were celibate or solitary or sometimes both, who always used that situation creatively. That creative resource has been discovered not only by writers and poets, but by painters, potters, sculptors, philosophers, nurses, researchers, weavers, trainers, teachers, who find solitude can help develop the imagination. It is the imagination that can facilitate invention and originality. It is the imagination that can make sense of suffering, it is the imagination that can bridge the gap between the external world and the individual psyche.

Though some women see regular sex or the security of a permanent partnership as the necessary condition for imaginative work, for others it is celibacy within Rilke's 'unconfined solitude which takes every day like a life, a spaciousness which puts no limit to vision and in the midst of which infinities surround'.[18]

What Rilke is pointing to is a second fruit of solitude, the fact that it offers enough time, proper time, for good work of any sort to grow. As Tillie Olsen movingly testifies in her book devoted to women's silences, substantial creative work demands time, and with rare exceptions the only women to achieve this are those who can work 'fulltime', in the sense that their chosen work should be their primary profession, practised habitually in time that is protected, free and undistracted. This is so unrealistic a description of most women's lives that for many it proves impossible. It took Katherine Anne Porter for instance twenty years to write *Ship of Fools* when she only needed two, but she spent the rest in 'trying to get to that table, to that typewriter, away from my jobs of teaching and trooping this country and of keeping house.'[19]

Katherine Porter's far from uncharacteristic story is borne out by the voices of many creative celibate women. Sarah, a playwright, told me:

In order to write good plays, I need time that stretches endlessly. I must make my own routines, control my work space. Such a plan was impossible when I brought up three daughters. I was at everyone's mercy. I was always shooing the children away then feeling guilty. I wrote bits of plays in odd corners of the house, or odd bits of the day. It felt fragmentary, ragged, incomplete even when it was finished. So I worked with that idea and made that a part of my writing style. Initially I devised dramas that focused on torn pieces of women's lives, little ragged scenes, jumbling up against other little ragged scenes.

Sarah's device of incorporating into the writing the domestic interruptions and the guilt had been used vividly by the American author Alta in a very thin and very exceptional novel, called *Momma: A Start on All the Untold Stories*:

i lose myself to fear, so this morning the headache, the chores: dirty dishes, library books to return (overdue of course) a boxful of mail to answer, & the need to write, to say it all, to say my life is so full of sinks full of dishes, bills on the mantle; i wait until this so-called 'work' is done, i wait to write . . . angel just sucked something up in the vacuum cleaner again & how dare i sit here writing instead of fixing the vacuum cleaner . . . (do i keep writing or get up & bang the tube until the tyrannical toy is loosened?) (how dare i say tyrannical toy? don't i love my children?)[20]

Women who do finally make it through tyrannical toyland and out the other side into solitude may fit sex into their work patterns, or they may entirely give it up. Sarah, the playwright, alternates periods of celibacy with periods of intense sexual activity, both programmed to her writing schedule.

'When I'm in the middle of a play, nothing else matters. Sex seems a waste of time. When the play is finished, then I usually go into a kind of hiatus, happy hysteria first, then a deep depression because I think of everything that might be wrong. Slowly I emerge. What's going on with the rest of the world? Who is out there? That's when I start making love again.'

For Marianne, a painter, living alone has always been an imperative condition of her work, but celibacy is more recent:

I'm an impossible person. I couldn't live fulltime with anyone, not that anyone would have me. In order to paint I need to feel nothing is closing in, that there is somewhere to put myself away where I cannot be reached. I have always lived alone. I put up with the occasional loneliness.

For a couple of years I had a lover and we matched some of each other's needs. He lived in town, I lived in the country. The light was important, and the hills. I didn't want him to live with me. For a time, making love felt good, until gradually I became more linked to his life. I had to stop concentrating on my work and start concentrating on his needs. I am quite a private person so it did not suit me. Space was essential. We talked about it . . . he understood. Then a curious thing happened. Unconsciously he began to leave more of his possessions at my house. I would find shirts, jackets, dressing-gowns, spare razors, odd socks . . . One day I realized clearly that the reason he felt he could do that was because we went to bed together. Lovers have rights. I expect I behave in his house in ways I would not behave elsewhere. I still wanted his companionship. But I need my strange little way of being solitary, controlling my hours, more than I need sex.

You do not have to sculpt or paint or write to use solitude creatively. You can use it to look at life's patterns, spin a new web, stop wasting your time or waste it in a way that suits you. May Sarton, who sees solitude as her 'real life' so that 'friends, even passionate love, are not my real life unless there is time alone in which to explore . . .', believes it is 'never a waste of time to be outdoors, and never a waste of time to lie down and rest even for a couple of hours.' It is then she says that images float up, then that she plans her work.[21]

Work, fine work, productive work. That is the key. This is not, commonly, what women are expected to give priority to. When Freud was asked what he thought constituted psychological wellbeing he said it was the ability to love and work. In looking at women's lives, our ability to love has been overemphasized at the expense of our ability to work. But solitude can provide women with the breeding ground not for babies but for fine work and self-definition.

Solitude can also help us to get in touch with our deepest feelings. It is difficult to discover exactly who we are when our lives are filled with domestic routines or sexual dramas. Many of us are biased towards perpetually giving ourselves to external purposes which, as Joanna Field points out in a thoughtful and introspective study called *A Life of One's Own*, are often 'artificial male purposes', except that we do not recognize them as such and believe they are our own.[22]

We find it easy to blind ourselves to what we really like, to drift into accepting our wants ready-made from others, and to evade the continual day to day sifting of values. In solitude we may be able to fasten introspectively upon what makes *us* happy without wondering whether it should or should not.

This may lead us to a desire to change our mental attitude, and the chance to do so can be another reward from a life alone. We might decide to alter some well-established pattern which no longer suits us. It is easier to do this alone because most of us have our sense of identity partially confirmed by those who think they know us and expect us to behave predictably. Good friends often set us in cement. This means that at the point when we are ready to give up smoking one will say:

'You have never been able to give up cigarettes for longer than two months!'

Or as we are contemplating flute lessons an ex-lover says: 'Darling, in all the years I've known you, you haven't understood a note of music. It will be a shocking waste of money.'

Worst of all, as we are setting ourselves a twelve point programme for punctuality, a well meaning brother or cousin says: 'We *expect* you to be an hour late every time, but we still love you.'

If this is what happens over the small mundane matters, imagine how hard it is to change from being sexually active to being celibate in the company of those who have an interest in your staying just as you are.

Changes of attitude may be needed most when our circumstances drastically alter: we may have broken up with someone we loved or lived with, or we may have had to face a death of someone we knew well. At this point, the meaning of our day to day life may have to be fundamentally reappraised. Solitude can help us in coming to terms with loss or bereavement.

Bereavement is not always about physical death. It can be about the emotional death of a relationship, a change in a partnership. We grieve over these things too. I have used my time alone to try to understand the transition from what I saw as a life partnership into what is now an intimate friendship lived in two separate houses, mine in the country, hers in town.

At first I did not know how to use my solitude. There was too much of it. I did not need to cook elaborate meals. I had a lot of toast fingers which I dipped into boiled eggs. I had three sherries instead of one when the sun had gone down over the yard arm. Then I stopped caring about either the sun or the yard arm and had my first sherry at quarter to five. The silence was eerie. The clatter of my single knife and fork an unwelcome cacophony.

I made my usual lists of what I would do when, then tore them up, as I realized I did not have to fit in with anyone's schedules. I knew I could leave long black hairs in the bath or talc on the bathroom mat without complaints, but curiously I stopped doing that. It hardly seemed worthwhile. I could do what I liked when I liked. But for the first time in years I was not sure what I liked, or what I wanted to do. I did not *use* time, I filled it in. I redecorated my new house. Every room. I outlined white doors with pink panels, I painted green lines on cream doors. I painted walls I had already wallpapered. I wallpapered over walls I had previously painted.

We had always had a gas fire in our study. There was no gas in my village. I was positively glad I could not have a gas fire. You cannot miss sitting with someone round a gas fire if there is no gas fire to sit round. There was a solid fuel boiler fire at one end of the sitting room, and a wall with a concealed fireplace the other end. I tore down the wall and opened up the fireplace. I sat alone round a log fire. Dammit, it wasn't the type of fire I was missing it was the type of person. I missed the challenge, the laughter, the utter loyalty, and the love, all of it on the premises. I knew it was still there but it was in another town divided by British Rail and daily lives spent separately.

It was obvious I was going to have to accept this challenge, rely on myself, be loyal to my work. I replastered the wall, and decided on sanity.

In the next stage of solitude, I went for long walks. I noticed plants and trees in greater detail. I began gardening. I became passionate about gardening: I bought gardening books, I went to gardening classes, I haunted garden centres. I felt good at something. At least plants came up all right if you fed and watered them. They did not make *demands*. They did not go into black moods. They did not refuse to say what was the matter with them. I could look up their symptoms in my plant book, and begin to put matters right.

After the first year, I learnt to stop eyeing tasks around the corner, the way some people look at paintings in a gallery, with one eye on the next painting, in a hurry to see them all. I learnt to linger. To analyse less, to stare longer. To live in the moment. I used to see obstacles as hurdles to leap over. Now I feel I have something to learn from them. Lying on the sitting room cushions, many evenings alone, reading, has given me a new way of approaching time. I try to use it to become present in my own life instead of always observing, or taking photos. I find this very hard.

Solitude, which has, with two short sexual interruptions, run concurrently with celibacy for me, has been the start of a journey towards understanding who I was in that couple and what mistakes I made. It has helped me see what at first I adamantly refused to see, that there can be an intense and passionate bond between two people who love each other without them necessarily making love or living together.

That journey from loss to transformation is by no means over, nor has it always been easy. During the second year, thoroughly accustomed to my solitude, nestling inside it, I had a drink with a good friend.

'Can you remember you once said you two would draw your old age pensions together? Doesn't that seem funny now!' she said.

Sometimes good friends need shooting. It did not seem funny that year. It hurt every time I thought about it. Two years further on I do not think about it much, but when I wrote that line, it hurt. These journeys of withdrawing from a life as a couple, reinventing the individual, take more time than sometimes we are prepared to acknowledge.

Journeys away from death take longer.

I have used this same period of celibate solitude to come to terms with the recent death of my mother.

Dead. What a permanent word dead is. You cannot come back from dead. You cannot change dead. It is the one word that is too late. My mother was in a nursing home where they never used the word, but every day several of the elderly occupants were engaged in dying and by nightfall two or more would be dead. My mother knew that. I knew that. We both understood that was why we had taken her out of the grim hospital ward, where elderly women stripped themselves naked and talked to people from an earlier life, and found this plant-filled place with a specially chosen room with a view over the landscaped garden, which she was by then too sick ever to see.

She had undergone a gruelling series of illnesses, heart problems, cancer, two minor strokes, an attempted suicide, then a major stroke, which caused her ultimately to lose her bodily functions one by one.

But not her mind. Never her mind. I watched her watching herself dying bit by bit, as we talked of books, of bus rides she might take when she 'got better', of the daily changes in her body, of her hatred of spilling food everywhere (she was a very fastidious woman), of her disbelief in her labelled incontinence.

When she could still talk above a whisper she told me she could not always find the bell when she needed to go to the toilet – her arm was too weak, her eyesight going, her voice too faint to shout for help – but she was not incontinent. I believed her and would rush about for commodes if the nurses were busy. They, the starched team of keepers and containers, would not listen. They put her in paddy pads to 'make life more tolerable'. Tolerable for whom? Not for her.

I thought before it occurred that if you sat and saw someone dying what you would concentrate on would be the life you had led with them or without them. But it did not happen like that. I found I lived the life she and I were currently engaged on. Feeding her sloppy protein milk fluid which was all she could swallow, mopping her up, putting her teeth in, terrified of getting it wrong, appalled at the intimacy. I constantly changed the green towel spattered with food round her neck for a fresh burgundy one. Green and burgundy, dark greens, dark reds, the colours of my childhood. Colours that today suffocate me.

We rarely talked of the past. It had not been good between us. In my solitude after visiting hours I learnt that how we feel about a person during their life does not necessarily correlate with how we shall respond to their dying or how we shall react to their death.

For me it was emotionally muddled because for nearly fifty years she had vehemently professed her disapproval and hatred of me. I did not know why as a child. I do not know why as an adult. Throughout my childhood she tried to control everything I did. If I disobeyed I would be severely punished. When I was sixteen the issue was my birthday party. She wanted me to have a respectable Jewish party in my parents' home with guests agreed upon with her, the kind of party I had had every January. I pointed out that I was now sixteen. I wanted something different. My friend Judy and I had decided upon a teen party with loud music and boys in a basement flat. My mother was appalled. If you cross me, she said, I shall never speak to you again. Obviously no mother could carry out such a threat. No child could believe anything so preposterous.

Frightened, I was, but I went ahead. The party was incredible. I felt free and happy. When I got home there was a note telling me she was no longer speaking to me.

She and I lived in the same house for nearly a year without her saying one word to me. For weeks, day after day, I screamed, and cried, and went down on my knees before her begging her to relent. She acted as if she no longer heard me or saw me. I was well fed and clothed. I was given books and she saw I was never late for school. But I was cast out as a daughter. I was cast into a world of silence. It took twenty years for me to recover from my belief that silence was hostile.

Now in the sunfilled nursing home, she and I sit in a comfortable silence. I think how open we are being in this situation. No more arguments. Dealing with the lead up to something we cannot change. We cannot change the past either. I cannot change the divorces, miscarriages by the wrong men, the abortion, the politics, the women friends, the banner waving, the marches, everything we disagreed upon. We cannot change the fact that for years she refused to see me. We cannot change the fact that at intervals over the years I would send her birthday cards or Mothers' Day cards, and at intervals she would send them back.

But something has changed. There are new facts. Suddenly in the eighteen months before her death she appeared to have changed her mind. As she became sicker, as I spent longer and longer hours by her bed, her reliance on me grew, and with it some affection and apparent pride in my achievements. Or was it merely tolerance, a self-deception rooted in her despair, disease and terrible need? I shall never know.

What I do know is that she appreciated my company, for she told me as she lay there what she had not told me thirty years before, that she herself had been unable to face sitting by my father's hospital bed while he lay dying. I remember, in that hospital in Ravenscourt Park three decades earlier, one Sunday afternoon and evening it was I who had sat and read *The Observer* out loud to a man who could no longer hear it but who insisted that as I worked for the scandalous *Daily Sketch*, we should minimize that enormity by reading the Qualities on Sunday.

On weekdays, travelling to work on the underground, my father would conceal the disreputable *Daily Sketch* inside his professional man's *Daily Telegraph* and surreptitiously (and, he would assure me later, very proudly) read my column. His office was near both

Billingsgate fish market, and Blooms' Jewish Delicatessen, and one
day he phoned me from work and said could he bring me home a
treat? Treats in a Jewish household are invariably food. I said I should
love a bagel spread with smoked salmon. When he arrived home, in
an act of typical wild generosity, he was holding a complete side of
smoked salmon and, bulging from his jacket pocket, a dozen bagels.

That Sunday, all generous acts, all gross faults behind him, my
father, a humorous and weak man with copperplate handwriting
and sensuous lips from which I shied away, lay inside an oxygen
tent and began to die. Though he was often late for appointments
he did not hang about for death. I finished *The Observer*, stared
inside the tent long and slowly, and thought:

'You have spoilt me and misunderstood me. You have made
me laugh and irritated me profoundly. I have always felt uneasy
anywhere near you. I have hungered for affection throughout my
childhood but I have never wanted you to touch me physically. I
have spent nineteen years in a house with you, and I do not know
who you are.'

I took the tube back to my mother's flat. He was dead two
hours after I arrived.

My mother's death took much longer. Many many months. The
way she died was like the way she lived, a harrowing drama. It was
filled with medical shifts, relapses, disguises. It was not unsuitable.
For most of my mother's life she had disguised herself in a variety of
blonde and brunette wigs. They were perched high or wide above her
very tiny frame. She was four foot something and fierce. You never
knew which wig she would wear on which day so you were never
quite sure what she would look like. It was disconcerting. Once I
sat three rows behind her in a Huyton College concert where my
daughter was in the choir and I did not recognize her, the distance
between us that year being more than three rows.

Now I sit by her bedside, in a chair touching the bed, as
near as anyone can get to her now, and comb back her thin
wispy white hair from her damp face. There are no more disguises.
She shuts her eyes, then she opens them again quickly. It is her new
way of acknowledging what is happening. She hardly talks now but
we have a range of codes going.

When I was very young, before she took to wigs, she had long
brown hair piled on top of her head. Once, just once, she let me
comb it, I think I even plaited it. Just that once. Perhaps I only like
to think I plaited it. Jenni, my friend, had long brown hair too. Hers

was sometimes in plaits, sometimes loose in a thick furry pony tail. When she was dancing she had it in a chignon. 'I have to look the part,' she said one day in that quiet melodic voice.

My mother is very slowly dying and I cannot keep my mind on it. I think of Jenni's death. Sudden. Horrible. Unfair. (Is death ever fair?) Took us all by shock. Jenni, the dancer, drowned having a fit over a bath while her newborn baby cried in the next room. She had been my friend all my adult years. They played her dance music at the funeral. Her students came. Throngs of them. Black, white, hopeful, eager, intensely sad that Jenni would no longer teach them. Honouring her as their heads moved to the music, trying not to tap their feet. Jenni would not have minded anyone tapping their feet. How bitter I felt that Jenni's baby boy would never know her as we did. I was glad he was not at the funeral. I did not want to see a tiny living baby, I wanted to see my friend.

Later my friend B and I packed up Jenni's clothes keeping some to wear in memory of her. I wore a brown and red patterned Indian silk shirt and skirt till it rent in shreds. I never understood how it fitted me. Jenni was half my size. A dancer's slim straight figure. Had she been pregnant when she bought it? Had she suddenly put on weight in those last four weeks when I hadn't seen her? Putting on weight would not have suited her. Why does it matter that I don't know? Why does it matter that I am not sure if I last saw her four weeks or five weeks before her death? I want it to be only four weeks, as if that would somehow bring her closer.

B took a beige trenchcoat of Jenni's. She kept it for years. It had a small pebble in one pocket which Jenni had picked up at the seaside. I sat by my mother and I wondered if the pebble was still in the trenchcoat pocket. I do not know because B and I no longer share a wardrobe. How funny that a pebble should make me acutely conscious of that fact. My mother is dying, Jenni is dead, B and I live separately. And all I can think of is that damn pebble. The pebble and pension books. I shall have to send my mother's pension book back to the social security office. Jenni died so young we never even talked of pensions. They were for other, older people. Older like B and I who according to the friend will draw them separately if we draw them at all. My mother is dying and I am thinking of other matters. Is not one death at a time enough to concentrate upon?

I did concentrate in my solitude outside visiting hours. I concentrated on coming to terms with my own feelings for her. Unattached, living alone, in the quiet house overlooking the woods,

I sat sturdily at the computer and separated out the longing for approval which I had systematically been denied as a child, the years of resentment I had felt for the suffering she had put me through, and the quite unfathomable loyalty and responsibility I felt to her now simply because a birth certificate (though not a single action) suggested she was my mother.

Is it that in a Jewish family, even if you go missing somewhere in the middle, you are always around towards the end?

Towards the very end I remember reading aloud to her from a large print book which the nursing home stocked for elderly residents. She could not see the pages so I am not sure why I so carefully chose it. Like choosing the room with the view of the garden it was a triumph of hope over realism. She did however become mildly immersed in the story which was written in the form of letters between a middle-aged married woman with literary aspirations and low self esteem, and a young bright Jewish American male academic also married with two small children. They lived several thousand miles apart at different sides of the US and they had not met. The woman had read a news-paper article by the bright young academic and had written to him on the strength of it. Thus did their correspondence start. Unlikely to meet, they let their feelings flow onto the pages and from an initial reserve they were soon expressing to each other whom they really were. Or perhaps whom they wished to be. I know from my own experience that a love affair by letter gives one an engaging licence. Half way through the book the couple plan to meet. My mother and I got quite excited. Before they could do so, my mother died.

I remember thinking: 'She will never know whether they liked each other once they had spent time together.'

It was a question that was the subtext of my days and evenings with her as we read or sat in silence. I think by the end my mother and I probably liked the reading and the sitting, and that was a start.

About the two people in the novel, I never knew either. I could not bear to finish the book. I gave it back to the library half read. As you see I have also blotted out the name of the title and the author. If you knew it and told me the name, I should probably cry.

Losing a mother, if you do not live in the same house with her, does not alter the material circumstances of your life, but for me it altered a great deal else. It altered the structure inside my head. It altered my imaginative life. It altered the picture of my past, changed the shape of things to come. It has both modified and expanded what I can create and how. I have changed my emotions from bitterness about my grim relationship with my mother to a feeling of acceptance along the lines: Well, my traumatic childhood was just the way it was. I no longer need to dwell on it.

I do not think I should have known this if I was still living in the hurly burly of a noisy family household, if I was still part of a sexually active couple. Other things would have been on my mind. I would have been pre-occupied with the tensions and delights of being in a partnership. On my own I had a chance to view the patterns of my life, to recognize that I could not change the mistakes I had made in the past, but I could open myself up to something different from today.

Thinking about my mother, whose life was ambivalent and whose death a mess, I am not sure if what we call 'mourning' ever comes to an end, but I do know that the process changes. At some point we stop talking to the dead, we stop being surprised that they won't phone or drop by, we stop stifling the mixture of white hot anger, loose ends left hanging, feelings we never resolved, conversations we did not get round to having, tears as much for ourselves as for them, tears that are often not even appropriate. Yes, the process of bereavement and loss changes, and solitude can facilitate that change.

'People are always trying to get you to stop talking about the person who has died, people are always suggesting you go out, mix more, try some entertainment, take your mind off it,' one celibate widow said.

There does seem to be an allowable portion of time, a few weeks, a couple of months, in which the bereaved person is allowed the luxury or necessity of overt grief, after which any outburst renders other people uncomfortable. They find it threatening, they need you to 'get over it' for their sakes. They talk endlessly about the importance of investing in the future. It is important: to survive we do have to make that investment, but we cannot hurry it. Often for fear of upsetting our family and friends if we cannot hasten the process we do at least fall silent.

Lilian, a celibate woman, widowed nine years ago, told me that her son who had been wonderful about driving her to the super-market, unendingly helpful about going through her finances, had never understood her need to talk about her husband. Never once, after the first two months, had he mentioned his father's name. The death was over, the name taboo.

Talking freely about the dead person is one way of diminishing the pain. Another way is by being alone, something bereaved people initially dread. Many celibate women however discover that after the first few months solitude may help.

Esther, an arts and entertainments officer, widowed after a deeply happy marriage lasting nearly half a century, said the initial difficulty for her was that:

> Couples were the norm in our lives. But after Danny died, I looked around and saw all these *young* women living on their own and making a real life. I knew that I had to be able to do that too. At first I relied on my family, who are constantly loving. I went away to one or other of them every weekend. But I got weary always being on trains at weekends, leaving my home because the children worried about my being on my own. *I am on my own.* I have learnt to accept this and see the good side. You can't do that in company. You have to be brave. You have to fall back on yourself. To my great surprise I have managed it. Every day I am surprised I cope as well as I do.

One way Esther copes is by immersion in her fulltime, responsible job. Another is by seeing friends regularly. 'Some of my widowed friends have matched up very fast with another partner,' she told me. 'I do not want that so there must be some strength in me.'

For Esther it is not sex that is missed in her continuing life of celibacy and solitude, it is what she calls 'the little intimacies'. In her bedroom are neat twin beds with a small enough space between them for the couple to hold hands.

'That's what I miss, not sex, the affection,' she said.

> Being able to reach out my hand at night and find he was reaching his hand across to me. That was our way of saying goodnight, knowing we would both be there in the morning. I still keep his bed made up. Sometimes one of the family sleeps in it when they come to visit. As I am getting undressed I talk to him. I tell him how the day went, and what shows we are planning, which exhibitions I am organizing. He loved paintings, he always took an interest in my job. It is those quiet times when I long for him to be here. 'My lovely Danny,' I say and begin this long conversation. How ridiculous I am being. I certainly don't believe in an afterlife, so goodness knows who I think I am talking to!

Once when I stayed in her apartment, I noticed that she stood up for her breakfast in the kitchen. She would walk about making her toast, then stand to spread the marmalade, finally still standing she would eat two slices quickly.

'Why do you do that?' I asked. 'There are two kitchen stools. You'll get indigestion if you don't sit down.'

'I can sit down for a hotel breakfast,' she said.

> We had wonderful holidays together in hotels abroad. But I don't know how to sit down for breakfast in my own home. Danny always brought me squeezed orange, toast and marmalade in bed. Every day, all those years, breakfast in bed, until they took him into hospital. Then when he came back for that last time, he couldn't do that. He apologized for being useless. I sound useless myself talking like that. But, yes, that's what I miss, the little important things that show what you mean to each other.

Not all bereaved celibate women had been as happy as Esther. Where marriage and sex had been unpleasant, solitude and celibacy came not as a learning process, but as a relief. One woman said:

> Why does everyone put widows in a box? Feel sorry for them. I had a terrible marriage, we loathed each other but we were brought up to stick it out, so we did. How I *did* stick it out. He got cancer of the bowel, ended up incontinent. There I was cleaning up the mess, emptying basins, using air freshener everywhere, taking sheets to the laundrette that I was ashamed to be seen with. 'You bloody wouldn't have done this for me!' I told him one night. Thank God for my widowhood. I have never had it so easy. I never believed all that stuff about women finding joy in sex and marriage, I'm finding more pleasure in a tray of tea and boiled egg in front of the telly than I ever found in that bed with him.

For some celibate women the death of someone close alters the imaginative shapes in their mind, as it did for me, but this is not the same as altering the daily structure of one's life which is what Esther and Lilian and those who lose a live-in partner have to face. For Lilian much of the adaptation was practical:

> There is no one there to take care of the bills. I had always been capable of doing it, but I didn't want to hurt him by suggesting it. So when he died I had it all to learn. Once John got fed up with battling with his broken typewriter and said he would take it to the menders. I took it away quietly and had it mended in

half an hour. Of course he never said anything! Men in my day did not like you to be able to cope. It upset their ego. But when they die you have to cope. I've learnt to go on public transport; he had always driven me everywhere. I've learnt to make major decisions about selling and buying houses. I had no idea I should have turned out so capable. Ultimately being so much on my own has helped me to get to grips with my loss. I have been forced to become selfish, to think about my self. The independence I have achieved may seem pathetic to some but to me it is alarming. I can please myself about programmes on TV or food or when I shall have my little walk. I am proud of how I now arrange my own days. You surprise yourself with what you can do.

The problems she faces are to do with being over seventy and always having lived in a couple.

At the funeral relations promise you can go and see them but they forget to ask you, if it's just you. It becomes too hard to go to ballroom dancing if you are not in a couple, so you have to find new hobbies that you can manage alone. I have never looked for another man, that side of things is not important. You lose so many friends when you are widowed. If you are not in a couple, they do not want to know. It is not sex I am looking for it is the perfect friend.

One celibate woman who did initially miss sex passionately has ended up with the perfect friend instead. Annie, widowed thirteen years, describes the first two years as devastating physically: 'People don't cuddle widows,' she pronounced.

If you've just lost your man and you have that need for sex real badly, if you can't get that, at least there ought to be cuddles. But there are never enough. In the first two years, if you have had that sexual connection so that when you and he enter a room and touch each other, you know just how far you'll go that night, that's what you miss.

I didn't look outside, I looked to the family for affection. I hoped my son would cuddle me, show me more physical love. But he didn't. Maybe it was because he got all that from his wife. Or maybe he thought I was so strong I didn't need it. He was a good boy, he drove me everywhere, he did my dishes, even the hoovering, but he left me to deal with my own physical needs. 'You're a survivor Mum,' he said. Well I am. I've survived. When I got the burning down there, I put all my sexual energies into being a nurse. I did shifts, double times, worked nights. After two years the burning and the sexual urges died down. I slowly began to realize you can have affection without sex. I came to it through Angela, a woman I nursed through a terrible illness in hospital. She's a widow too. When she recovered we used to go for walks together, exercise the dogs, go to the films. We live two streets away. When I was sick last year, she came twice a day every day trotting down the road with two plastic buckets. One had my dinner in, one my pudding. That's love for you. In hospital I've wiped her bum, and I've mopped up her vomit. I'd do it again if she ever got sick. That's love for you too. But I wouldn't tell her that. She's not a person of many words. She's not a person of many hugs either. I suspect her own marriage was all washing the shirts, doing the laundry, setting the table. I can't imagine her having urges. She didn't look to her husband for those loving connections, so maybe she doesn't look to anyone else for them. But they are there. Underneath. We have bought a pony between us now. 'Our' pony we say proudly. We buy books together and write both our names in. Some are kept on her shelf, some on mine. It's a partnership in which we each live alone, we don't worry about men, and we have the perfect friend.

Friendship is more than an important source of delight for celibate women who live alone. It is a linchpin. Non-genital passion is the oddball love for women living outside two accepted paradigms: the model of coupledom and the model of genital congress.

Women who have suffered loss and bereavement, who have found a new passion within friendship, even though they did not necessarily choose their celibate state, also found, as did the positive Sensual and Ascetic Celibates of this study, strength, self-definition, purpose and connected autonomy. Celibate and solitary women are women who disturb the social order; they are also women who have found something to celebrate.

CONCLUSION

A Passion for Celibacy

WHAT then is Passionate Celibacy and how far has it moved away from the shorthand description often applied to it, of abstention from genital activity? That was the first question I explored in this study. It has become clear that the ideal of passionate celibacy, although it incorporates a movement away from genital sexual behaviour, is even more about a rejection of the sexual and material roles which women are still required to play. Celibacy stands firm as a revolt against a set of male definitions about women's sexuality in a society that is genitally focused and geared to coupledom.

These explorations have shown that not all forms of celibacy can be considered passionate celibacy. When a woman wants but cannot obtain a genitally active relationship, there is nothing either purposeful or passionate about what she may call her 'celibate' state. It is not a situation she has chosen, it may only be temporary. Unchosen and unrelated to autonomy, it cannot be classed as passionate celibacy. However, it is interesting that sometimes a purely circumstantial celibacy may change and move towards a more self-chosen, autonomous celibate position. I believe that every form of female celibacy can be regarded as embryonic passionate celibacy, and therefore as a form of politics, in the sense that it does not serve male interests and is a radical departure from convention.

In our society at present all forms of celibacy exist at varying levels of awareness. Some women are accidentally celibate. They fall into celibacy then stay there. Others as we have seen are unwilling celibates; of these, some who become distressed at long periods of genital inactivity usually manage to change their mode of sexuality. Others who find celibacy productive sometimes settle for it and find it an increasingly fruitful experience. Some women decide to take a short break from genital activity and emotional dependence on other people then become celibate for a lengthy sustained period. Some women are celibate as a matter of what they call 'temperament', but they are largely indifferent to any of the political or social implications of their behaviour. Some women, however, are fully aware and highly motivated celibates. They have made a positive decision to take on celibacy either for a long period or for life. They identify themselves as celibate. They do so for a variety of reasons, which are usually rooted in a desire for connected autonomy and independence. Through this they can be seen to develop a group identity. Some of these live in non-genital couples or with relatives, but the majority live on their own, finding productive the links between celibacy and solitude in their fight against the genital myth.

It is this last group whom I call Passionate Celibates. Their choice of sexual expression is manifesting itself as a new form of consciousness for women. It has become a source of power and encouragement for celibate women previously labelled sick, prudish or frigid. Passionate celibacy can be seen as one type of female autonomous sexuality, which does not serve the interests of the genital mythmakers. As an alternative sexual strategy that takes power away from men, it allows women their own choices about what to do with their bodies. By defining celibacy as passionate, as a form of sexuality, women are creating choices that contradict oppressive patriarchal definitions.

The genital mythmakers inside a coercive couple-focused society have defined women's sexuality with a rigid role structure. Celibate women are contesting these fixed notions. Men do not like women to withdraw from the sex game – a power game in which women are the players whose very powerlessness is eroticized. Penalties can be exacted for withdrawal from sexual behaviour as men have defined it, and from the male value system that upholds it. Throughout history, men have judged women's ideas according to the sexual status of the women concerned. The technique is to bring a woman's character into disrepute by means of her sexuality so that her ideas do not have to be addressed. If, for instance, a woman can be labelled promiscuous then her ideas can be categorized as 'unreliable'. If a woman can be labelled as 'lesbian' or 'deviant' then her ideas can be dismissed as 'abnormal' or 'neurotic'. If a celibate woman can be labelled 'prudish' or 'frigid' or 'twisted' then her ideas can be similarly devalued.

When one group of people take strong measures to obstruct or to distort the actions taken by another group, you can be certain that those actions have become threatening to the group in power.

I have already described the ways in which celibacy is a threat to the genital mythmasters and to the sexual mores of our time. Men have responded to the threat by ensuring celibacy has not been easy for women to choose. Celibacy as a mode of sexual practice, as a positive option for women, has not been on an open agenda, available to be freely chosen.

The notion of 'choice' with regard to sexuality is problematic. In general, society looks at sexual practice as something that is 'inherent' or 'essential'. The sexual, from this standpoint, is seen as having fixed, unchanging characteristics grounded in biology. From an essentialist view, culture is not seen as having much influence on sexuality, therefore external factors and the matter of 'choice' become marginal.

In this study, by taking the alternative approach to essentialism, by viewing sexuality as socially constructed, celibacy can be seen as part of a sexual practice whose cornerstone is choice, rooted of course in social, psychological, political and emotional factors. If one can choose one's sexuality and can freely decide on a form of 'sexual' behaviour that lies outside traditional definitions of what *is* sexual, then one can choose celibacy as a form of sexuality, which may become part of a contemporary passionate politics.

If this book enables us to add celibacy to our existing definitions of what is sexual for women, and if it empowers women to practise celibacy freely and with pride, it will have served its purpose.

Notes

•••|├────────➤┤✿┤┤•────────┤|••

Introduction: Celibacy is not Hereditary

1. 'True Trash' from *Wilderness Tips*, Margaret Atwood (Bloomsbury, London, 1991).
2. Simon Long, Beijing, reporting on the official Xinhua News Agency story, 1991.
3. *The Change: Women, Ageing and the Menopause*, Germaine Greer (Hamish Hamilton, London, 1991), pp. 3–4.
4. *Reflecting Men at Twice Their Natural Size*, Sally Cline and Dale Spender (André Deutsch, London, 1987).
5. *Eunuchs for Heaven*, Uta Ranke-Heinemann, (Trans.) John Brownjohn (André Deutsch, London, 1990), pp. ix–x.
6. *Ibid.*, p. 2, quoting Diogenes Lasertius *Lives of the Philosophers VIII*.
7. *Ibid.*, p. 2.
8. *Ibid.*, quoting Michel Foucault *The History of Sexuality*.
9. *Collins English Dictionary*, (Collins, London, 1979), p. 243.
10. *Just Desserts: Women and Food*, Sally Cline (André Deutsch, London, 1990).
11. Sally Cline and Dale Spender, *op. cit.*
12. Germaine Greer, *op. cit.*
13. *Sex is Not Compulsory*; Liz Hodgkinson (Sphere, London, 1986), pp. 28–31; *Humour Therapy in Cancer, Psychosomatic Diseases, Mental Disorders, Crime, Interpersonal and Sexual Relationships*, Branko Bokun (Vita Books, London, 1986).
14. *Solitude*, Anthony Storr (Fontana, London, 1989).
15. *Sex: Facts, Frauds and Follies*, Thomas Szasz (Basil Blackwell, Oxford, 1981), p. 19.

1. Genital Messages

1. *The Butcher*, Alina Reyes (Methuen, London, 1991).
2. Charlotte Brontë referring to her father's curates, dismissing the idea of marriage. Quoted in *Strong-minded Women and Other Lost Voices from Nineteenth Century England*, (Ed.) Janet Horowitz Murray (Penguin, Harmondsworth, 1982), p. 116.
3. *The Joy of Sex*, Alex Comfort (Quartet Books, London, 1972).
4. *The Fight for Acceptance: A History of Contraception*, Clive Wood and Beryl Suitters (Medical and Technical Publishing Company, Aylesbury, 1970).
5. *Human Sexual Response*, William Masters and Virginia Johnson (Little, Brown and Company, Boston, 1966).
6. *Human Sexual Inadequacy*, William Masters and Virginia Johnson (J. A. Churchill, London, 1966).

7. *Nothing Natural*, Jenny Diski (Methuen, London, 1986), pp. 28–31.
8. *Sita*, Kate Millett (Virago, London, 1977), pp. 7–10.
9   *The Swimming Pool Library*, Alan Hollinghurst (Penguin, Harmondsworth, 1988), pp. 5–31. First published by Chatto & Windus, 1988.

2. Genital Manipulations

1. Sally Cline and Dale Spender, *op. cit.*; *The Beauty Myth*, Naomi Wolf (Vintage, London, 1990), p. 136.
2. Sally Cline, *op. cit.*
3. *A Feminist Dictionary*, (Eds.) Cheris Kramarae and Paula A. Treichler (Pandora Press, London, 1985), p. 414.
4. 'Sex and Reference', Janice Moulton in (Ed.) *Sexist Language*, Mary Vetterling-Braggin (Littlefield Adams and Co., Boston, 1981), pp. 184–5, cited in Cheris Kramarae and Paula A. Treichler, *op. cit.*, p. 414.
5. *The Hite Report: A Nationwide Study of Female Sexuality*, Shere Hite (Macmillan, New York, 1976), p. 196.
6. *The Myth of the Vaginal Orgasm*, Anne Koedt (New England Free Press, Somerville, Mass., 1970).
7. *Man Made Language*, Dale Spender (Routledge and Kegan Paul, London, 1980); *Gyn/Ecology: The Metaethics of Radical Feminism*, Mary Daly (Beacon Press, Boston, 1978); 'Perceptions of Female and Male Speech', Cheris Kramarae in *Language and Speech* 20, No. 2, April/June 1977, pp. 151–161; 'International Shitwork', Pamela Fishman in *Heresies: A Feminist Publication on Arts and Politics* No. 2, May 1977, pp. 99–101; *Language and Sex: Difference and Dominance*, (Eds.) Barrie Thorne and Nancy Henley (Newbury House, Rowley House 1975), pp. 184–203; *Language and Woman's Place*, Robin Lakoff (Harper and Row, New York, 1975); *Feminism and Linguistic Theory*, Deborah Cameron (Macmillan, London, 1985).
8. *Womanwords*, Jane Mills (Virago, London, 1991).
9. *Women in Love: A Cultural Revolution in Progress*, Shere Hite (Alfred A. Knopf, New York, 1987), p. 202.
10. Jane Mills *op. cit.*, p. 199.
11. *The Spinster and Her Enemies: Feminism and Sexuality 1880–1930*, Sheila Jeffreys (Pandora Press, London, 1985), pp. 86–93.
12. *Victorian Spinsters*, Rosemary Auchmuty (Australian National University, Unpublished PhD thesis, 1975), p. 19, cited in Sheila Jeffreys, *op. cit.*, pp. 35–36.
13. Jane Mills, *op. cit.*, p. 199.
14. Sheila Jeffreys, *op. cit.*, pp. 35–36.
15. *The Poison of Prudery*, Walter Gallichan (T. Werner Laurie, London, 1929), p. 184.
16. *Pure Lust*, Mary Daly (The Women's Press, London, 1984).
17. *The Oxford English Dictionary* (Oxford University Press, Oxford, 1982).
18. *Collins Dictionary of the English Language*, (Ed.) Patrick Hanks (Collins, London, 1979), p. 582.
19. *A New Dictionary of Terms Ancient and Modern of the Canting Crew* (1700), cited in Jane Mills, *op. cit.*, p. 99.
20. *Webster's Ninth New Collegiate Dictionary* (Springfield, Merriam-Webster Inc., 1988).
21. Thomas Szasz, *op. cit.*, pp. 7, 8.
22. Sheila Jeffreys, *op. cit.*, p. 164.
23. *Ibid.*

24. *Frigidity in Women in Relation to her Love Life*, William Stekel (1926) cited in Jane Mills, *op. cit.*, p. 99.
25. *Intercourse*, Andrea Dworkin (Arrow Books, London, 1988), p. 147.
26. *Ibid.*, p. 146.
27. *Ibid.*, p. 148.
28. William Masters and Virginia Johnson, *op. cit.*
29. Anne Koedt, *op. cit.*
30. 'There's Glory For You', Dorothy Hage in *Aphra: The Feminist Literary Magazine* Vol. 3, No. 3, Summer 1972, pp. 2–14.
31. Dale Spender, *op. cit.*
32. Thomas Szasz *op. cit.*, p. 70.
33. *Gyn/Ecology: The Metaethics of Radical Feminism*, Mary Daly (Beacon Press, Boston, 1978), pp. 155–56.
34. *The Women's History of the World*, Rosalind Miles (Paladin, Grafton Books, London, 1988), p. 115.
35. '*The functions and disorders of the reproductive organs in childhood, adult age, and advanced life, considered in their physiological, social and moral relations*', Dr William Acton (1875) cited in *Strong Minded Women*, Janet Horowitz Murray (Penguin, Harmondsworth, 1982), pp. 127, 128.
36. *The Horrors of the Half-known Life: Male Attitudes Towards Women and Sexuality in Nineteenth Century America*, G. J. Barker-Benfield (Harper and Row, New York, 1976), p. 125.
37. *Ibid.*, p. 125.
38. 'Authority and Masturbation: Some Remarks on a Bibliographical Investigation' R. A. Spitz in *Year Book of Pyschoanalysis* Vol. 9 (International Universities Press, New York, 1953), p. 123.
39. *On the Curability of Certain Forms of Insanity, Epilepsy and Hysteria in Females*, Isaac Baker Brown (1866), cited in Janet Horowitz Murray, *op. cit.*, pp. 131–132.
40. Thomas Szasz, *op. cit.*, p. 77.
41. *Woman's Experience of Sex*, Sheila Kitzinger (Penguin, Harmondsworth, 1983), p. 25.
42. Naomi Wolf, *op. cit.*, p. 144.
43. *Empire of the Senseless*, Kathy Acker (Pan Books, London, 1988), pp. 11–12. Reprinted by permission of the William Morris Agency Inc. on behalf of the author. Copyright © 1988 by Kathy Acker.

3. Celibacy Begins in the Mind

1. 'The Gift of Sexuality in the Spirit of Celibacy', Sister Hana Zarinah in *Lesbian Nuns: Breaking Silence*, Rosemary Curb and Nancy Manahan (Warner Books, New York, 1985), p. 130.
2. Sally Cline and Dale Spender, *op. cit.*
3. 'A Time to Refrain from Embracing', Polly Blue, in *Sex and God*, (Ed.) Linda Hurcombe, (Routledge and Kegan Paul, New York, 1987), p. 55.
4. *Ibid.*, p. 55.
5. *Ibid.*, p. 69.
6. *Ibid.*, p. 55.
7. *Ibid.*, p. 55.
8. *Gyn/Ecology: The Metaethics of Radical Feminism*, Mary Daly (Beacon Press, Boston, 1978), p. 3 of Introduction.
9. Polly Blue, *op. cit.*, p. 55.
10. *Ibid.*, p. 66.
11. *Ibid.*, p. 67.

12. *Ibid.*, p. 64.
13. *Ibid.*, p. 68.
14. Rosemary Curb and Nancy Manahan, *op. cit.*, p. 130.
15. *Ibid.*, p. 130.
16. *Ibid.*, p. 130.

4. Spirituality? A Simple Life? Or Just Sheer Spite?

1. United Nations Figures, 1975–1985.
2. *Working Your Way to the Bottom: The Feminization of Poverty*, Hilda Scott (Pandora Press, London, 1984).
3. Sally Cline and Dale Spender, *op. cit.*; *Father-Daughter Incest*, Judith Lewis Herman (Harvard University Press, Cambridge, Mass., 1981); *The Conspiracy of Silence*, Sandra Butler (Bantam Books, New York, 1979); *Sexual Abuse of Children in the United Kingdom*, Beezley Mrazek, P. M. Lynch and A. Bentovim, (Unpublished manuscript, 1981), cited in 'Violence Against Women', Jalna Hanmer in *The Changing Experience of Women* Unit 15 (Open University Press, Milton Keynes, 1993).
4. Sally Cline and Dale Spender, *op. cit.*, p. 177.
5. 'Self-reported Likelihood of Sexually Aggressive Behaviour: Attitudinal Versus Sexual Explanations', John Briere and Neil M. Malamuth in *Journal of Research in Personality* Vol. 37, 1986, pp. 315–318; *I Never Called It Rape*, (Harper and Row, New York, 1988), p. 83.
6. *Women's Spirituality: Resources for Christian Development*, (Ed.) Joann Wolski Conn (Paulist Press, New York, 1986), p. 2.
7. *Ibid.*, p. 3.
8. 'Family Structure and Feminine Personality', Nancy Choderow in *Woman, Culture and Society*, (Eds.) M. Z. Rozaldo and L. Lamphere (Stanford University Press, Stanford, 1974), pp. 43–44.
9. *Reproduction of Mothering*, Nancy Choderow (University of California Press, Berkeley, 1978), pp. 150, 166, 167.
10. *Identity: Youth and Crisis*, Erik Erikson (W. W. Norton, New York, 1968).
11. *In a Different Voice*, Carol Gilligan (Harvard University Press, Cambridge, Mass., 1982), p. 16.

5. Convent Girls and Impossible Passions

1. *There's Something About a Convent Girl*, (Eds.) Jackie Bennett and Rosemary Forgan (Virago, London, 1991), p. 37.
2. *Jean Rhys*, Carole Angier (André Deutsch, London, 1990), p. 25.
3. Jackie Bennett and Rosemary Forgan, *op. cit.*, p. 90.
4. Carole Angier *op. cit.*, p. 25.
5. Jackie Bennett and Rosemary Forgan *op. cit.*, p. 27.
6. *Birth Control in Jewish Law*, D. M. Feldman (New York University Press, New York, 1968), in *Sex: Facts, Frauds and Follies*, Thomas Szasz (Basil Blackwell, Oxford, 1981), p. 104.
7. *Ibid.*, p. 110.
8. Polly Blue *op. cit.*, pp. 69–70.
9. *Alone of All Her Sex: The Myth and the Cult of the Virgin Mary*, Marina Warner (Picador, London, 1985), p. 54.
10. *Ibid.*, p. 55.
11. *Ibid.*, p. 55.
12. *Ibid.*, p. 56.
13. *The Gospel According to Woman*, Karen Armstrong (Elm Tree Books,

London, 1986).
14.   *The Female Eunuch*, Germaine Greer (MacGibbon and Kee, London, 1970), p. 218.
15.   Karen Armstrong, *op. cit.* p. 247.
16.   *The Oxford English Dictionary*, (Oxford University Press, Oxford, 1982).

6. Celibacy is More Than Chastity

1.   *Collins Dictionary of the English Language*, (Ed.) Patrick Hanks (Collins, London, 1979), p. 257.
2.   *The Second Sex*, Simone de Beauvoir (Alfred A. Knopf, New York, 1957), cited in *Womanwords*, Jane Mills (Virago, London, 1991), p. 42.
3.   'The Nature of Women in Society', Introduction to *Defining Females:The Nature of Women in Society*, (Ed.) Shirley Ardener (John Wiley, New York, 1978), p. 36.
4.   *Womanwords*, Jane Mills (Virago, London, 1991), p. 43.
5.   Shere Hite, *op. cit.*, pp. 225–270; *The New Sex Therapy*, Helen Singer Kaplan (Brunner-Mazel, New York, 1974); *Understanding the Female Orgasm*, Seymour Fischer (Bantam Books, New York, 1973); Naomi Wolf, *op. cit.*, p. 147; Sally Cline and Dale Spender, *op. cit.*, pp. 96–109.
6.   *The Treasury of Humorous Quotations*, (Ed.) Evan Esar (English Ed. Nicolas Bentley (Phoenix House, London, 1951), p. 131.
7.   *Ibid.*, p. 61.
8.   *Ibid.*, p. 147.
9.   'Sacred ritual' is an apt phrase of Sheila Jeffreys' in *anticlimax*, Sheila Jeffreys (The Women's Press, London, 1990), p. 315.
10.   Dale Spender, *op. cit.*
11.   *Language, Thought and Reality: Selected Writings of Benjamin Lee Whorf*, (Ed.) John B. Carrol (MIT Press, Cambridge, Mass., 1976).
12.   *Single Minded: Aspects of Chastity*, Michael Adams (Four Courts), pp. 37–38.
13.   *Ibid.*, p. 49.
14.   *Ibid.*, p. 52.
15.   *Adam, Eve and the Serpent*, Elaine Pagels (Penguin, Harmondsworth, 1990), p. 80.
16.   *Ibid.*, p. 78.
17.   *Ibid.*, p. 79.
18.   *A New Song: Celibate Women in the First Three Christian Centuries*, Jo Ann McNamara (Harrington Park Press, New York, 1985), pp. 1, 2, 3.
19.   'The Conversion of Women to Ascetic Forms of Christianity', Ross Kraemer, Signs 6, 1981, pp. 298–307.
20.   *Marriage as a Trade*, Cicely Hamilton 1909 (The Women's Press, London, 1981).
21.   *Ibid.*, p. 35.
22.   *Ibid.*, p. 35.
23.   *Ibid.*, p. 35.
24.   *Ibid.*, p. 36.
25.   *Ibid.*, p. 35.
26.   *Ibid.*, p. 36.

7. Perpetual Virgins

1.   *If You Can't Live Without Me, Why Aren't You Dead?!*, Cynthia Heimel (Fourth Estate, London, 1991), pp. 97–99.

2. *Ibid.*, pp. 97–99.
3. *Collins Dictionary of the English Language*, (Ed.) Patrick Hanks (Collins, London, 1979), p. 1618.
4. Cicely Hamilton, *op. cit.*, p. 35.
5. Audrey Slaughter in *She* magazine, October 1990.
6. *Ways of Seeing*, John Berger (Penguin, Harmondsworth, 1988), p. 47.
7. 'True Trash' in *Wilderness Tips*, Margaret Atwood (Bloomsbury, London, 1991), p. 9.
8. *Ibid.*, p. 10.
9. *Ibid.*, p. 13.
10. *Ibid.*, p. 10.
11. *Ibid.*, p. 17.
12. *Ibid.*, p. 27.
13. *Ibid.*, p. 36.
14. *Ibid.*, p. 34.
15. *Ibid.*, p. 34.
16. *Ibid.*, p. 32.
17. *Ibid.*, p. 36.
18. Nawal el Saadawi (1982) in Cheris Kramarae and Paula A. Treichler, *op. cit.*, p. 473.
19. *Alone of All Her Sex: The Myth and the Cult of the Virgin Mary*, Marina Warner (Picador, London, 1976), p. xxi.
20. *Ibid.*, p. xx.
21. *Jean Rhys*, Carole Angier (André Deutsch, London, 1991), p. 25.
22. *A New Song: Celibate Women in the First Three Christian Centuries*, Jo Ann McNamara (Harrington Park Press, New York, 1985). p. 2.
23. *Ibid.*, p. 3.
24. *Ibid.*, p. 3.
25. *Ibid.*, p. 3.
26. *Ibid.*, p. 3.
27. *Ibid.*, p. 4.
28. *Ibid.*, p. 56.
29. *Acts of Paul and Thecla*, a second century popular romance cited by Jo Ann McNamara, *op. cit.*, p. 68.
30. Jo Ann McNamara, *op. cit.*, p. 36.
31. Jo Ann McNamara, *op. cit.*, pp. 5, 68, 71–2.
32. *Pure Lust*, Mary Daly (The Women's Press, London, 1984), p. 262.
33. *The Trial of Joan of Arc Being the Verbatim Report of the Proceedings from the Orleans Manuscript*, (Trans.) M.S. Scott (Associated Booksellers, Westbrook, Conn., 1956), p. 79.
34. *Ibid.*, p. 110.
35. *Intercourse*, Andrea Dworkin (Arrow Books, London, 1988), p. 111.
36. *Ibid.*, p. 99.
37. *Ibid.*, p. 100.
38. *A Passion for Friends: Toward a Philosophy of Female Affection*, Janice Raymond (The Women's Press, London, 1986), p. 69.
39. *Ibid.*, p. 69.
40. Sozomen quoted in *Prostitution and Society*, Fernando Henriques (Citadel, New York, 1962), p. 23.
41. *Ibid.*, p. 41.
42. Letter of Martin Luther, 6 August 1524, quoted in *Not in God's Image: Women in History from the Greeks to the Victorians*, (Eds.) Julia O'Faolain and Laura Martines (Harper, New York, 1973), p. 196.

43.   Albert Ellis, *The Journal of Sex Research* Vol. 5, No. 1, February 1969, pp. 41–9.

8. Endangered Species

1.   *Chaste Liberation: Celibacy and Female Cultural Status*, Sally Kitch (University of Illinois Press, Urbana and Chicago, 1989), p. 8.
2.   'Timewatch: The Shakers', BBC2, 17 October 1990.
3.   *Ibid.*
4.   *Ibid.*
5.   Sally Kitch, *op. cit.*, p. 6.
6.   *Intercourse*, Andrea Dworkin (Arrow Books, London, 1988), p. 127.
7.   Sally Kitch, *op. cit.*, pp. 7, 8.
8.   Sally Kitch, *op. cit.*, p. 7.
9.   Sally Kitch, *op. cit.*, p. 7.
10.   Sally Kitch, *op. cit.*, p. 8.
11.   *The Shaker Holy Land: A Community Portrait*, Edward R. Horgan (Harvard Common Press, Harvard, Mass., 1982), pp. 8–9, cited in Sally Kitch, *op. cit.*, p. 139.
12.   Edward R. Horgan, *op. cit.*, pp. 8–9.
13.   Edward R. Horgan, *op. cit.*, p. 10.
14.   *The American Shakers: From Neo-Christianity to Presocialism*, Henri Desroche, (Trans. and Ed.) John K. Savacool (University of Massachusetts Press, Amherst, Mass., 1971), p. 29.
15.   'The Testimony of Christ's Second Appearing', Benjamin Youngs et al., quoted in *Gleanings from Old Shaker Journals*, (Comp.) Clara Endicott Sears (Houghton Mifflin; Riverside Press, Boston, 1916), pp. 13–14.
16.   Sally Kitch, *op. cit.*, p. 9.
17.   'Timewatch: The Shakers', BBC2, 17 October 1990.
18.   Sally Kitch, *op. cit.*, pp. 32, 33.
19.   Sally Kitch, *op. cit.*, p. 48.
20.   Sally Kitch, *op. cit.*, p. 54.
21.   Sally Kitch, *op. cit.*, p. 34.
22.   Sally Kitch, *op. cit.*, p. 36.
23.   Sally Kitch, *op. cit.*, p. 136.
24.   *The Motherhood of God*, Anna White (Press of Berkshire Industrial Farm, New York, 1903), pp. 21–22.
25.   *God, – Dual*, Nicholas Briggs (East Canterbury, New Hampshire), p. 3, cited in Sally Kitch, *op. cit.*, p. 54.
26.   'Should All Be Shakers?', Frederick W. Evans in *The Shaker Manifesto* 8 April 1878, p. 92.
27.   'Timewatch: The Shakers', BBC2, 17 October 1990.
28.   *Ibid.*
29.   *Shakers, Correspondence Between Mary F. Carr of Mt Holly City and a Shaker Sister Sarah Lucas of Union Village*, (Ed.) R. W. Pelham (Union Village, Ohio, 1868), p. 21.
30.   *The People Called Shakers*, Edward D. Andrews (Dover Publications, New York, 1963), pp. 232–35.
31.   'Timewatch: The Shakers', BBC2, 17 October 1990.
32.   Sally Kitch, *op. cit.*, p. 9.
33.   'Shaker Demographic 1840 to 1900', William Bainbridge in *Journal for the Scientific Study of Religion* 21, 1982, p. 355.
34.   'Woman's Mission', Anna White in *The Manifesto*, (21 January 1891),

pp. 3–4.

35.   'Sketches of Shakers and Shakerism' from *Synopsis of the Theology of the United Society of Believers in Christ's Second Appearing*, G. Avery (Weed Parsons Printers, New York, 1883), p. 12.

36.   *Celibacy from the Shaker Standpoint*, Frederick W. Evans (Davies and Kent, New York, 1866), p. 8.

37.   'Dani Sexuality: A Low Energy System', Karl G. Heider in *Man* (New Series) Vol. 2, No. 2, p. 188, cited in *Sex and Destiny*, Germaine Greer (Secker and Warburg, London, 1984), p. 86.

38.   *Ibid.*, p. 87.

39.   *Ibid.*, p. 204.

40.   'Longevity of Virgin Celibates', G. Avery in *The Celibate Shaker Life*, Elijah Myrick (Mount Lebanon, 1889), p. 8.

41.   *Sex and Destiny*, Germaine Greer (Secker and Warburg, London, 1984), p. 102.

42.   *Just Desserts: Women and Food*, Sally Cline (André Deutsch, London, 1990).

43.   *Human Sexual Behaviour: Variations in the Ethnographic Spectrum*, Donald S. Marshall and Robert C. Suggs (Basic Books, New York, 1970).

44.   *Sexual Conduct: The Sources of Human Sexuality*, John Gagnon and William Simon (Aldine, Chicago, 1973).

45.   *The Myth of the Vaginal Orgasm*, Anne Koedt (Know Inc. Women's Printing Collective, 1970).

9. Celibate Sisters

1.   *Chaste Liberation: Celibacy and Female Cultural Status*, Sally Kitch (University of Illinois Press, Urbana and Chicago, 1989), pp. 63, 187.

2.   *Surpassing the Love of Men: Romantic Friendships and Love Between Women from the Renaissance to the Present*, Lillian Faderman (Junction Books, London, 1981), p. 191.

3.   'A Woman's Community in Texas', George Pierce Garrison in *The Charities Review* 3, November 1983, p. 29.

4.   'Mrs McWhirter and Her Community of Celibate Women in Washington: They Migrated There from Belton, Texas: How They Work and Prosper in their New Home', *The Waco Weekly Tribune*, 20 July 1901, George Pierce Garrison Papers, Barker Texas History Center, The General Libraries, The University of Texas at Austin.

5.   Mainly their constitution, printed in 1902; several interviews; the testimony of Martha McWhirter at her daughter's divorce; a manuscript about McWhirter's spiritual experience. Also Sally Kitch, *op. cit.*

6.   Sally Kitch, *op. cit.*, p. 103.

7.   Sally Kitch, *op. cit.*, p. 49.

8.   'The Woman's Commonwealth of Washington', in *Margarita Gerry Ainslee's Magazine*, September 1902, p. 138.

9.   Martha McWhirter quoted in 'Sanctificationists of Belton', Eleanor James in *The American West* 2, Summer 1965, p. 68.

10.   Testimony of Martha McWhirter, quoted in *Haymond v Haymond, Interrogatories*, Nos. 8, 10.

11.   Martha McWhirter quoted in 'The Woman's Commonwealth: Separatism, Self, Sharing', Gwendolyn Wright in *Architectural Association Quarterly* 6, Fall-Winter 1974, p. 370.

12.   Testimony of Ada Haymond, 'Haymond v Haymond', *Southwestern*

Reporter, p. 91.
13.	Sally Kitch, *op. cit.*, p. 107.
14.	'Story of Women's Hotel One of Most Interesting in Life of Historic Belton', John R. Lumsford Temple (Texas). Telegram, 24 November 1929, George Pierce Garrison Papers, *op. cit.*
15.	'The Woman's Commonwealth of Washington', *op. cit.*
16.	Martha McWhirter quoted in *Life and Spiritual Experience of Martha McWhirter, Leader and Founder of the Woman's Commonwealth*, p. 14, paper probably written by Margarita Gerry, cited in Sally Kitch, *op. cit.*, p. 106.
17.	Sally Kitch, *op. cit.*, p. 104.
18.	Sally Kitch, *op. cit.*, p. 108.
19.	'The Woman's Commonwealth', A. H. Mattox in *Social Service*, 4 November 1901, p. 170.
20.	Sally Kitch, *op. cit.*, p. 108.
21.	*Gatesville (Texas) Star Messenger* 24 April 1908.
22.	Sally Kitch, *op. cit.*, pp. 151, 166.

10. Creative Solitude

1.	*The School of Genius*, Anthony Storr (André Deutsch, London, 1988), p. 11.
2.	*Ibid.*, p. 93.
3.	Gloria Steinem in an interview with Yvonne Roberts, *The Observer*, January 12 1992, talking about her book *Revolution from Within* (Bloomsbury, London, 1992).
4.	*Stevie Smith Selected Poems*, (Ed.) James MacGibbon (Penguin, London, 1978), p. 18.
5.	from 'Dirge', in *The Collected Poems of Stevie Smith* (Penguin 20th Century Classics) by permission of James MacGibbon.
6.	*The Holiday*, Stevie Smith, Introduction by Janet Watts (Virago, London, 1979), p. ix; *The Collected Poems of Stevie Smith*, (Penguin, Harmondsworth, 1985), p. 186.
7.	*Stevie Smith Selected Poems*, (Ed.) James MacGibbon (Penguin, Harmondsworth, 1978), p. 282.
8.	*Emily Brontë: A Chainless Soul*, Katherine Frank (Hamish Hamilton, London, 1990), pp. 1, 2.
9.	*Ibid.*, p. 13.
10.	*The Complete Poems of Emily Jane Brontë*, (Ed.) C.W. Hatfield (Columbia University Press, New York, 1941), p. 128.
11.	*Ibid.*, p. 163.
12.	Katherine Frank, *op. cit.*, pp. 1, 2.
13.	*The Franchise Affair*, Josephine Tey (Penguin, London, 1948), pp. 15, 250, 251.
14.	*My Day*, Jean Rhys (Frank Hallman, New York, 1975).
15.	'Close Season for the Old', in *My Day*, Jean Rhys (Frank Hallman, New York, 1975).
16.	*Jean Rhys: Letters 1931–66*, (Eds.) Francis Wyndham and Diana Melly (Penguin, Harmondsworth, 1985), p. 12.
17.	*My Day*, Jean Rhys (Frank Hallman, New York, 1975).
18.	*Silences*, Tillie Olsen (Virago, London, 1980), p. 12.
19.	*Ibid.*, p. 13.
20.	*Momma: A Start on All the Untold Stories*, Alta (Times Change Press, New York, 1974), pp. 7, 8.

21.   *Journal of a Solitude*, May Sarton (The Women's Press, London, 1973), pp. 1, 14, 15.
22.   *A Life of One's Own*, Joanna Field (Marion Milner) (Virago, London, 1986), p. 18.

Bibliography
and Further Reading

Abbott, Sidney and Love, Barbara *Sappho was a Right-on Woman: A Liberated View of Lesbianism* (Stein and Day, New York, 1973).

Acker, Kathy *Blood and Guts in High School, plus two* (Picador/Pan Books, London, 1984).

Acker, Kathy *Empire of the Senseless* (Picador/Pan Books, London, 1988).

Ardener, Shirley (Ed.) *Defining Females: The Nature of Women in Society* (Croom Helm in association with the Oxford University Women's Studies Committee, London, 1978).

Armstrong, Karen *The Gospel According to Woman, Christianity's Creation of the Sex War in the West* (Elm Tree Books, London, 1986).

Bancroft, Anne *Weavers of Wisdom. Women Mystics of the Twentieth Century* (Arkana, Penguin, Harmondsworth, 1989).

Barfoot, Joan *Gaining Ground* (The Women's Press, London, 1980).

Barry, Kathleen *Female Sexual Slavery* (New York University Press, New York, 1984).

Beauvoir, Simone de *After 'The Second Sex' (Conversations with Simone de Beauvoir and Alice Schwarzer)* (Pantheon, New York, 1986).

Benevento, Nicole (Ed.) *Building Feminist Theory: Essays from Quest, A Feminist Quarterly* (Longman, New York, 1981).

Bengis, Ingrid *Combat in the Erogenous Zone* (Quartet Books, London, 1974).

Bennett, Paula *Emily Dickinson: Woman Poet* (Harvester Wheatsheaf, Brighton, 1990).

Bennett, Jackie and Forgan, Rosemary (Eds.) *There's Something about a Convent Girl* (Virago, London, 1991).

Bernard, Jessie S. *The Future of Marriage* (Yale University Press, New Haven, 1972).

Bernard, Jessie S. *The Future of Motherhood* (Dial Press, New York, 1974).

Bernard, Jessie S. *The Female World* (Free Press, New York, 1981).

Blumstein, Philip and Schwartz, Pepper *American Couples: Money, Work, Sex* (William Morrow & Co., New York, 1983).

Bode, Janet *View from Another Closet. Exploring Bisexuality in Women* (Hawthorn Books Inc., New York, 1976).

Botwin, Carol *Is there Sex after Marriage* (Bantam Books, London, 1990).

Bowles, Gloria and Duelli Klein, Renate (Eds.) *Theories of Women's Studies* (Routledge & Kegan Paul, London, 1983).

Brecher, Ruth and Edward *An Analysis of Human Sexual Response* (Panther, London, 1968).

Brown, Judith C. *Immodest Acts. The Life of a Lesbian Nun in Renaissance Italy* (Oxford University Press, New York and Oxford, 1986).

Brownmiller, Susan *Against Our Will* (Simon & Schuster, New York, 1984).

Bullough, Vern L. *Sexual Variance in Society and History* (University of Chicago Press, Chicago, 1980).

Bunch, Charlotte et al. *Building Feminist Theory: Essays from Quest, A Feminist Quarterly* (Longman, New York, 1981).

Bunch, Charlotte *Feminism in the '80s. Facing Down the Right* (The Inkling Press, Denver Colorado, 1981).

Bunch, Charlotte *Passionate Politics. Feminist Theory in Action. Essays 1968–1986* (St. Antin's Press, New York, 1987).

Butler, Josephine *Women's Work and Women's Culture* (Macmillan, London, 1869) (ix), cited in *The Feminist Dictionary*, p. 140, Kramarae, Cheris and Treichler, Paula A. (Eds.) (Pandora, London, 1985).

Caplan, Pat (Ed.) *The Cultural Construction of Sexuality* (Routledge & Kegan Paul, London, 1989).

Carpenter, Edward *The Intermediate Sex* (George Allen & Unwin, London, 1908).

Cartledge, Sue and Ryan, Joanna (Eds.) *Sex and Love: New Thoughts on Old Contradictions* (The Women's Press, London, 1983).

Clark, Lorenne and Lewis, Debra *Rape: The Price of Coercive Sexuality* (The Women's Press, Toronto, 1977).

Cline, Sally and Spender, Dale *Reflecting Men at Twice Their Natural Size* (André Deutsch, London, 1987).

Cline, Sally *Just Desserts: Women and Food* (André Deutsch, London, 1990)

Clunis, D. Merilee and Green, G. Dorsey *Lesbian Couples* (Seal Press, Seattle, Washington, 1988).

Cohen, Steve; Green, Stephanie; Jones, Gay; Merryfinch, Lesley; Slade, Janet and Walker, Maggie *The Law and Sexuality. How to Cope with the Law if You're not 100% Conventionally Heterosexual* (Grass Roots Books Ltd. and Manchester Law Centre, Manchester, 1978).

Comfort, Alex (Ed.) *The Joy of Sex. A Gourmet Guide to Lovemaking* (Quartet Books, London, 1974).

Conn, Joann Wolski *Women's Spirituality. Resources for Christian Development* (Paulist Press, New Jersey, 1986).

Connor, Steven *Postmodernist Culture. An Introduction to Theories of the Contemporary* (Basil Blackwell Ltd., Oxford, 1989).

Corea, Gene *The Mother Machine* (Harper & Row, New York, 1985).

Corea, Gene; Duelli Klein, R.; Hanner, J. et al. *Hutchinson Education in Association with the Explorations in Feminism Collective* (Pergamon Press, London, 1986).

Coveney, Lal; Jackson, Margaret; Jeffreys, Sheila; Kay, Leslie and Mahony, Pat *The Sexuality Papers. Male Sexuality and the Social Control of Women* (Hutchinson in association with the Explorations in Feminism Collective, London, 1984).

Covina, Gina and Galana, Laurel (Eds.) *The Lesbian Reader* (Amazon Press, California, 1975).

Coward, Rosalind *Female Desire. Women's Sexuality Today* (Paladin, London, 1984).

Cruikshank, Margaret *Lesbian Studies, Present and Future* (The Feminist Press, New York, 1982).

Curb, Rosemary and Manahan, Nancy *Lesbian Nuns: Breaking Silence* (Warner Books & The Naiad Press Inc., New York, 1985).

Daly, Mary *Gyn/Ecology: The Metaethics of Radical Feminism* (The Women's Press, London, 1979).

Daly, Mary *Pure Lust: Elemental Feminist Philosophy* (The Women's Press, London, 1984).

Daly, Mary *Beyond God the Father: Toward a Philosophy of Women's Liberation* (Beacon Press, Boston, 1985).

Davenport-Hines, Richard *Sex, Death and Punishment. Attitudes to Sex and Sexuality in Britain since the Renaissance* (Collins, London, 1990).

Davis, Angela *Women, Race and Class* (The Women's Press, London, 1982).

Dworkin, Andrea *Our Blood* (The Women's Press, London, 1982).

Dworkin, Andrea *Right-Wing Women: The Politics of Domesticated Females* (The Women's Press, London, 1983).

Dworkin, Andrea *Ice and Fire* (Secker & Warburg, London, 1986).

Dworkin, Andrea *Intercourse* (Arrow Books, London, 1988).

Dworkin, Andrea *Letters from a War Zone, Writings 1976–1987* (Secker & Warburg, London, 1988).

Ehrenreich, Barbara and English, Deidre *Witches, Midwives and Nurses: A History of Women Healers* (Glass Mountain Pamphlet No. 1, Compendium, London, 1974).

Ehrenreich, Barbara and English, Deidre *Complaints and Disorders: The Sexual Politics of Sickness* (Glass Mountain Pamphlet No. 2, Compendium, London, 1974).

Ehrenreich, Barbara and English, Deidre *For Her Own Good: 150 Years of the Experts' Advice to Women* (Pluto Press, London, 1979).

Ehrenreich, Barbara *The Hearts of Men: American Dreams and the Flight from Commitment* (Anchor Press/Doubleday, New York, 1983).

Eichenbaum, Luise and Orbach, Susie *What Do Women Want? Exploding the Myth of Female Dependency* (Fontana/Collins, Glasgow, 1984).

Eichler, Margrit *The Double Standard: A Feminist Critique of Feminist Social Science* (St. Martin's Press, New York, 1980).

Ellis, Havelock *Psychology of Sex* (William Heinemann, London, 1944).

Erkhardt, Anke A. and Money, John *Man & Woman, Boy & Girl: Differentiation and Dimorphism of Gender Identity from Contraception to Maturity* (Johns Hopkins University Press, Baltimore, 1972).

Ettore, E. M. *Lesbians, Women and Society* (Routledge & Kegan Paul, London, 1980).

Faderman, Lillian *Surpassing the Love of Men: Romantic Friendship and Love between Women from the Renaissance to the Present* (Junction Books, London, 1980).

Feminist Review (Ed.) *Sexuality: A Reader* (Virago, London, 1987).

Finkelhor, David and Kersti, Yllo *License to Rape: Sexual Abuse of Wives* (Holt, Reinhart & Winston, New York, 1986).

Firestone, Shulamith *The Dialectic of Sex* Revised Edition (Bantam, New York, 1971).

Fitzgerald, Maureen; Guberman, Connie and Wolfe, Margie (Eds.) *Still Ain't Satisfied: Canadian Feminism Today* (The Women's Press, Toronto, 1982).

Fitzgerald, Penelope *Charlotte Mew and Her Friends* (Collins, London, 1984).

Fleming, Lee (Ed.) *By Word of Mouth: Lesbians Write the Erotic* (Gynergy Books, Charlottetown, 1989).

Ford, C. S. and Beach, F. A. *Patterns of Sexual Behaviour* (University Paperbacks, Methuen, London, 1965).

Forster, Margaret *Significant Sisters: The Grassroots of Active Feminism, 1839–1939* (Alfred A. Knopf, New York, 1985).

Foucault, Michel *The History of Sexuality. Vol. 1: An Introduction* (Trans.) Robert Hurley (Pantheon, New York, 1978).

Foucault, Michel *The History of Sexuality. Vol. 2: The Uses of Pleasure* (Trans.) Robert Hurley (Pantheon, New York, 1985).

Foucault, Michel *The Care of the Self* (Pantheon, New York, 1987).

Freedman, Estelle B.; Gelpi, Barbara C.; Johnson, Susan L. and Weston, Kathleen M. (Eds.) *The Lesbian Issue: Essays from SIGNS* (The University of Chicago Press, Chicago, 1982).

Freeman, Jo *The Politics of Women's Liberation* (Longman, White Plains, New York, 1975).

Friday, Nancy *My Secret Garden: Women's Sexual Fantasies* (Quartet Books, London, 1975).

Friday, Nancy *Women on Top: How Real Life has Changed Women's Sexual Fantasies* (Hutchinson, London, 1991).

Friedman, Scarlet and Sarah, Elizabeth (Eds.) *On the Problem of Men: Two Feminist Conferences* (The Women's Press, London, 1982).

Fritz, Leah *Thinking like a Woman* (Win Books, New York, 1975).

Gawain, Shakti *Creative Visualization* (Bantam New Age Books, London, 1979).

Gilligan, Carol *In a Different Voice: Psychological Theory and Women's Development* (Harvard University Press, Cambridge, Mass., 1982).

Gossip (Journal) Nos. 3, 4, 5 and 6 (Onlywomen Press, London).

Grahn, Judy *Another Mother Tongue: Gay Words, Gay Worlds* (Beacon Press, Boston, 1984).

Greer, Germaine *Sex and Destiny: The Politics of Human Fertility* (Secker & Warburg, London, 1984).

Greer, Germaine *The Change: Women, Ageing and the Menopause* (Hamish Hamilton, London, 1991).

Griffin, Susan *Pornography and Silence* (The Women's Press, London, 1981).

Hamilton, Cicely *Marriage as a Trade* (The Women's Press, London, 1981).

Hanks, Patrick *Collins Dictionary of the English Language* (Collins, London, 1979).

Hanmer, Jalna and Saunders, Sheila *Well-Founded Fear: A Community Study of Violence to Women* (Hutchinson in association with the Explorations in Feminism Collective, London, 1984).

Harding, Sandra and Hintikka, Merrill B. (Eds.) *Discovering Reality: Feminist Perspectives on Epistemology, Metaphysics, Methodology and Philosophy of Science* (D. Reidel Publishing, Holland, 1983).

Hartsock, Nancy C. *Money, Sex and Power: Toward a Feminist Historical Materialism* (Northeastern University Press, Boston, 1985).

Heath, Stephen *The Sexual Fix* (Macmillan, London, 1982).

Heimel, Cynthia *If You Can't Live Without Me, Why Aren't You Dead?* (Fourth Estate, London, 1991).

Henley, Nancy M. *Body Politics: Power, Sex and Nonverbal Communication* (Prentice-Hall Inc., New Jersey, 1977).

Hite, Shere *The Hite Report: A Nationwide Study of Female Sexuality* (Macmillan, New York, 1976).

Hite, Shere *The Hite Report on Male Sexuality* (Alfred A. Knopf, New York, 1981).

Hite, Shere and Colleran, Kate *Good Guys, Bad Guys and Other Lovers: Every Woman's Guide to Relationships* (Pandora, London, 1989).

Hoagland, Sarah Lucia *Lesbian Ethics* (Institute of Lesbian Studies, California, 1988).

Hochschild, Arlie Russell *The Managed Heart: Commercialization of Human Feeling* (University of California Press, Berkeley, 1983).

Hodgkinson, Liz *Sex is not Compulsory* (Sphere Books Ltd., London, 1986).

Hollinghurst, Alan *The Swimming Pool Library* (Penguin, Harmondsworth, 1988).

Holly, Lesley (Ed.) *Girls and Sexuality: Teaching and Learning* (Open University Press, Milton Keynes & Philadelphia, 1989).

Holmstrom, Lynda Lytle and Burgess, Ann Wolbert *The Victim of Rape: Institutional Reactions* (Transaction Books, New Brunswick, 1983).

Hooks, Bell *Feminist Theory: From Margin to Center* (South End Press, Boston, Mass., 1984).

Hopkins, June *Perspectives on Rape and Sexual Assault* (Harper & Row, London, 1984).

Humm, Maggie *The Dictionary of Feminist Theory* (Harvester Wheatsheaf, Brighton, 1989).

Hunter College Women's Studies Collective *Women's Realities, Women's Choices: An Introduction to Women's Studies* (Oxford University Press, Oxford, 1983).

Hurcombe, Linda (Ed.) *Sex and God: Some Varieties of Women's Religious Experience* (Routledge & Kegan Paul, London, 1987).

Hutcheon, Linda *A Poetics of Postmodernism: History, Theory, Fiction* (Routledge & Kegan Paul, London, 1988).

Jackson, Stevi *On the Social Construction of Female Sexuality* (Women's Research & Resources Centre Publications, London, 1978).

Jagger, Alison M. and Struhl, Paula Rothenberg *Feminist Frameworks: Alternative Theoretical Accounts of the Relations between Women and Men* (McGraw-Hill Book Company, New York, 1978).

Jagger, Alison M. *Feminist Politics and Human Nature* (Rowman & Littlefield, Totowa, N.J., 1988).

Janssen-Jurreit, Marie Louise *Sexism: The Male Monopoly on History and Thought* (Farrar, Straus & Giroux, New York, 1976).

Jeffreys, Sheila *The Spinster and Her Enemies: Feminism and Sexuality 1880–1930* (Pandora Press, London, 1985).

Jeffreys, Sheila *Anticlimax: A Feminist Perspective on the Sexual Revolution* (The Women's Press, London, 1990).

Jones, Carol & Mahoney, Pat (Eds.) *Learning Our Lines: Sexuality and Social Control in Education* (The Women's Press, London, 1989).

Karlen, Arno *Sexuality and Homosexuality* (MacDonald, London, 1971).

Kennedy, Mopsy Strange *The Sexual Revolution Just Keeps on Coming, Mother Jones*, 25–9 December 1976.

Kessler, Suzanne and McKenna, Wendy *Gender: An Ethnomethodological Approach* (John Wiley & Sons Inc., New York, 1978).

Kinsey, Alfred C. et al *Sexual Behavior in the Human Female* (W. B. Saunders & Company, Philadelphia, 1953).

Kitch, Sally L. *Chaste Liberation: Celibacy and Female Cultural Status* (University of Illinois Press, Illinois, 1989).

Kitzinger, Sheila *Women's Experience of Sex* (Penguin, Harmondsworth, 1985).

Kramarae, Cheris and Treichler, Paula A. *The Feminist Dictionary* (Pandora, London, 1985).

Lennert, Midge & Willson, Norma (Eds.) *A Woman's New World Dictionary* (Lomita, California, 51% Publications Pamphlet, Special Collections, Northwestern University Library, Evanston, Illinois, 1973).

Linden, Ruth Robin et al. (Eds.) *Against Sadomasochism: A Radical Feminist Analysis* (Frog in the Well, California, 1982).

Loulan, Jo Ann *Lesbian Sex* (Spinsters/Aunt Lute, San Francisco, 1984).

Loulan, Jo Ann *Lesbian Passion: Loving Ourselves and Each Other* (Spinsters/Aunt Lute, San Francisco, 1987).

MacGibbon, James (Ed.) *Stevie Smith: Selected Poems* (Penguin, Harmondsworth, 1978).

Mailer, Norman *The Prisoner of Sex* (Sphere Books, London, 1972).

Manning, Rosemary *A Time and A Time* (Calder & Boyers, London, 1971).

Manning, Rosemary *A Corridor of Mirrors* (The Women's Press, London, 1987).
Marks, Elaine and Courtivron, Isabella de (Eds.) *New French Feminism: An Anthology* (Schocken Books, New York, 1981).
Martin, Del and Lyon, Phyllis *Lesbian Woman* (Bantam, New York, 1972).
McEwan, Christian and O'Sullivan, Sue (Eds.) *Out the Other Side: Contemporary Lesbian Writing* (Virago, London, 1988).
McNamara, Jo Ann *A New Song: Celibate Women in the First Three Christian Centuries* (Harrington Park Press, New York, 1985).
Meulenbelt, Anja *For Ourselves: From Women's Point of View: Our Bodies and Sexuality* (Sheba Feminist Publishers, London, 1981).
Miller, Henry *Tropic of Capricorn* (Grafton Books, London, 1966).
Millett, Kate *Sexual Politics* (Doubleday, New York, 1970).
Millett, Kate *Sita* (Virago, London, 1977).
Mills, Jane *Womanwords: A Vocabulary of Culture and Patriarchal Society* (Virago, London, 1991).
Morgan, Robin *The Anatomy of Freedom* (Martin Robertson, Oxford, 1983).
Morgan, Robin (Ed.) *Sisterhood is Global: The International Women's Movement Anthology* (Penguin, London, 1985).
Murray, Janet Horowitz *Strong-Minded Women, and Other Lost Voices from Nineteenth Century England* (Penguin, Harmondsworth, 1984).
Nestle, Joan *A Restricted County: Essays and Short Stories* (Sheba Feminist Publishers, London, 1987).
O'Barr, Jean F. *Signs: Journal of Women in Culture and Society* Spring 1988, Vol. 13, No. 3 (The University of Chicago Press, Chicago, 1988).
Olsen, Tillie *Silences* (Virago, London, 1980).
Onlywomen Press *Love Your Enemy? The Debate Between Heterosexual Feminism and Political Lesbianism* (Onlywomen Press Ltd., London, 1981).
Ortner, Sherry B. And Whitehead, Harriet (Eds.) *Sexual Meanings: The Cultural Construction of Gender and Sexuality* (Cambridge University Press, Cambridge, 1981).
Osman, Sona, 'A to Z of Feminism', *Spare Rib*, 27–30 November 1983.
Pagels, Elaine *The Gnostic Gospels* (Penguin, Harmondsworth, 1982).
Pagels, Elaine *Adam, Eve and the Serpent* (Penguin, Harmondsworth, 1990).
Pankhurst, Sylvia *The Suffragette Movement* (Virago, London, 1977).
Paul, Diana Y. *Women in Buddhism: Images of the Feminine in Mahayana Tradition* (University of California Press, California, 1985).
Patton, Cindy and Kelly, Janis *Making It: A Woman's Guide to Sex in the Age of AIDS* (Firebrand Books, New York, 1987).
Raeburn, Antonia *Militant Suffragettes* (New English Library, London, 1974).
Raeburn, Antonia *The Suffragette View* (David & Charles, London, 1976).
Ranke-Heinemann Uta *Eunuchs for Heaven: The Catholic Church and Sexuality* (Trans.) John Brownjohn (André Deutsch, London, 1990).
Raymond, Janice *A Passion for Friends: Towards a Philosophy of Female Affection* (The Women's Press, London, 1986).
Red Collective *The Politics of Sexuality in Capitalism* (Red Collective and Publications Distribution Co-operative, London, 1973).
Reich, Wilhelm *The Sexual Revolution* (Vision Press Ltd., London, 1951).
Reiter, Rayna R. (Ed.) *Toward an Anthropology of Women* (Monthly Review Press, New York, 1975).
Rich, Adrienne *The Meaning of Our Love for Women is What We Have Constantly to Expand* (Out & Out Books, Pamphlet Series: No. 1, New York, 1977).
Rich, Adrienne *Women and Honor: Some Notes on Lying* (Motheroot Publications/Pittsburgh Women Writers, Pittsburgh, 1977).

Rich, Adrienne *Compulsory Heterosexuality and Lesbian Existence* (Onlywomen Press Ltd., London, 1981).

Root, Jane *Pictures of Women: Sexuality* (Pandora Press, London, 1984).

Rosaldo, Michelle Zimbalist and Lamphere, Louise (Eds.) *Woman, Culture and Society* (Stanford University Press, Stanford, 1974).

Ruether, Rosemary Radford *Religion and Sexism: Images of Women in the Jewish and Christian Traditions* (Simon & Schuster, New York, 1974).

Rule, Jane *Lesbian Images* (Peter Davies, London, 1975).

Russell, Diana E. H. *Rape in Marriage* (Macmillan, New York, 1982).

Sarton, May *As We Are Now* (The Women's Press, London, 1983).

Sarton, May *Journal of a Solitude* (The Women's Press, London, 1985).

Sayers, Janet *Sexual Contradictions: Psychology, Psychoanalysis and Feminism* (Tavistock Publications, London, 1986).

Schaef, Anne Wilson *Women's Reality: An Emerging Female System in a White Male Society* (Winston Press, Minneapolis, Minn., 1987).

Sheba Collective (Eds.) *More Serious Pleasure: Lesbian Erotic Stories and Poetry* (Sheba Feminist Publishers, London, 1990).

Sherfey, Mary Jane M.D. *The Nature and Evolution of Female Sexuality* (Vintage Books, New York, 1973).

Showalter, Elaine *The Female Malady: Women, Madness and English Culture 1830–1980* (Virago, London, 1987).

Smith, Barbara *Towards a Black Feminist Criticism* (Out & Out Books, Pamphlet Series).

Sniton, Ann; Stansell, Christine and Thompson, Sharon (Eds.) *Desire: The Politics of Sexuality* (Virago, London, 1984).

Sontag, Susan *Aids and its Metaphors* (Allen Lane, London, 1988).

Spalding, Frances *Stevie Smith: A Critical Biography* (Faber & Faber, London, 1988).

Spender, Dale *Man Made Language* (Routledge & Kegan Paul, London, 1980).

Spender, Dale (Ed.) *Men's Studies Modified: The Impact of Feminism in the Academic Disciplines* (Pergamon Press, Oxford, 1981).

Spender, Dale *Women of Ideas and What Men Have Done to Them: From Aphra Behn to Adrienne Rich* (Ark, London, 1982).

Spender, Dale (Ed.) *Feminist Theorists: Three Centuries of Women's Intellectual Traditions* (The Women's Press, London, 1983).

Spender, Dale *For the Record: The Making and Meaning of Feminist Knowledge* (The Women's Press, London, 1985).

Spender, Dale *Personal Chronicles: Women's Autobiographical Writings* Women's Studies International Forum, Vol. 10, No. 1, (Pergamon Press, Oxford, 1987).

Spender, Dale *The Writing or the Sex?* (Pergamon Press, Oxford, 1989).

Stanley, Liz (Ed.) *Feminist Praxis: Research, Theory and Epistemology in Feminist Sociology* (Routledge & Kegan Paul, London, 1990).

Stanko, Elizabeth A. *Intimate Intrusions: Women's Experience of Male Violence* (Routledge & Kegan Paul, London, Boston, Melbourne & Henley, 1985).

Steinem, Gloria *Outrageous Acts and Everyday Rebellions* (Jonathan Cape, London, 1984).

Stimpson, Catharine R. *Where the Meanings Are: Feminism and Cultural Spaces* (Methuen, London, 1988).

Stone, Lawrence *The Family, Sex and Marriage* (Harper & Row, New York, 1977).

Stone, Merlin *Ancient Mirrors of Womanhood Vol. 1, Our Goddess and Heroine Heritage* (Sibylline Books, New York, 1979).

Storr, Anthony *The School of Genius* (André Deutsch, London, 1988).

Szasz, Thomas *Sex: Facts, Frauds and Follies* (Basil Blackwell, Oxford, 1980).

Tannen, Deborah *You Just Don't Understand: Women and Men in Conversation* (Virago, London, 1991).

Tilly, Louise A. and Scott, Joan W. *Women, Work and Family* (Holt, Rinehart and Winston, New York, 1978).

Todd, Janet *Women's Friendship in Literature* (Columbia University Press, New York, 1980).

Tsuzuki, Chushichi *Edward Carpenter 1844–1929: Prophet of Human Fellowship* (Cambridge University Press, Cambridge, 1980).

Tuchman, Gaye; Daniels, Arlene Kaplan and Benet, James *Hearth & Home: Images of Women in Mass Media* (Oxford University Press, New York, 1978).

Vance, Carole S. (Ed.) *Pleasure and Danger: Exploring Female Sexuality*, (Routledge & Kegan Paul, London, 1984).

Vetterling-Braggin, Mary (Ed.) *Sexist Language: A Modern Philosophical Analysis* (Littlefield, Adams & Co., 1981).

Warner, Marina *Joan of Arc: The Image of Female Heroism* (Weidenfeld & Nicholson, London, 1981).

Warner, Marina *Alone of All Her Sex: The Myth and the Cult of the Virgin Mary* (Picador, London, 1985).

Weeks, Jeffrey *Coming Out: Homosexual Politics in Britain, from the Nineteenth Century to the Present* (Quartet Books, London, 1977).

Weeks, Jeffrey *Sexuality and its Discontents: Meaning, Myths and Modern Sexualities* (Routledge, London, 1985).

Whisler, Sandra M. 'The Celibacy Letters', *Heresies 3:4*, (Issue 12, pp. 26–8, 1981).

Whitehead, Alfred North *Process and Reality: An Essay in Cosmology* (Harper & Bros., New York, 1929).

Wittig, Monique and Zeig, Sande *Lesbian Peoples: Materials for a Dictionary* (Virago, London, 1980).

Wolf, Naomi *The Beauty Myth* (Vintage, London, 1991).

Wolff, Charlotte *Bisexuality: A Study*(Quartet Books, London, 1977).

Wright, Stephen (Ed.) *Different: An Anthology of Homosexual Short Stories* (Bantam Books, New York, 1974).

Index

abortion 59, 83, 100, 108, 119, 244
Abortion Act 59
Acker, Kathy 67–8, 258
Acton, William 62
Adams, Michael 153, 260
Adler, Larry 120
Adler, Marmoset ix, 120, 245
advertising 25, 29, 60–1, 65, 85, 139
affection 9–10, 14, 30, 58, 65, 73–4, 76, 78, 85, 99, 139, 147, 149, 155, 218, 220, 224, 245, 249, 251–2
age 2, 6, 9, 13, 69, 100, 211, 221, 223, 236
AIDS 16–17, 27, 41, 91, 100–102
alienation 60–1, 69, 106, 124, 168, 220
  emotional 28–9, 137
Alta 238, 264
Amana Inspirationists 196
Ambrose, Father 135–6
Amis, Kingsley 40
Amis, Martin 40
ancient world 4–5, 152, 183, 185–6
anger 28, 92, 106, 205, 217–18
Angier, Carole 259, 261
anxiety see sexual anxiety
approval 14–16, 22
Ardener, Shirley 146, 260
Aristotle 5
Armatrading, Joan 120
Armstrong, Karen 136, 259–60
artists 192–3, 204, 210, 231–9
  see also writers
Ascetic Celibates 4, 14, 58, 109, 127, 140, 142, 144, 150–1, 156–9, 162, 193, 252
asexuality 14, 71, 81, 84, 134
assertion 66, 115, 149, 162
Atwood, Margaret 173–7, 190, 256, 261
Augustine, St 135–6, 143, 159–60
autonomy 9, 11, 20–1, 28, 42, 53, 65, 81, 84, 89, 111–17, 123, 131, 139, 151, 154, 157–8, 163, 186, 188, 195, 202, 222, 233, 235, 252
  female view 111–17, 157–8
  male view 111–17, 158
  see also connected autonomy
Avery, Giles 208, 211, 263

backlash 169
  see also feminism; male control; power
Baker Brown, Issac 63

battering 85, 97
  see also violence
Baudricourt, Robert de 187
beauty 1, 6, 65–6, 161, 199
Belling, Davina 24
Bennett, J. and Forgan, R. 259
Berger, John 61
bereavement 7, 100, 228–9, 240–1, 248, 250–2
Bernadette of Lourdes, St 123
Biggs, Nicholas 202
Binchy, Maeve 126
bisexuality 30, 138, 193
black women 12, 179
  see also women of colour
  people 59
Blue, Polly 86–8, 258–9
Blue Velvet (film) 59
bodies
  women's 8, 60–1, 64, 66, 71, 122, 128, 147, 172, 176, 179, 181, 183, 212
  men's 183
  objectification of women's 60, 65–6, 139, 169
Boylan, Clare 122
Breaking Glass (film) 24
British Museum 147
Brontë, Charlotte 26, 256
Brontë, Emily 232–3
Buddhism viii, 55, 58, 108–9
Butler, Josephine 48

campaigns 48–9, 51–2, 54, 66, 140, 160
Canadian Broadcasting Corporation vii, 9
Carter, Angela ix
Catholicism 108, 121–31, 135–6, 181–2, 195–6, 223
celibacy 1–5, 7–13, 21, 24, 73, 76–7, 87, 94, 102–3, 107, 118, 141, 143, 150–1, 153, 159, 161–2, 167, 177, 183, 191, 195, 199–200, 203–5, 208–11, 214–15, 217–18, 225, 227–9, 231–4, 237–8, 240, 242, 252–5
  as anti-consumerism 162, 193–4
  as anti-sex 55, 73, 160, 197, 199, 225
  as deviance 76, 224
  as disease 3–4, 17–18, 42, 49, 64
  as disinterest 223–4
  as failure 26, 53–4, 77, 84, 86, 144–6
  as form of consciousness 186, 233, 254
  as negative market value 29, 213

as oddness 42, 76, 78, 87
as prudery 46−9
as rebellion 108, 188
as repression 26, 141, 153, 210, 224
as self-protection 100
as solitude 20, 121, 156, 158
as symbol 20, 194, 196−7, 212, 225−6
ascetic celibacy *see* Ascetic Celibates
begins in the mind 45, 71−90, 131, 143, 153, 156
calmness 17, 19, 64, 80, 110
causes of 12, 72, 98, 110−17, 161, 197−8
definitions 5, 43−4, 76−8, 123, 153, 193
female 2, 4, 14, 21−2, 43, 47, 52, 54, 80−1, 117, 144, 160−2, 164, 179, 194−5, 202, 210, 216−17, 221−2, 225−6, 228, 235, 237−8, 249−50, 251
is not hereditary 1−22
male view of 47, 161, 163−4
male 34, 117, 135, 210
passionate *see* passionate celibacy
sensual *see* Sensual Celibates
sexual 14, 16, 22, 83, 120, 128−31, 144, 253−5
spiritual 109, 123−9, 134, 139, 216
see also spirituality
timely 16, 127, 134, 141, 151
celibate
break 99, 101, 110, 254
choices 10−12, 19, 21, 25, 39, 43, 46−7, 53−4, 57−8, 80, 82, 135−6, 148, 202, 204, 226, 235
coming out 42, 54−9, 75, 139
communities 13, 104, 196, 209; Christian 128−31, 158, 160, 162, 186, 191−209, 214−26; Shaker 191−209, 211−12, 214−18, 221−4; women's 215−26
couples (partners) 57, 73, 77−9, 85−6, 95, 116, 133−4, 183, 185, 218−19
identity 110, 116, 161−2, 183, 195
lifestyle 14, 76, 128−31, 133, 144, 151−4, 158−9, 162−3, 167, 182−3, 189, 191−212, 214−226
marriage 48, 54, 72−4, 85, 93
messages 70
perspective 21, 71, 127, 182, 226
philosophy 43, 71−2, 124, 143, 151, 153, 158−60, 162, 194, 196, 198, 200−1, 203, 207−9, 211−12, 214−15, 218, 221, 224−5
priesthood 4, 135−6, 195, 208, 211
relationship 76, 85, 203
spirit 71
wife 55−7, 76−7, 218
women *see* celibacy, female
celibates 8−10, 12−13, 18, 80, 104, 184
ascetic *see* Ascetic Celibates
new media 141
previous eras 2, 59, 162−3, 182−3, 191−204, 214−26
sensual *see* Sensual Celibates
unwilling 82, 253
see also sexual inactivity
censorship 59
Charles VII 187
chastity 5, 9, 21, 26, 43, 51, 88, 110, 122−3, 125, 127, 129, 135−6, 143−64, 167, 172, 179, 181−2, 186, 189, 201, 208, 212
ascetic 212

purposeful 143, 151, 153−4, 157, 194
sensual 149
useless 151, 161
chastity belts 146−7, 179
chauvinism 71
childbearing 184, 197, 202, 206
childcare 84, 194, 202, 223−4
Choderow, Nancy 113−14, 259
Christian spirituality 104−5
women 4, 104, 107, 183
world, early 4, 9, 46−54, 143, 145−7, 152, 159, 162, 182−3, 195
Christianity 4, 62, 87, 105, 126−7, 136, 143, 145, 159, 183−4, 217−18
see also spirituality
Church 106−8, 126, 128, 135−6, 182, 184, 186, 195−6, 217−18
Cixous, Hélène 229
Clements, Father 195
Cline, Sally 2, 9, 75, 150, 256−60, 263
clitoris 7, 62−4
coitus *see* sexual congress
Comfort, Alex 26, 190, 256
communication 65, 95, 133, 137
see also language
companionship 12, 85, 91, 149, 156−8, 229, 234, 239, 244
celibate 65, 95, 133
confessional literature 25, 28, 40
Congreve, William 152
Conn, Joann Wolski 104, 259
connected autonomy 21, 110−117, 146, 254−5
see also autonomy
connections 21, 25, 113, 115, 129, 135, 145, 158, 163, 195, 199, 201
consumer society 1−2, 6, 26, 29, 103
consumers, sexual 1, 3, 7, 13, 21, 65, 137, 139, 213−14
Contagious Diseases Act 48
contraception 26−7, 56, 83, 102, 225
control 23, 54, 58, 62, 124, 135, 140, 144, 151, 158−9, 162, 172−3, 181, 183, 210, 219, 222
male 165, 167, 171, 178−9, 188−90, 202, 219
parental 243−4
social 146−8, 179, 195
convents 121−31, 141−2, 158, 181, 211
Corinthians 185, 218
Cosmopolitan magazine 23
cosmetic surgery 6, 38, 61−70
couples 7, 11, 13, 15, 19, 35, 57, 64−5, 73, 76−80, 97,100, 134, 154−6, 174−5, 206, 210, 222, 226−7, 229−31, 235, 242, 249, 251, 254−5
see also celibate couples
creative solitude 227−52
creativity 9−10, 21, 195, 206−7, 210, 227, 232, 237−8
crones 2, 12
cuddling *see* affection
Curb, Rosemary 88, 258−9

Daily Sketch 244
Daily Telegraph 244
Daly, Mary 49, 62, 86−7, 186, 257−8, 261
Dani, the 209−13
Daochu, Long 2
death 197, 205, 211, 231, 233, 236, 240, 242,

244–8, 250
dependence 11, 20, 28, 30, 115, 139–40, 163, 197, 200, 208, 218, 223, 227, 254
desire 8, 9, 13, 18, 129, 141, 161, 202, 212, 226
    heterosexual 29–30, 163, 204
    lesbian 29, 130
Desroche, Henri 197
diets 1, 60, 65
disability 10, 19, 64, 100, 161
disease 10, 17–18, 27, 49–51, 54, 64, 161, 164, 223
    see also celibacy as disease
Diski, Jenny 30–3, 257
divorce 10, 12, 97, 106, 228
domination 23, 27, 30, 36, 53, 65, 135, 152, 194, 200, 202, 212
Doolittle, Elderess Antoinette 204
Dressed to Kill (film) 59
drugs 101
duty 124–5
Dworkin, Andrea 52, 188, 194, 258, 261–2

economics 1, 65, 91, 95–6, 103, 110, 145, 163–4, 180, 197, 200, 207, 218–20, 223, 225–6
education 48, 64, 121, 124–5, 161, 203–4, 206–7
Elizabeth, Sister 192
Ellis, Albert 190, 262
Elmy, Elizabeth Wolstenholme 48–9
emotions 29, 64, 69, 71, 79, 88, 95, 103, 131, 134, 137, 150–1, 157, 161, 177, 180, 185, 227, 229, 231, 240, 247, 254–5
    emotional needs 71, 153–4, 160, 163
enemies, men as 9
energy 10–11, 18, 22, 83, 94, 104, 124, 140, 150–1, 158–9, 210, 213–14
Engels, Friedrich 145
equality 20–1, 30, 37–8, 48, 65–7, 94, 146, 160, 191, 194–6, 198–9, 202–4, 206–9, 216, 219, 223
Erikson, Erik 114, 259
erogenous zones 41, 71
erotica 7, 61, 66, 129, 140, 147, 211
    erotic needs see lust
essentialism 254–5
Evans, Elder Frederick W. 203–4, 208, 262–3
exploitation 66

Faderman, Lillian 263
family see relatives
femininity 6, 8, 11, 25, 47, 49, 123–4, 141, 144–5, 163, 181, 188, 201, 206–7, 232
feminism 6, 12, 16, 20, 22–3, 28, 47, 49–54, 71, 81, 87, 148–9, 160, 165–6, 169, 196, 204, 221–2, 225–6
Field, Joanna 239–40, 265
films 24–5, 59
Fischer, Seymour 150
food 10, 120, 124, 124–21, 223, 235, 240, 243
    disorders 6, 29, 60; anorexia 29; bulimia 29
Foucault, Michel 5, 256
Frank, Katharine 232–3, 264
freedom 9, 21, 27–8, 52, 56, 60, 71–2, 79, 89, 91, 94, 112, 114, 118, 131, 142, 146, 153, 156–63, 194, 202, 218
Freud, Sigmund 53, 210–11, 213, 228–9
Friday, Nancy 23–4

friendship 9, 11, 13–14, 88, 91, 93, 103, 110, 116, 119–20, 133–4, 153, 155, 182, 203, 218, 223–4, 231, 240, 242–6, 249, 251–2
    romantic 26, 149
frigidity 19, 22, 25, 42–3, 46, 49–54, 136, 142, 254
    definitions of 49–50

Gagnon, J. and Simon, W. 213, 263
Gallichen, Walter 49, 257
Garrison, George P. 216, 263
gay see homosexual
gay rights 22, 102, 119
gender 162, 183, 195, 207–8, 216, 222
    identity 20, 113, 162
genital
    abstention 1, 5, 22, 43–5, 48–54, 59, 72, 81, 83, 136, 143–4, 150–1, 154–64, 179, 193, 196, 201, 209–10, 215, 218, 225–6, 253
    activity 1, 5, 7–8, 14–15, 48, 57, 72–3, 79, 100, 109–10, 116, 118, 126, 130–1, 133–4, 144, 150, 153, 157, 161–2, 168, 193, 196, 200–1, 210, 212–13, 223–4, 253–5
    appropriation era 6, 26, 28, 48, 53, 168, 190
    behaviour 45, 71–2, 85
    culture 30, 47, 61, 64, 66–7, 69, 71, 84, 103, 121, 126, 144, 157, 191, 196, 213, 222, 226
    fixated society 25, 27, 53, 64, 76, 157, 193, 214, 216
    focus 79, 130–2, 253
    manipulations 21, 24–7, 36–70, 157
    messages 21, 23–37, 59, 62, 64, 69–71, 80, 157
    myth 2, 5–9, 11–12, 14, 16–22, 29, 39, 41, 44, 48, 60, 69, 71, 98, 121, 136–9, 144–53, 157, 162, 164–7, 172–3, 177–8, 184, 186, 189, 195, 197, 214, 217, 220, 225, 227–8, 232, 254–5
    mythmakers/masters 19, 25, 27–8, 39, 42–3, 47, 49–50, 52–3, 60–1, 64–5, 93–4, 98, 117, 143–4, 149–50, 152, 183, 194, 227, 229, 254–5
    perspective 2, 23, 69, 73, 136, 225
    pressure 49, 80
    standard 21, 215–16
    trap 8, 15, 172, 210
genitals 1, 15, 23–4, 61, 63, 71–3, 78, 85, 101, 143, 160–1, 185, 198, 211, 227
Gilligan, Carol 115, 259
green politics 2–3
Greer, Germaine 2, 13, 125, 137, 210–11, 256, 260, 263
Gregory's Girl (film) 24
grief 28, 87, 197, 217
guilt 7, 11, 21, 23, 39, 56, 76–7, 126, 238

Hadrian, Emperor 5
Hage, Dorothy 54
Hamilton, Cicely 163–4, 167–8, 260–1
Haymond, Ada 220, 263
health 4–6, 10, 17–19, 25–6, 69
Heider, Karl 209–11, 263
Heimel, Cynthia 165–6, 176, 260
Henriques, Fernando 188, 261
Herman, Judith 98
heterosexuality 8, 12–13, 20–21, 24–5, 29–30, 49–51, 54, 60, 99, 116, 137–8, 160, 201, 212,

225–6, 229
  compulsory 6, 25, 97, 229
Himerius of Tarragona 4
Hippocrates 5
Hite, Shere 39, 43, 149–50, 257, 260
HIV 100–102
Hodgkinson, Liz viii, 256
Hollinghurst, Alan 34–5, 257
Hollywood 24
homeopathy 108
homosexuality 6, 25, 83, 89, 96, 99, 102, 212
Honey magazine 168, 174
Horgan, Edward 197, 262
hugging see affection

ideas
  impersonal 228–9
  women 254
identity 9, 114, 183, 240
  group 254
ideology 48, 52, 64, 71, 121, 128, 225
Idomeneo 35
Ignatius of Antioch 185
illness 10–11, 16–17, 22, 51–2, 100, 242–5, 252
images 59, 65–7, 69, 85, 112
  female 29–30, 60, 199
imagination see creativity
immigration 179
incest 67–9, 85, 96–7, 138, 147, 161
  see also violence
independence 9, 11, 20–2, 30, 45, 48, 53–4, 58,
  81, 111–17, 123, 126, 135, 140, 142, 149,
  151–2, 158, 162–4, 195–6, 202, 216–17, 220,
  227, 232–3, 254
  see also autonomy
insecurity 9, 26, 65
integrity 87, 153
interdependence 30, 55, 128, 207
intimacy 13–14, 20, 102, 113–14, 116, 119,
  140–1, 149, 151, 158, 223–4, 229, 240, 249
invisibility 45–6, 65

James, Alice 237
jealousy 15–16, 95, 134, 138, 223, 226
Jeffreys, Sheila 47, 52, 257, 260
Jerome, Father 135–6
Jesus 4, 8, 104, 125, 135, 162, 208
Jewish
  culture 105, 119, 121–5, 127–8, 141, 245
  family 121, 124–5, 127, 247
  woman 12, 121, 126–7, 182
  see also Judaism
Joan of Arc 187–8
Jong, Erica 28
Judaism 105, 127–8

Kaplan, Helen 150
Kinsey, Alfred 26–7, 190
kissing 25, 85, 125, 149, 157
Kitch, Sally 215, 217, 220, 262–4
Kitzinger, Sheila 64, 258
Koedt, Anne 39, 53, 213, 257–8, 263
Koreshans, the 20
Kramarae, C. and Treichler, P. 38, 257, 261

labelling 24, 46, 48, 76–7, 117, 135, 144, 152,

161, 176
language 25, 38, 39, 40–6, 49, 152, 183, 199
Lee, Ann 193–4, 197–200, 204–5, 217–18
legitimacy 15–16, 20, 25, 36, 49, 84, 127, 145, 152
lesbianism/lesbians 6–7, 12–13, 16, 22, 24, 26, 28,
  30, 40, 80, 87, 91, 99–100, 116, 137–8, 154–7,
  170, 179, 212, 224–6, 254
Long, Simon 2, 257
loneliness 137, 228, 230–4, 236
love 8, 15–16, 18, 28, 34, 67–9, 107, 121, 124,
  126, 128–30, 132, 134, 140, 149, 153, 155, 161,
  168, 175, 197, 200–2, 204, 206, 214, 217–18,
  223–4, 229, 231, 234
lovers 9, 15, 35, 78, 80, 116, 138, 140, 150, 152,
  203, 239–40
Lucas, Sarah 204
lust 48, 51, 71, 118, 126, 134–6, 160, 175,
  198–202
Luther, Martin 189

Mace, Sister Aurelia 204
McNamara, Jo Ann 162, 182–3, 186, 195, 260–1
McWhirter, George 217–19
McWhirter, Martha 215–22, 263–4
Mailer, Norman 28, 40
Malamuth, Neil 98
male reflection mechanism 2, 9, 58, 124, 150, 155,
  214, 230, 234–5, 251
Manahan, Nancy 88
Manning, Rosemary 237
Maring community, the 209
marriage 4, 7–9, 12–13, 47–8, 51–2, 57, 63, 72,
  74, 76, 158, 160, 162–4, 182–3, 185–6,
  195–7, 201, 203, 206, 209, 216, 218–20,
  222–5, 230, 234–5, 249–51
  see also celibate marriage
Marshall, O. and Suggs, R.C. 263
Masters, W. and Johnson, V. 26–7, 53, 256, 258
masturbation 14, 26, 29, 63–4, 81, 84–6, 93, 96,
  125, 145, 148–51, 156, 161, 196
media 7–8, 17, 23–5, 59, 66, 149, 200, 203–5
medical profession 19, 57, 61–70, 214
Medical Society 63
meditation 107, 110, 118, 212
men, dissatisfaction with 91–2, 95–6, 98–9, 110,
  184
The Men's Room 23
menopause 2, 57, 59, 161
menstruation 64, 147, 161
mental illness 1, 18–19, 25–6, 37, 49–50, 54–9,
  63–4, 210, 220, 229–30
Mew, Charlotte 237
Mildred, Sister 193
Miles, Rosalind 62, 258
Miller, Henry 28, 40, 69
Millett, Kate 33–4, 257
Mills, Jane 43, 46, 257–8, 260
misogyny 66, 104, 106, 196
monogamy 180
Monroe, Harriet 237
motherhood/mothers 10, 12, 30, 113, 116, 119,
  123, 166, 184, 195, 205, 215, 224, 242–8
Ms magazine 98, 230–1
Mulford, Wendy ix
mysticism 51, 107, 137, 232–3
mythmakers/masters see genital mythmakers/

masters

naming *see* celibate definitions, naming
National Institute for Mental Health 98
New Lebanon community, the 203–4, 211
Nietzsche, Friedrich 152
normative attitudes 76, 80, 84, 114, 209, 211–13,
  216, 227, 229, 234, 254
nuns 18, 71, 81, 88–9, 121–5, 127–31, 134–5,
  140–1, 153, 155, 158–60, 189, 195, 208, 211,
  223
nymphomania 50, 224

Oakley, Ann 23
Observer 244–5
Oedipus 229
Olsen, Tillie 237, 264
oppression *see* subordination, power
oral sex 25
orgasm 26–7, 29–30, 32, 39, 53, 60, 64, 92, 95,
  127, 137–9, 149–51, 210–11, 228
  clitoral 7, 27, 39, 53, 150, 213
  obligatory 17, 21, 25, 29, 38, 53, 150, 155
  vaginal 27, 53, 213
Other People's Money (film) 24
Ovid 152

Pagels, Elaine 158–9, 260
Pankhurst, Christabel 48
parenting 12, 15, 147, 197
partners/partnerships 7–8, 10–22, 13, 15, 21, 27,
  29, 64, 73, 76, 86, 93–5, 98, 101, 116, 127, 132,
  137, 140, 146, 150, 153–4, 222–3, 228, 236,
  240, 248, 252
  see also celibate partners, couples
passion 13, 21, 34, 38, 65, 87, 91, 108, 110,
  117–42, 157, 163, 180, 200, 212, 217, 222–3,
  226, 228, 242, 252
  celibate 24, 121
  genital 5, 156
passionate celibacy (self chosen) 7–8, 10–11,
  20–2, 28, 40, 42, 49, 51, 54–7, 59, 64–5, 69,
  72–3, 82, 86, 127–8, 131, 138, 140–1, 146,
  148, 162, 178, 186–7, 253–5
patriarchy 43, 62, 64, 105, 135, 163, 232, 254
Paul, St 136, 185–6
peace movement 88, 119
Peck, Gregory 24
penetration/penetrative sex 24–5, 40, 45, 50, 52,
  54, 58, 74, 92, 95, 145, 149–50
penis 2, 9, 83, 147, 170–1, 214
  enhancement 1–2
permissive society *see* sexual revolution
Petticoat magazine 168
Philip the Evangelist 183
Philosophers of Stoa 5
pill, the 26–7
Plato 5
Playboy magazine 60
politics 2–3, 22, 51, 53, 61, 66, 85, 87, 98, 119,
  169, 187, 216, 244, 254–5
pornography 7, 23, 59, 65–7, 85, 213
pornographic culture 25, 37, 59–61, 67, 69, 98
Porter, Katherine 237
possession/non-possession 58, 71–2, 79, 88–9, 95,
  131–2, 134, 145, 152, 180–1, 223, 226

Potter, Beatrix 237
power 1, 6, 9, 12, 20, 25, 28, 30, 34, 36, 48, 85,
  104, 125, 156, 162–4, 179–80, 185, 194–6,
  202, 208, 216, 226, 255
  of access 25
  female 216, 222, 254
  male 2, 22, 24, 28, 40, 52, 61, 147, 171, 206,
    254
  spiritual 5, 13
  see also control, male
Pratt, Ada 224–5
pregnancy 161, 175, 177, 185
pride 46, 65, 87
prostitution 6, 25–6, 51, 165–6, 170, 174, 188–9,
  195
prudery/prudes 25, 42–3, 46–51, 136, 170
  definition of 46–7
Puritanism 22, 46, 49, 54
purity 143, 147, 152, 181, 183, 186, 215, 225
Pythagoras 4

rape 7, 23, 30, 32, 37, 51, 61, 66, 97, 99, 138, 147,
  152
  date 51, 99
Ranke-Heinemann, Uta 256
rapture 103, 137, 139
Raymond, Janice 261
rejection 9, 11, 28, 150–2, 157, 159, 221
relatives 119–25, 127–8, 132, 191, 200–4,
  206–9, 215–16, 218, 223–4, 232–52
religion 4, 9, 51, 61–2, 81, 103–4, 106–7,
  121–31, 136, 153, 158–60, 162, 167, 182, 185,
  187–9, 191–209, 217–19, 222–3, 226
reluctance 52, 54, 149
Reyes, Alina 24, 256
Rhys, Jean 124–5, 182, 235–7, 264
Rigoletto 120
Rilke, Rainer Maria 237
Robbins, Harold 28, 40
romance 32, 35, 39, 103, 120–1, 137, 139, 163,
  200
Royal Literary Fund vii

Sabbathday Lake community 192–3, 203–6, 209,
  214
sadomasochism 6, 32, 59–61, 65–7
Sanctificationist Sisters, the 9, 20, 215–26
Sarton, May 239, 265
Scheble, Martha 221, 225
Scott, Hilda 96, 259
security 11, 15, 74, 116, 161, 177, 220, 237
seduction 24, 175
self-determination 5
  see also autonomy; independence
self-worth 9, 29, 48, 65, 127, 152, 154–6, 161,
  178, 220
semen 5, 100–1
Sensual Celibates 14, 16, 84–5, 109, 140, 142, 196,
  252
sensuality 133, 174
separation 10, 12, 20, 28, 86, 94, 107, 114, 137–9,
  158, 194, 208, 212, 219, 222
sex
  as commodity 29, 55, 60, 65, 103
  as conversation 29, 41–3, 213
  as cure 25, 64

as panacea 93
as performance 7, 29, 73−4, 92, 144, 149
as power 22−3, 29−30, 35−6, 49, 52, 61−2,
    67, 186
see also power
as promiscuity 42, 75; male 168; female 254
see also promiscuity
as violence see violence
sex education 99
sexism 104, 106, 114, 152
Sex, Lies and Videotape (film) 61
sex, safe 27, 41, 101
sex therapy 17, 27, 64
sexual
    abuse 48, 51, 95−7, 147, 160−1, 197, 218
    see also violence
    activity 1−3, 6−8, 10−12, 14, 17−19, 21−2,
        24−6, 28, 30, 35, 37−40, 55, 58, 61, 69,
        74−6, 78, 81−2, 84, 89, 92−4, 102−3,
        105−8, 121−3, 125−7, 132, 135−8, 144,
        146, 149−50, 154−8, 160−1, 163, 165−6,
        172, 177, 184, 186, 188, 195−7, 200, 203,
        207, 210−16, 220, 223, 225, 229, 237−40,
        242, 248, 250−2, 255
    activity as disease 26, 100
    anxieties 7−8, 30, 39, 65, 91−2, 95, 100, 131
    availability 6, 44, 150, 163, 200
    boredom 57, 91−3, 95, 149
    breaks 48−9, 54, 58, 91, 93−6, 110, 141, 152,
        209
    see also celibate breaks
    conduct 4, 25, 28, 102
    congress 1, 4−8, 25, 29−30, 37−40, 43, 48, 50,
        52−3, 55, 58, 63−4, 67−8, 72, 96, 100, 106,
        127, 129, 131−3, 135, 137−8, 143, 149−50,
        152, 155−7, 164, 166−8, 175, 184, 187−8,
        191, 193−5, 197, 200, 205, 209−10, 212,
        222, 226−7
    see also penetration/penetrative sex
    disorder 17, 51, 200
    dissatisfaction 56, 58, 63, 65, 92, 110, 132−3,
        161
    double standard 26, 144, 146, 217
    dualism 25, 140
    fantasies 23−4, 26, 29−30, 32, 93, 141, 212
    focus see genital focus
    harassment 7, 97
    see also violence
    history 101−2, 138
    inactivity 6, 10, 12, 71, 79, 82, 143, 153, 253
    liberation 8, 28
    liberation era 6, 26, 48, 53, 81, 148
    see also genital appropriation era
    messages 3, 25, 37, 61
    mores 255
    needs 93, 132, 140, 143, 149
    orientation 9
    pleasure 4, 29, 52, 54, 62, 64, 127, 131, 139, 147,
        149, 154, 213−14, 225
    pressure 58, 89−90, 169, 172
    see also violence
    problems 95
    relationships 11, 13, 37, 48, 72, 79−80, 89, 93,
        146, 154, 156−8, 160−1, 163, 179, 182, 194,
        201, 218, 228−9
    revolution see sexual liberation era; genital

    appropriation era
    sexuality 14, 16, 21−2, 24−5, 46, 71, 80, 83, 85,
        94, 167, 172, 181, 197, 210−11, 214, 253−5
    as choice 255
    as socially constructed 255
    compulsory 28−9, 107, 155, 201, 205, 213−14
    female 53, 60−2, 65−6, 127, 129, 135−6,
        140−1, 143, 147−9, 153, 161, 254−5
    male 52, 145
sexually transmitted diseases 41, 100−101
Shackman, Harriet viii, 119
Shakers, the 9, 20, 191−209, 211−12, 214−18
    see also celibate communities, Shakers
Shaker and Shakeress magazine 204
'Sharm El Sheikh' 120
She magazine 261
Sheppard, Ba ix, 240, 246
sickness see disease
simple life 91−117, 161, 192−3
sin 4, 51, 108, 122, 125−7, 135−6, 153, 158, 160,
    193, 200−2, 215, 217
singlehood 5, 7−8, 13, 19, 21, 47, 63, 79−80,
    131−3, 141, 151, 153, 166, 197, 202, 216, 222,
    228, 234−5
Siricius, Pope 4
Six Day War 120
Slaughter, Audrey 168, 261
slave 35, 47, 52, 145
sluts 165−6, 169, 176−7, 183
Smith, Stevie 231−2, 237, 264
Smith, Vic ix, 119
social
    class 12, 220
    order 2, 25, 227, 252
    reality 20, 25
    status 20, 47, 113, 226; women's 191, 194−6,
        200, 202−7, 209, 215−16, 220, 226, 253−5
Soranus of Ephesus 5
Soderberg, Steven 61
solitude 7, 20, 78−9, 87, 91, 94, 100, 110, 118,
    227−52, 254−5
space 10, 55, 70, 91, 94−5, 100, 103, 118, 132,
    134, 139, 151, 157, 227, 235, 239, 241
spiritual growth 91−117, 161−2
spirituality 18, 21, 54−5, 66, 69, 81, 87−117,
    121−4, 126, 128−9, 131, 133, 136−7, 139−40,
    142, 150, 153, 159, 162, 167, 181, 184, 186,
    191−209, 216−18, 222−3, 226
spite 12, 91−117, 161
Stanley, Abraham 197
Steinem, Gloria 230, 264
Stekel, William 52
stigma 13, 17, 26, 28, 51, 54, 77, 140, 182
Stoa 5
Storr, Anthony 20, 229−30, 256, 264
submission 27, 32, 38, 48, 52, 62, 65, 67, 86, 123,
    127, 152, 194, 197, 212, 214
subordination 6, 28, 35, 48, 52, 86, 105, 164, 187,
    254
    eroticisation of 48, 85
suffragettes 9, 48−9, 197
Swiney, Francis 48−9
symbolism 61, 63, 191, 215
Szasz, Thomas 22, 51, 62−4, 127, 256−8

taboos 148–50, 248
Taoism 103
Teresa of Avila, St 123, 127
Tertullian, Father 195
Tey, Josephine 233–5, 264
Thecla 185–6
threats 59, 138
Tie Me Up! Tie Me Down! (film) 59
Tightrope (film) 59
Timewatch: the Shakers (BBC2) 262
True Romance magazine 149, 174

United Society of Believers, the 198
unity (between sexes) 20, 35, 194, 208, 223, 226

value 14, 16, 58, 65, 150, 157, 193, 196, 201, 208,
  216, 224–6, 254
Verdi, Giuseppe 120
vibrators 7, 101, 141, 151
violence 1, 7, 29–30, 32, 59, 61, 64–7, 74, 85, 91,
  96–8, 110, 119, 147, 161, 198, 200, 216, 219
virginity 9, 21, 135–6, 143, 146–7, 165–90
  as conquest 179–90
  as handicap 165–90
  perpetual/purposeful 165–90
  transitional 165–90
virginity tests 179
virgins 86, 135, 141, 145, 162, 165–90, 195, 206
  perpetual 141, 164–90
  transitional 141, 165–90

vows 88–9, 128–30, 132, 208
vulnerability 30, 140, 161

War of Independence 198
Warner, Marina 135, 181, 259, 261
Watervliet community 198, 205
Weaver, Harriet Shaw 237
weight 6, 29, 37–8
White, Anna 202, 208, 262–3
whores see prostitution
widows, celibate 7, 10, 12, 91, 162, 183–4, 195,
  228, 248–52
witchcraft 12–13
Wolf, Naomi 257–8, 260
Women Against Violence Against Women 67
women of colour 179
  see also black women
Women's Movement 60, 74, 86, 165, 168
Woolf, Virginia 118
work (employment) 1, 9, 55–6, 59, 63, 93–4, 96,
  110, 133–4, 139, 153–5, 159–61, 164, 197,
  201, 206–9, 216, 219–24, 226, 239, 241
worship 107, 144, 192, 198, 207, 212
writers ix, 3, 75, 124–5, 208, 230–9, 247
Wyndham, F. and Melly, D. 236, 264

Xenophon 5

Zarinah, Sister Hana 71, 88, 131, 258